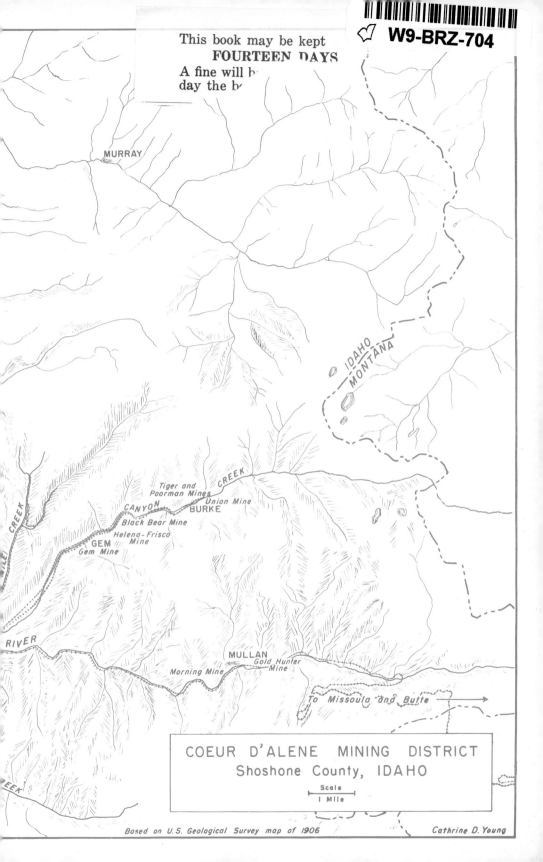

W9-BRZ-704

MURRAY

IDAHO
MONTANA

Tiger and
Poorman Mines
CANYON CREEK
Union Mine
BURKE
Black Bear Mine
Helena-Frisco
Mine
GEM
Gem Mine

MULLAN
Gold Hunter
Mine
Morning Mine

MILE CREEK

RIVER

CREEK

To Missoula and Butte

COEUR D'ALENE MINING DISTRICT
Shoshone County, IDAHO

Scale
1 Mile

Based on U.S. Geological Survey map of 1906   Cathrine D. Young

The Coeur d'Alene
Mining War of 1892

OREGON STATE MONOGRAPHS

Studies in History

JOSEPH W. ELLISON, *Consulting Editor*

1. Opening and Penetration of Foreign Influence in Samoa to 1880, by Joseph W. Ellison.
2. Coeur d'Alene Mining War of 1892, by Robert Wayne Smith.

1892

The Coeur d'Alene
Mining War of 1892

A CASE STUDY OF AN INDUSTRIAL DISPUTE

By Robert Wayne Smith
Professor of History, Oregon State University

31685

OREGON STATE UNIVERSITY PRESS

Design by Richard Koe

Printed at
Oregon State University
Corvallis, Oregon

THOSE WERE TROUBLOUS TIMES in the Coeur d'Alenes last summer; there is no doubt that some of the miners went to deplorable extremes. But the provocation was great and passion ran high. Many of those who were leaders in this notable struggle of labor against capital have already suffered the loss of their liberty for longer or shorter periods, and without exception, we believe, have bowed to the law and endured their imprisonment like men. When an impartial history of the great Coeur d'Alene strike shall be written, it will be found that mixed with not a little that was ugly and horrible there was yet a great deal of honor and honesty and heroism.

—From an editorial in the Anaconda (Montana) STANDARD
March 30, 1893

Preface

THE READER of *The Coeur d'Alene Mining War of 1892* deserves a word of introduction and explanation: an introduction to the theme of this monograph, and an explanation why it is being published almost twenty-four years after it was written.

In introducing the theme, I must take my readers back to the years 1929 to 1933, a period during which I taught history in the public high school of Wallace, Idaho. Early I became aware of the tumultous and violent labor struggles of 1892 and 1899 which had converted the Coeur d'Alene mining district into a veritable battlefield. Later I became aware that the deep divisions within the community created by those long-ago controversies still existed; that the citizens of the 1930's still took sides on social, economic, and religious questions more or less as their predecessors had done in the 1890's. Piqued by curiosity, I asked many questions, and my queries generally received evasive or irritated replies. Citizens of Wallace simply were not discussing the past with strangers. "We're trying to forget those things," they told me.

I devoted two years of intensive study to the history of the Coeur d'Alene mining district. I utilized the libraries of Spokane, Boise, and Berkeley. I read the newspaper files in Spokane, Boise, and Butte. I uncovered scores of documents filed away in the case records of the state and federal courts. I finally won the confidence of a few surviving participants in the events of the 1890's.

Narrowing my study to the great mining labor controversy of 1892, I brought it to a conclusion in 1937, and presented it as a doctoral dissertation in history at the University of California (Berkeley). In this phase of my labor I was directed by the late distinguished Professor Frederic Logan Paxson. My dissertation bore the title *The Idaho Antecedents of the Western Federation of Miners, 1890-1893*.

After a brief unsuccessful attempt to have the dissertation published, I laid it aside. I was soon deeply involved in college teaching and in studies in other fields.

The years have passed—almost a quarter of a century. A few historians and economists have utilized my dissertation; I receive occasional inquiries from interested persons; a few libraries in the Pacific Northwest have acquired copies on microfilm. One librarian remarked: "Idaho material is hard to come by."

During these years, to the best of my knowledge, no significant new study of the Coeur d'Alene mining conflicts has been written or published.

A possible exception is the excellent history of the Western Federation of Miners entitled *Heritage of Conflict,* by Professor Vernon H. Jenson, published by Cornell University Press in 1950. Professor Jenson has a clear and interesting chapter on the Coeur d'Alene conflict of 1892, and his brief account parallels the general lines of my dissertation.

In these twenty-some years, also, most of the participants in the events of the 1890's who were living in the 1930's have died. Their witness has ended.

For a number of reasons I consider this historical study of mine still significant and worthy of publication. It may well be the definitive word on this dramatic incident in the history of organized labor in the mining West. It relates the development, step by step, of a fundamental controversy in the mining industry in a relatively isolated area. The entire community becomes involved in the struggle; there is no neutral group of bystanders. The conflict runs to its tragic conclusion, developing on the way interesting collateral stories of federal military intervention and the manipulation of public opinion.

I am pleased to accept the invitation of the Faculty Publications Committee of Oregon State College to publish my manuscript as a monograph in history. I send it to the press practically unchanged from its original form. One glaring, illogical fault I corrected. I hope that it may prove to be valuable to the student of the history of the West and informative to the general reader.

Corvallis, Oregon
1 December, 1960

Table of Contents

The Coeur d'Alene
Mining War of 1892

The Coeur d'Alene Mining District

T HE COEUR D'ALENE mining district, a region rich both in natural resources and in human history, lies in the mountain wilderness of Shoshone
County in northern Idaho. Situated just to the west of the Bitter Root
divide, the Coeur d'Alene mountains form a lateral continuation of that
divide. Rising from springs and glacial lakes high in the hills, a network
of creeks course downward through the steep canyons and unite their
waters in the North and South Forks of the Coeur d'Alene River.* Forests
of pine, fir, and larch clothe the mountain slopes, while heavy stands of
cedar grow in the valley bottoms. Above the forest belt rises a series of
rocky summits which attain altitudes between 6,000 and 7,000 feet above
sea level, whereas the river bottom lands rest at elevations 2,000 to 3,000
feet above the sea. Snow lies deep over the whole region four or five
months of the year, and lingers in protected basins and on shady slopes
high in the hills for an equal additional space of time. Water flows in the
creeks and rivers all year long. Excesses of snow coupled with chinook
winds in the winters have brought snow slides roaring down into the valleys, and long continued drought in the summers, aided by lightning, has
sent disastrous fires raging through the timbered hills.

This mountain solitude remained for centuries the hunting ground
of the Indian, without permanent habitation and with only slight exploita-
tion of the natural resources contained therein. However, within the last
century a stirring human drama has been enacted within the valleys of the
Coeur d'Alene. Exactly who the first white man was and when he first set
foot and eye upon the Coeur d'Alene cannot be known for a certainty.
But in the 1840's Jesuit missionaries came into the region from the east

* See map on end papers.

and built a mission which still stands on a hill overlooking the Coeur d'Alene River below Cataldo.[1] Then, in the 1860's, a party of engineers and soldiers of the United States Army under the command of Captain John Mullan, cut a military road through the Coeur d'Alene valley.[2] This was the Mullan Road which ran from Fort Walla Walla, on the Columbia River, to Fort Benton, on the Missouri, and crossed from Idaho into Montana territory by the St. Regis (Sohon) Pass. A thin stream of immigration and travel and military movement trickled through the Coeur d'Alene along the Mullan Road, but none of it lingered within the mountain canyons. In 1879 the United States established a military post, Fort Sherman, upon the shores of Coeur d'Alene Lake.[3]

A prospector, Andrew J. Prichard by name, working alone in the Coeur d'Alene gulches in 1879, 1880, and 1881, and with a party of associates in 1882, discovered placer gold in paying quantities along the tributary streams of the North Fork. Gold had been found in the Coeur d'Alene region before—particularly during the Mullan Road construction—but Prichard's discovery was the first to receive wide publicity. The Northern Pacific Railroad in 1883 was just completing its transcontinental line which ran down the Clark Fork River in Montana and approached the Coeur d'Alene country within twenty-five or thirty miles. The railroad seized upon the news of Prichard's rich find, and issued a circular which magnified the facts and carried the name of Coeur d'Alene all over the United States. As a consequence of such advertising, the north side of the Coeur d'Alenes received a "rush" of some 6,000 or 8,000 men in the winter of 1883-84. The center of this stampede was the camp of Eagle City, at the confluence of Eagle and Prichard Creeks. Other camps which sprang into existence in the same winter were Murray and Littlefield on Prichard Creek, and Delta at the confluence of Beaver and Trail Creeks. The tale of that first big winter in the Coeur d'Alenes is almost fabulous—the eager thousands of miners milling about the camps week after week waiting for the snow to melt so that they could begin work in the placer diggings.[4]

When spring finally came in 1884 it was found that all the desirable placer ground had been staked and the claims filed by the early comers. Many of the disappointed fortune seekers left the country in disgust, cursing it as they went. Others set out across the divide and prospected the gulches tributary to the South Fork of the Coeur d'Alene. On the South Side, the prospectors found not yellow gold gleaming in the creek gravels, but a black, shiny, crystalline substance lying exposed upon the hillsides. It was galena, or sulfide of lead, and it also contained silver in varying proportions and sometimes zinc. Lead carbonate also appeared on the surface of the ground in rusty red

[1] A full and interesting account of this episode is contained in Edmund R. Cody, *History of the Coeur d'Alene Mission of the Sacred Heart* (Caldwell, Idaho: Caxton Printers, Ltd., 1930), 45 pp.
[2] Captain John Mullan, U.S.A., *Report on the Construction of a Military Road from Fort Walla Walla to Fort Benton* (Washington, D. C., Government Printing Office, 1863); also John M. Henderson, William S. Shiach and Harry B. Averill, *An Illustrated History of North Idaho* (. . . Western Historical Publishing Company, 1903), pp. 760-763.
[3] Henderson, Shiach and Averill, 765.
[4] Henderson, Shiach and Averill, part VI, ch. 1, pp. 981-995, deal rather fully and accurately with the early gold mining phase of Coeur d'Alene development; also a Master of Arts thesis at the University of Idaho, by Robert Wayne Smith, *History of Placer and Quartz Gold Mining in the Coeur d'Alene District* (Moscow, Idaho, unpublished thesis, 1932), 124 numbered leaves.

masses.[5] At first prospectors were inclined to pass over these base ores with contempt, so eager were they for gold bearing sands and gold bearing quartz ledges. However, a few miners recognized the value of the lead-silver deposits and staked their claims and filed for possession at the courthouse of Shoshone County. The Tiger mine on Canyon Creek was the first lead-silver claim to be entered from the South Side. John Carton and Alameda Seymour were the discoverers and they date their location as of May 2, 1884.[6]

Within the two years 1884 and 1885, practically every lead-silver mine of any consequence in Coeur d'Alene history was discovered and legally possessed. In Canyon Creek, the Tiger and the Poorman, the Frisco, the Black Bear, the Badger, the Gem, and the Granite; in the upper South Fork valley, near the townsite of Mullan, the Morning and the Gold Hunter; in isolated Nine Mile canyon, the Custer; down the South Fork and high on a hill, the Polaris, rich in silver; and, greatest of all, up Milo Gulch, in the shadow of Kellogg Peak, the Bunker Hill and Sullivan.[7] Concerning the great value of these Coeur d'Alene lead-silver discoveries, Walter Renton Ingalls, in his book *Lead and Zinc in the United States,* wrote, "In the course of time those veins became the most important source of lead in North America, a position which they still hold."[8]

While the development of the gold properties on the North Side continued at a rapid pace, the lead-silver deposits on the South Side lagged far behind. And for a simple reason: whereas a single miner or a small partnership could operate a placer claim and extract the gold with simple tools and hand labor, a ledge of galena ore required much more complex organization and technical operation. Tunnels had to be driven into the hillside to cut the vein of ore; solid rock had to be blasted and in most places the walls and roof of the tunnel had to be supported by timbers. The ore was brought down by blasts of dynamite; then it had to be loaded on cars and wheeled to the mouth of the tunnel. Waste rock came with the ore and the two must be separated. Far from the simplicity of washing out gold in a sluice or a pan, was the smelting of lead-silver ores in complex furnaces. Either an expensive smelter must be built or the ore be sent away to a smelter already established. In the early years of lead mining in the Coeur d'Alenes the latter practice prevailed; building a smelter was out of the question. Yet transporting the ore to a smelter was almost as baffling a problem at first. The mines had to wait for railroad construction. But this was not all. Much of the ore which the mines yielded was low grade, that is, the proportion of lead and silver in the mass of rock with which they were compounded was so low that it would not pay the mine to ship it to a distant smelter. Therefore, concentrating mills had to be erected at most of the mines where by pulveriz-

---

[5] For a thorough discussion of the mineral resources of the Coeur d'Alenes see *The Geology and Ore Deposits of the Coeur d'Alene District,* by Frederick Leslie Ransome and Frank Cathcart Calkins, U. S. Department of the Interior, United State Geological Survey. Professional Paper 62 (Washington, D. C., Government Printing Office, 1908); and *Geology and Ore Deposits of Shoshone County, Idaho,* by Joseph B. Umpleby and E. L. Jones, Jr., U. S. Department of the Interior, United States Geological Survey bulletin 732 (Washington, D. C., Government Printing Office, 1923).
[6] Henderson, Shiach and Averill, 994.
[7] *Ibid.,* 993-994.
[8] Walter Renton Ingalls, *Lead and Zinc in the United States* (New York, Hill Publishing Company, 1908), p. 164.

ing the ore and washing it with small jets of water and agitating it upon smooth and corrugated table surfaces a concentrated ore could be obtained; that is, by the action of the water and gravity, the heavy metal bearing ore was separated from the lighter waste rock.[9]

It should be evident from the foregoing description of lead-silver mining that such a game could not be played by a single miner, and seldom even by a group of partners. Extensive capital was required with which to buy costly machinery, pay a large force of laborers, defray heavy expenses of transportation, and carry on the enterprise while awaiting the proceeds from the smelter. Lead-silver mining demanded the corporation. Gradually, one by one, the Coeur d'Alene lead-silver mines were bought up and developed by corporations which drew their resources from hundreds of stockholders scattered throughout the country. It was a far different growth from the pell-mell "rush" to the gold diggings.

As a corporation began to develop a mine and to employ laborers in the tunnels, the shops, and the concentrating mill, a mining town or camp would spring into existence. A few stores, saloons, gambling houses, and brothels made up the business district of the camp while the shacks in which the miners and laborers lived straggled up and down the canyon and perched upon the hillsides. These mining camps whose buildings were uniformly of wood and generally without architectural grace presented a drab and monotonous picture. The contour of the Coeur d'Alene hills further restricted the camp's development. Most of the camps were built upon the narrow bottoms of canyons and gulches where the creek and the (generally the only) street ran parallel the length of the camp, and where, when the railroad came, it, too, had to be squeezed in on the same narrow bottom. In the five years following the discovery of galena on the South Side, 1884 to 1889, six mining camps grew up to achieve post offices and relative permanence. Wardner, in Milo Gulch, was supported by the Bunker Hill and Sullivan, the Last Chance, the Sierra Nevada, and the Stemwinder mines; Osburn, situated on a broad prairie of the South Fork, drew support from a group of small mines, including the Polaris; Wallace, at the confluence of Nine Mile, Canyon, and Placer Creeks with the South Fork, had no big mines in the immediate vicinity, but won its living as a trading and transportation center; Gem, four miles up Canyon Creek, housed the workers at the Gem, Frisco, Black Bear, and Badger mines; Burke, three miles farther up Canyon Creek, was supported by the Tiger and Poorman mines; and Mullan, up toward the headwaters of the South Fork, had the Morning mine on one side and the Gold Hunter mine on the other.

A final significant feature of the Coeur d'Alene district is its absolute dependence upon one single industry—mining. From the early gold rush of '83 down to the present day this condition has existed. There are no extensive farms in the Coeur d'Alene valleys—only a few tiny gardens or hayfields. There are no manufacturing plants unconnected with the mining in-

---

[9] For a more comprehensive account of the 19th century methods of milling lead-silver ores, see Ingalls, pp. 164 ff; also Arthur F. Taggart, *Handbook of Ore Dressing* (New York, John Wiley and Sons, Inc., 1927), 1679 pp., a standard reference book.

dustry in the Coeur d'Alene towns. The storekeepers and amusement operators in the towns depend for their business upon the patronage of miners or other employes of the mines and their families. The first concern of an adult resident of the Coeur d'Alenes when he opens his morning newspaper is the current price of lead, silver, and zinc. Coeur d'Alene children in their play dig miniature tunnels, raises, and stopes in gravel banks and even in snowdrifts. Samples of ore adorn the windows of stores and brokerage houses, and one hears everywhere the gossip of mines, stocks, dividends, assessments. In such a community it should not seem strange that a labor controversy which brought the mining industry to a complete standstill for half a year should become the concern of every person in the district. There was no neutral or indifferent group in the Coeur d'Alenes when industrial warfare broke out in the 1890's.

2

The Coeur d'Alenes in 1890-1891

THE YEAR 1890 and the first half of 1891 form an important period for the Coeur d'Alene district. The late eighties had been years of pioneering and of fundamental development in the lead-silver mines. By 1890 the properties were beginning to assume the permanence of mature enterprises and were yielding profits to their owners. This year and a half period is also significant as the last long period of industrial peace in the district, and in order to understand the situation after industrial war was declared a general survey of the Coeur d'Alenes in 1890-91 is essential.

In 1890 the eleventh federal census showed the population of Idaho to be 84,385.[1] Shoshone County had 5,383 inhabitants.[2] Most of Shoshone County's population lived in the Coeur d'Alenes; perhaps 500 dwelt in the Clearwater, the St. Joe, and other remote areas of the county. Ten years earlier, before the Coeur d'Alene gold rush, the census had reported only 469 inhabitants in Shoshone County.[3] Within the county, the precincts on the South Fork of the Coeur d'Alene contained almost 4,000 of the residents of Shoshone—3,993 to be exact. They were distributed as follows:

Wallace precinct	....	913
Wardner "	....	858
Mullan "	....	818
Burke "	....	482
Gem "	....	339
Kellogg "	....	324
Osburn "	....	259

Wallace was the only organized town within the county, and of its precinct population 878 lived within the town limits.[4]

---

[1] *Compendium of the 11th Census: 1890*, Part I, Population, U. S. Dept. of the Interior, Census Office (Washington, D. C., Government Printing Office, 1892), p. 2.
[2] *Ibid.*, I, p. 14.
[3] *Compendium of the 11th Census; 1890*, Part I, p. 14.
[4] *Ibid.*, I, pp. 107-108.

Wardner, Gem, and Burke were distinctively canyon camps. Each was located in a narrow mountain-walled canyon and they ran all to length, with but little breadth. Contemporary photographs show the clusters of small wooden buildings confined within the limited area of bottom land. Contemporary descriptions add a few colorful details:

> The town proper [of Wardner] is built in the upper portion of the narrow gulch named Milo; the grade, which is very steep, gives the impression of always climbing a hill. . . . Above the town in plain sight are the celebrated Sullivan and Bunker Hill mines.[5]

> Gem was a camp of two or three stores and half a dozen saloons. The three mines, the Gem, Helena-Frisco and Black Bear, which supported the camp, were near by, so that the men boarded in town. About 500 miners worked in these three mines, besides hundreds of other surface workers; hence the little camp was a lively place after night when the saloons and gambling halls were running full blast.[6]

> Situated away up at the head of the canyon, where the mountains rise on either side steep and precipitous, Burke is a town of one street, and a narrow one at that, up which the Northern Pacific railroad runs; and by the first of the month the Union Pacific will be side by side with it, crowding the foot passengers on the narrow three-foot sidewalks into the stores.

> For half a mile or more the stores front the street on both sides; while the rear portions are either dug out of the banks or blasted from the solid rock.[7]

Somewhat different in appearance were Wallace, Mullan, and Osburn,[*] which might be cataloged as mountain meadow towns, since they were built in places where the South Fork canyon widened out into grassy and swampy flats grown up with impressive cedar groves. The swamps were drained and the cedars cut down eventually, and in their places rose more rows of wooden buildings paralleling muddy or dusty streets and board sidewalks. Osburn and Wallace were also unique in being residence and business towns rather than mining camps, properly speaking. The roads to Murray, the county seat, wound northward from Osburn and Wallace, so that many lawyers, county officials, and mine executives lived in these towns where they could be close to the scenes of mining activity and still close to the road to the county seat. This inconvenience of the county seat's remote location (20 miles from Wallace, 16 miles from Osburn) was slightly lessened by the holding of occasional terms of the district court at Osburn.[8] This description of Wallace in 1892 will serve as an illustration of the mountain meadow camps:

> The town of Wallace, prettily located at the junction of Placer, Nine Mile and Canyon Creeks with the South Fork of the Coeur d'Alene River, is the largest town in the mines, claiming about 2,500 population. . . . One bank, many stores and saloons, several good hotels, a creamery, two newspapers, two steam laundries, two hospitals, two churches, one public school, railway repair shops,

---

[5] *Spokane Review* (Spokane, Washington), January 1, 1892, p. 19, from a feature article by Eugene Klein, entitled "South Fork Mines. The Greatest Silver-Lead Camp in the World."
[6] Charles A. Siringo, *A Cowboy Detective* (Chicago, W. B. Conkey Company, 1912), p. 137.
[7] *Spokane Review*, September 26, 1890, p. 6, from a feature article by Bailey Avery, entitled "Richest Camp of All."
[*] See photographs among illustrations.
[8] *Spokane Review*, June 1, 1890, p. 10, tells of the opening of a special summer term of the territorial district court on May 30, 1890, at Osburn.

many pretty residences, electric lights and other modern improvements, including an ample fire department . . . go to make it not only habitable, but an agreeable place to reside.[9]

Mining flourished in 1890 and early 1891. By 1891 there were forty developed mines in the district, of which twenty-six were classed as producers. Thirteen concentrating mills were in operation, with an aggregate capacity of 2,000 tons of ore a day. By far the largest of these mills was that of the Bunker Hill and Sullivan at Wardner which could grind out 450 tons a day.[10] Other large mines operating concentrators were the Last Chance and the Stemwinder at Wardner; the Tiger, the Poorman, the Gem, the Frisco, and the Granite in Canyon Creek; the Morning and the Gold Hunter at Mullan. Two additional mines were turning out good quantities of ore but had not yet erected concentrators, namely, the Sierra Nevada at Wardner, and the Custer, up Nine Mile Creek north of Wallace. The value of the ore taken out of the Coeur d'Alene mines in 1890 was about $10,000,000,[11] and some of the mines paid good dividends to their stockholders.[12] The Bunker Hill and Sullivan Company kept its property inactive for about half of the year 1890 because of a lawsuit involving the title,[13] and the Morning mine was forced to close in December of 1890 when the Spokane and Wallace banking enterprises of Warren Hussey collapsed. With these two exceptions mining was nearly continuous throughout the period.

Vital to the mining industry was the problem of transportation. By 1891 the railroad facilities in the district had become almost adequate. The Northern Pacific operated a narrow gauge railroad from the Old Mission on the Coeur d'Alene River up the South Fork to Wallace and on up Canyon Creek to Burke. At the Old Mission passengers and freight were transferred to steamboats which carried their cargoes down the river and Coeur d'Alene Lake to the small town of Coeur d'Alene City, in Kootenai County, whence all were again transferred to trains running to Spokane, Washington, via Hauser Junction. From Wallace to Spokane it was six or seven hours by this route. The Union Pacific (Oregon Railroad and Navigation Company) ran a standard gauge line from Tekoa, Washington—a station on the Pendleton to Spokane line—across the upper end of Coeur d'Alene Lake and up the river and the South Fork clear to Mullan. The Union Pacific was also engaged in building a line up Canyon Creek to Burke in 1890. However, the most extensive piece of railroad construction in 1890 and 1891 was the Coeur d'Alene cutoff of the Northern Pacific Railroad. This line swung eastward from Mullan across the Bitter Root divide in long graceful loops, descended the St. Regis valley in Montana, and joined the Northern Pacific main line near

[9] *Ibid.*, January 1, 1892, p. 19, from a feature article by Eugene Klein entitled "South Fork Mines. The Greatest Silver-Lead Camp in the World."
[10] Walter Renton Ingalls, *Lead and Zinc in the United States*, p. 164; also the annual report (1891) of the Spokane Mining Exchange, as tabulated in the *Spokane Review*, January 6, 1892, p. 3.
[11] Estimate by A. J. Dunn, of Wallace, in the *Spokane Review*, January 1, 1891, p. 31.
[12] The mines which gave to the press information on dividends and profits in 1890 and 1891 were the Gold Hunter, the Badger, the Frisco, the Poorman, and the Last Chance.
[13] This suit was terminated on August 12, 1890, by a decision of the district court at Osburn. This decision gave victory to the "Lackawanna" group headed by Simeon G. Reed of Portland, Oregon, over the "Mammoth" group headed by Mike Flaherty and John M. Burke. Details in the *Spokane Review*, August 13, 1890, p. 2.

Missoula. The new cutoff was completed December 22, 1890.[14] but regular passenger and freight service did not begin until August 14, 1891.[15]

Within the district wagon roads were almost as important as railroads. By 1890, all the towns in the Coeur d'Alenes had been connected with roads, such as they were. The old Mullan Road, improved, was the "Main Street" of the district, from Wardner to Mullan. Two tortuous roads connected the South Fork camps with the county seat, Murray. These roads led north from Osburn and Wallace; they ascended Two Mile and Nine Mile Creeks respectively, and both dropped down into a common route in Beaver Creek. From Murray and from Burke wagon roads crossed over into Montana, utilizing Thompson and Glidden passes respectively, and joining in Prospect Creek valley into a common road to Thompson Falls, Montana.

What sort of life went on in the Coeur d'Alene communities? The labor of mining was hard and the hours were long, yet there seems to have been much gaiety and lively recreation for the dwellers of the camps. Early in 1891 electric lighting was just reaching the Coeur d'Alenes, and Wardner, Wallace, and Mullan vied with each other in the number of arc lights at street intersections.[16] In all the camps the saloons and gambling houses served as clubs and centers for gatherings of men. The number of saloons in these small communities is always amazing; Wallace had twenty-eight in 1890.[17] An old proverb in the mining camps runs to the effect that although food may become scarce there is always whiskey enough for all contingencies. The miners were hard drinkers, perhaps as a reaction from the hazardous nature of their work. Dancing was a popular recreation in the Coeur d'Alene towns; the special holiday balls given at Christmas and New Year's were elaborate affairs which lasted from 9 o'clock in the evening until almost dawn.[18] The big holiday of the year, however, was the Fourth of July when the whole district generally united in a grand celebration.[19] There would be a parade, followed by races of all sorts, orations in the afternoon, and a big dance at night. But the supreme event of the day was the hard rock drilling contest in which experienced miners competed against each other in drilling holes as deeply as possible into blocks of rock within a given time. This drilling was of two kinds, single-handed and double-handed. In the former case, a single miner held the drill against the rock with one hand and drove it with blows of a sledge held in the other, whereas in the double-handed drilling teams of two men competed, one man holding and directing the drill and the other wielding the sledge.

In the summer season baseball teams from Wardner, Wallace, Mullan, and Osburn played games on Saturdays and Sundays and holidays. Gem and Burke did not figure in these contests chiefly because there was no space for a diamond in their canyon. Even Wardner and Wallace were cramped for

[14] A golden spike ceremony at Look-out Pass, described in *Spokane Review*, December 23, 1890, p. 2.
[15] *Spokane Review*, August 16, 1891, p. 8.
[16] *Ibid.*, July 8, 1891, p. 4; and July 30, 1891, p. 2, credits Wardner with the first arc lights and Wallace with the most.
[17] *Spokane Review*, June 18, 1890, p. 6.
[18] *Ibid.*, December 26, 1891, p. 5, tells of holiday festivities at Mullan.
[19] The 1890 celebration was held at Wallace. Wm. H. Clagett and Willis Sweet gave the orations. The *Spokane Review*, July 5, 1890, p. 1, carried the detailed story.

playing space, so that most of the games were played at Osburn and Mullan. Local patriotism and the miners' gambling spirit put heavy stakes on these baseball games. However, even more money was bet upon horse races which were held frequently on a quarter mile "straightaway" track at Osburn— probably the only location on the South Fork where so long a straight stretch could be found. At one famous race held on a Sunday afternoon, October 25, 1891, William H. Stokes' "Dollie" carried off a prize of $1,000, while about $10,000 changed hands in private wagers among the five hundred spectators.[20] Boxing matches enlivened the long winter season and gave amusement to the men in the camps. Wallace, in the spring of 1890, mustered twenty-five sportsmen with interest and leisure enough to organize a rod and gun club and to prepare traps east of town for regular shooting.[21] Probably half the population of Shoshone County fished and hunted without the formalities of a club.

The intellectual life was not neglected in the larger camps. Elementary schools existed and gave elaborate public programs.[22] Newspapers appeared weekly under able editors. Wallace led in this field in 1890 with two weekly journals, the *Wallace Press,* Democratic in politics and edited by Adam Aulbach, and the *Wallace Miner,* Republican and edited by the brothers A. J. and J. L. Dunn. Wardner had its *Wardner News,* Mullan its *Mullan Tribune,* and Osburn its *Coeur d'Alene Statesman.* On the North Side the *Coeur d'Alene Sun* appeared weekly at Murray. There was also considerable travel in and out of the district. The railroads gave cut rate excursions to Spokane, Helena, Missoula, and also brought in throngs of visitors from those cities on similar excursions. Upon one of these excursions the people of Wallace erected at the corner of Sixth and Bank Streets a pyramid of ore with samples from almost every mine in the district, to the great delight of the visiting excursionists.[23]

Some important events occurred in 1890—important to the Coeur d'Alenes —which should be considered at the beginning of this historical study. First, Idaho became a state by action of Congress and President Harrison on July 3, 1890, a circumstance which gave occasion for a double celebration the following day. In October the first state government was elected. It was Republican in party complexion. George L. Shoup, of Salmon City, headed the slate as governor. Shoup's personal friend, Norman B. Willey, of Warren, Idaho County, became lieutenant governor. When the legislature met in December, that body sent Governor Shoup to the United States Senate, and Norman B. Willey became the governor who had to deal with the Coeur d'Alene crisis in 1892. In Shoshone County the local government also housed a Republican majority. Two notable exceptions were Richard A. Cunningham, sheriff, and W. S. Sims, coroner, both of whom were to figure prominently in forthcoming events. At Washington, D. C., in March, 1891, President Harrison made two appointments of vital significance. He named James H. Beatty, of

[20] *Spokane Review,* October 28, 1891, p. 7.
[21] *Ibid.,* April 16, 1890, p. 9.
[22] *Spokane Review,* October 14, 1891, p. 7, reported 730 pupils in the schools of Coeur d'Alenes, distributed as follows: Wardner 230, Wallace 139, Kellogg 108, Burke 56, Kingston 53, Mullan 52, Murray 31, Osburn 23, Littlefield 22, Delta 16.
[23] *Ibid.,* August 26, 1891, p. 3.

Hailey, the judge of the United States Circuit Court for the District of Idaho, and Joseph Pinkham the United States marshal for Idaho.[24]

Congress in the summer of 1890 passed two laws which exerted a favorable influence upon the mining industry in the Coeur d'Alenes. On July 14 came the Sherman Silver Purchase Act which authorized the Secretary of the Treasury to buy 4,500,000 ounces of silver each month. Under this act, government purchases of silver would aggregate $50,000,000 annually, whereas under the Bland-Allison Act the figure lay somewhere within the limits of $24,000,000 to $48,000,000. The Sherman Act was supported by almost every senator and representative from the western states regardless of party, and it was considered by many to be merely a step on the way to the free and unlimited coinage of silver—a solution dear to the heart of the mining West. On October 4, President Harrison signed the McKinley Tariff Act which carried among its thousands of provisions a duty upon lead ores imported into the country. The lead ore provision was directed principally against Mexican lead-silver ores, and it gave the Coeur d'Alene mines a valuable protection.

On Sunday, July 27, 1890, the town of Wallace burned to the ground with the loss of the entire business district and most of the residences. This fire was not the first destructive blaze in the district,[25] nor the last, but it was one of the worst. Block after block of wooden buildings flamed to the sky, while the town reservoir soon ran dry and left the fire fighters helpless. Fortunately, only one life was lost.[26] The Wallace fire is significant because it demonstrates the vitality of the district at that early date. Smoke had not yet ceased to rise from the ruins before piles of new lumber appeared on the ground and the process of rebuilding had commenced.[27] Wallace declined, courteously but proudly, all offers of money and supplies from outside the district. Her neighbor towns, particularly Mullan, Osburn, and Wardner, rushed to her aid. The cash subscription raised at Osburn ran to a total of $1,297 and was headed by Simeon G. Reed, chief owner of the Bunker Hill and Sullivan mine, in the sum of $500. It also carried substantial contributions by John Hays Hammond, Victor M. Clement, and other prominent citizens.[28] Mullan raised $600 in cash within twelve hours of the outbreak of the fire.[29] From Mullan and Wardner relief crews raced to burning Wallace with railroad flatcars loaded with fresh baked bread, fresh cooked hams and roasts, and a thousand gallons of steaming coffee. The records say that the Mullan men arrived first, as they should have done, since the distance is less and all down hill. Even with these advantages they beat the Wardner men by only a small margin.[30]

[24] Henderson, Shiach and Averill, *An Illustrated History of North Idaho*, pp. 1021-1022, tabulates conveniently the election returns of 1890 in Shoshone County on national, state, and county tickets.
[25] Wardner had suffered a disastrous fire on January 4, 1890, in which 25 buildings burned with losses estimated at close to $70,000. *Spokane Review*, January 5, 1890, p. 1.
[26] *Ibid.*, July 29, 1890, p. 1.
[27] *Spokane Review*, July 30, 1890, p. 1.
[28] *Ibid.*, July 31, 1890, p. 6.
[29] *Ibid.*, August 1, 1890, p. 7.
[30] A really thrilling story of open-hearted generosity, as related in the *Spokane Review*, August 1, 1890, p. 7. A certain Frank Smith, of Mullan, hiked from Wallace to Mullan after the fire, cooked all Sunday night, rode back on the flatcar and served food all Monday morning.

In the fall of 1890 the miners of the Coeur d'Alenes organized four local miners' unions, and in the middle of December they gave to the district the first rumbling of impending industrial warfare when they went on strike at the Tiger mine at Burke. Before the summer of 1891 had passed, the whole mining district had become conscious of the miners' unions and their varied activities.

Also in the middle of December, 1890, the Wallace National Bank closed its doors, thereby giving local business men who were just recovering from the fire another serious setback. Worse even than the tie-up of deposits was the effect of this failure upon mining. Warren Hussey, cashier of the bank, was also chief owner of the Morning mine at Mullan. The mine was tied up in the bankruptcy proceedings and closed down. The Morning mine, one of the largest and richest of the Coeur d'Alene mines, was destined to remain idle for over a year.

Despite the threat of labor trouble and the unfortunate collapse of Hussey, however, the outlook for the Coeur d'Alenes seemed rosy indeed at the beginning of 1891. The *Spokane Review* in its special New Year issue described with rapture the great mines and their unlimited wealth now to be poured out upon a happy populace and to be spent quite liberally in Spokane. With only a slight exaggeration the *Review* speaks of 3,000 miners and $1,000 a day dividends in the big mines.[31] A day later, however, the *Review* carried another comment on the Coeur d'Alenes which stands in vivid contrast to the optimistic holiday "blurb." Mr. Alfred M. Esler, manager of the Helena and Frisco Mining Company, had just learned that the men in the Badger mine had struck for higher wages for carmen and shovelers underground. In his indignation Mr. Esler gave to the press a statement characteristic of his peppery nature and one bearing a portentous prophecy for the future. "The greatest thing we have to contend with now," said Esler, "is the miners' union !"[32]

[31] *Spokane Review,* January 1, 1891, pp. 9, 11, 31. For years this newspaper made a practice of issuing a special number on New Year's Day devoted to the booming of the city and its adjacent region and industries.
[32] *Ibid.,* January 2, 1891, p. 5.

3

Miners' Unions
in the West

THE MINERS' UNION which A. M. Esler declared "the greatest thing we have to contend with now," although a recent organization in the Coeur d'Alenes, was not a new phenomenon in the West generally. For more than twenty years, since 1867 in fact, a miners' union had existed continuously at Virginia City, Nevada. Leadville, Colorado, had a vigorous union of miners in 1879. And a year before this last date, the Butte City, Montana, Miners' Union was organized.[1]

So significant in the history of the Coeur d'Alene labor struggle is the part played by the Butte Miners' Union that a brief consideration of that union is pertinent at this point. In the summer of 1878, an attempt was made at Butte to lower the wages of miners in certain mines, particularly in the Alice and the Lexington mines. On June 13, 1878, a small group of indignant miners, under the leadership of A. C. Witter, organized the first union of workingmen in Butte, in order to oppose this wage cut. With a nucleus of 115 union members, a strike was organized and carried through to a successful termination.[2] Then and there—at Butte, Montana, and late in the summer of 1878—a wage scale was drawn up and accepted by both parties to the dispute which would pay $3.50 a day to all men working underground.

After achieving its initial success the miners' union at Butte might have rested upon its laurels and quietly disintegrated. But such was not the case. Under energetic leaders the union built up its membership and undertook a constructive line of activities. At its third anniversary celebration in 1881, the Butte Miners' Union had 800 members.[3] Twelve years later, in 1893,

---

[1] These dates and a few details upon each organization are found in *A Report on Labor Disturbances in the State of Colorado, from 1880 to 1904, Inclusive,* 58th Cong., 3rd S., S. Doc. 122 (Washington, Government Printing Office, 1905), p. 35.

[2] *The Weekly Miner* (Butte, Montana), June 11, 1878, p. 8; June 18, 1878, p. 5; July 30, 1878, pp. 4, 5. Also *The Weekly Miner,* June 17, 1879, p. 5, for a retrospective article a year later. And *The Miners' Voice* (Butte, Montana), I, 6 (June, 1935), p. 1, a historical article entitled "Our Anniversary."

[3] *The Daily Miner* (Butte, Montana), June 14, 1881, p. 3. The union had organized originally as the Butte Workingmen's Union and had admitted mechanics and other workers. In 1881, however, it had reorganized as the Butte Miners' Union and limited its membership to those who worked underground.

there were 4,600 dues-paying members,[4] and it was acknowledged to be the most powerful organization of laborers in the West. From initiation fees, regular dues, special hospital dues, and other sources of income, the union built up a large fund from which hospital care, sick benefits, and burial expenses were provided for members who fell sick, were injured, or died while at work. Every year, on the thirteenth of June, the union miners took a holiday, paraded the streets of Butte and marched to the heights of Walkerville in an impressive demonstration of strength. The annual anniversary ball given by the union on the evening of the same day became a social event of prime importance, so much so, indeed, that the Union Hall could not contain the throng.[5]

The Butte Miners' Union did not confine its activity to maintaining the $3.50 wage scale and offering social services to its members in Butte. It carried on, in addition, a sort of missionary campaign throughout the mining regions of the West. Wherever Butte miners went to work they spread the gospel of unionism, and whenever the opportunity arose new miners' unions came into existence. Thus, to the Butte union can be traced the origins of the miners' unions in other Montana camps, such as Philipsburg,[6] Granite, Barker, and Castle, and also those in the Wood River district of Idaho,[7] and still later the Coeur d'Alenes.

At this point one may inquire why the necessity for miners' unions in the camps of the West. The obvious reason at Butte, as given above, was the maintenance of a favorable wage scale. But back of the wage question lay a fundamental and formidable problem—the tyranny of the corporation. The utility of the corporation in large scale and complex lode mining has already been pointed out. Useful and necessary as were the organization and financial power of the corporations, these institutions brought with them serious abuses. In the mining camps the company-owned store was often the only store, so that the miners were obliged to buy their food and clothing and other supplies from the company and at the company's prices. Unmarried miners were often obliged to live and eat at the company bunkhouse and boarding house. In some of the camps the companies owned and operated saloons. These adjuncts of the mining corporation frequently laid a heavy and unfair toll upon the miners and their families. And often, it must be admitted, the grievance lay not upon the corporations as corporations, but rather upon the personal greed of the individual managers, who collected a private dividend over and above the legitimate profit for the company. At any rate, the company store, boarding house, and saloon became issues against which the miner's unions fought.

A still more sinister phase of corporation activity was the false economy practiced by ambitious mine managers in their efforts to produce profits. No one can deny the pressure put upon a manager by a board of directors and

---

[4] *Anaconda Standard* (Anaconda, Montana), May 19, 1893, p. 8.
[5] The anniversary celebrations can be followed in the Butte newspapers which carried large advertisements and long accounts of the annual event.
[6] According to *The Weekly Miner*, October 8, 1878, p. 5, the Philipsburg miners' union was organized only four months later than the Butte union.
[7] James H. Hawley, in his *History of Idaho, the Gem of the Mountains* (Chicago, The S. J. Clarke Publishing Company, 1920), p. 244, gives an interesting though rather vague account of miners' union activity on Wood River in May, 1884. The Wood River unions, according to Hawley, were organized by Butte miners.

a big group of stockholders residing outside the mining district and clamoring for dividends upon their investments. Hence came the pressure for lower wages. In their efforts to trim expenses and produce dividends, many managers skimped upon essential safeguards of life and limb. Insufficient timbering would be provided, and the result—a cave-in of the tunnel with injury and perhaps death to a miner or group of men. It cost money to operate the ventilating fans which kept the air circulating in the stopes and tunnels where men were working with dynamite. Let the manager cut down on the operation of the fans and gas poisoning resulted. Pneumonia from exposure in wet places and miner's consumption (silicosis) from breathing rock dust in dry places—these were hazards which the miner had to risk and to which the mining companies gave little concern. When the company provided a doctor, he was likely to be one whose services could be had for a small retaining fee and who worked hastily and carelessly upon his patients.

Toward the mining community the corporation was often patronizing or defiant, according to whichever technique seemed more effective in obtaining desired results. An example of each attitude is easily found in the period of this study. In Wardner, Idaho, the Bunker Hill and Sullivan company dominated the community and won the good will of the town government by granting special privileges and by dispensing other favors. The town fire bell was suspended from one of the company's tramway towers. Also, the company provided both a lot and a building for the meetings of the town fire company and the town council.[8] Citizens whose interests were not identical with those of the corporation resented these favors, viewing them as the exertion of undue influence upon the town government.

At Butte, Montana, a city ordinance prohibited the open roasting of copper ores, which formerly had covered the town with noxious sulfurous fumes, and required all smelters to do their roasting in kilns provided with smokestacks at least seventy-five feet high. In December, 1891, the Boston and Montana company began roasting its ores in the open, pouring a terrific smudge over the town. Within forty-eight hours, fifteen deaths had occurred and many citizens were confined to their beds; at least some of these casualties were due to the fumes. The city got an injunction against the company; the citizens in mass meeting demanded relief; finally, the mayor ordered a gang of one hundred men to pour sand upon the smoking heaps of ore until the fires were snuffed out.[9]

In the face of these evils growing out of corporation mining, the majority of experienced and bona fide miners in more than one camp came to realize that only through organization, through cooperation together, and through united opposition when opposition was necessary, could their condition be improved. The maintenance of high wages, the breaking down of the corporation's commercial monopoly, the protection of life and limb while on the job, the proper care of sick and injured, and the decent burial of the dead—these were the ideals of miners' unionism and the mainsprings of union activity.

---

[8] A Wardner dispatch in the *Spokane Review*, April 6, 1892, p. 2, reveals these and other details of the close relationship of corporation and community.
[9] *Spokane Review*, December 15, 16, 17, 1891, front page news dispatches from Butte.

As the miners associated together in the quest of these objectives the social and fraternal aspects of unionism began to develop—dances, parties, parades, etc.—until eventually the Union Hall became the center of community life.

With the realization of some of their aims, such as high wages, or safe conditions—often after a long and bitter struggle against the corporation—the union miners generally felt that all who enjoyed the benefits obtained by union activity should pay for them. Hence came the demand that all the miners in the camp join the union. Since the improvement came as the result of united action, perhaps by united suffering, the man who would not join the union, pay his dues, and support the union in its next crisis, was considered a "sponge," disloyal to his fellow workers and to the community, and unworthy of association. This feeling explains many a dark and mysterious event wherein otherwise admirable miners were escorted to the limits of the camp and sent on their way with a warning never to return.[10]

---

[10] This analysis of the case against the corporation and of the union reaction comes not from the reading of specific references, but from long discussions with veteran miners in scattered localities in the mining Northwest. Among those interviewed were Jerome J. Day and John Wourms, of Wallace, Idaho; Edward Boyce, of Portland, Oregon; J. A. Harrington, of Boise, Idaho; Timothy Nolan, of Butte, Montana.

4

Miners' Unions of the Coeur d'Alenes

The first miners' union in the Coeur d'Alene district was organized at Wardner on November 17, 1887. Of this pioneer union little is known because it was organized secretly and likewise carried on most of its activity secretly. The reason for such secrecy lay in the antiunion policy of the Bunker Hill and Sullivan mine where union organizers and union members were discharged whenever their identity became known. In the winter of 1887-88, the union miners at the Bunker Hill and Sullivan mine led a strike against that company and partially defeated a scheme to reduce wages. Miners' wages were restored to $3.50 a day, but carmen and shovelers were to be paid only $3.00 a day.[1] Following this early strike at the Bunker Hill and Sullivan mine, a distinction continued to exist between miners' and muckers' wages throughout the district, the figures remaining $3.50 and $3.00 per day respectively.

As the big lead-silver mines of the South Fork were developed late in the 1880's, conditions favorable for unionism began to appear in the mining camps. The evils associated with corporation mining began to be experienced and resented. In Burke the only stores were those of the Tiger and Poorman mines, where in addition to monopoly prices the miners were charged a one percent discount on their pay checks. These checks were drawn on the Old National Bank of Spokane, and the company preferred to follow this check and discount system rather than carry a cash balance of $30,000 a month for the payroll. Gem and Wardner also felt the extortion of the company store. In Burke a suit of gum (waterproof rubber) clothes, necessary for all miners

[1] This information regarding the Wardner union comes from a paper by Edward Boyce, entitled *The Crime of the Century—Worse than Siberian Cruelties under the American Flag,* 56th Cong., 1st sess., S. doc. 25 (Washington, Government Printing Office, 1900), pp. 1-2. Also, in a letter dated August 18, 1936, Mr. Boyce named the Wardner union's first officers: Tom Butler, president; Dan Condon, vice-president; Dan Kennedy, secretary; Patrick O'Rourke, treasurer. Boyce had been a member of this early union.

who worked in wet mines, such as the Tiger and the Poorman, cost $19 or
$20 in the company store, whereas in Butte under free competition an identi-
cal suit sold for only $11. Residents of Burke often bought large quantities
of staple foods, such as flour, sugar, and potatoes, in Spokane and had deliv-
ery made under cover of darkness in order to escape the high prices of the
company store. Every large mine in the district—and several small ones,
too—had its boarding house and bunkhouse where the unmarried miners were
obliged to live. A room in the bunkhouse cost $8 a month, and the meals in
the boarding house cost $1 a day.[2]

A series of accidents in the mines, some of them fatal, occurred in 1890,
at the Empire State, Frisco, Gold Hunter, and Last Chance mines.[3] At the
same time, considerable philosophic discussion appeared in the newspapers of
the district over the security of the miner and the justice of his compensation.
One writer, in considering the prospector, said:

> . . . These are the men who pave the way for capital. They toil in winter snows
> and under the blazing sun of summer, and too often their reward is not com-
> mensurate with their great service to capital and the world.[4]

Another contributor expressed this view:

> The frequent and fatal accidents that befall the unhappy laboring man from
> time to time, in mines and upon the railroad, leads us to express the conviction
> that the laborer and the poor man are not always given a fair deal in this free
> republican commonwealth. As civilization reaches a higher plane and wealth in-
> creases, respect for the laboring man seems to diminish, and little care is taken
> to shield him from danger and discomfort.[5]

The result of the increasingly serious situation and of the humanitarian
agitation was a powerful drive for union organization in all the camps of the
Coeur d'Alene in the fall of 1890. Gem and Burke organized in October, and
Mullan in November.[6] The old union at Wardner was revived. Union leaders
from Butte were reported to have participated in this work, but no names of
organizers have come down to the present day.[7] These men probably did their
work secretly and consciously avoided publicity. Within a few months almost
all of the underground workers of the Coeur d'Alene camps were enrolled
in the four miners' unions.[8]

These local unions professed themselves to be voluntary associations of
underground miners whose purposes were the maintenance of high wage

[2] Information on company stores and boarding houses comes from newspaper interviews given
by Thomas O'Brien to the *Spokane Review,* May 13, 1892, p. 1, and the *Anaconda Standard,* May 29,
1892, p. 8.
[3] *Spokane Review,* April 1, 1890, p. 12; April 5, 1890, p. 6; July 27, 1890, p. 2; December 23,
1890, p. 7.
[4] *Ibid.,* April 18, 1890, p. 10, from a feature article on the mines of Canyon Creek.
[5] *Ibid.,* September 16, 1890, p. 4, portion of an editorial copied from the *Coeur d'Alene Statesman*
of Osburn.
[6] These dates were given by Thomas O'Brien in his affidavit dated May 27, 1892, and filed before
the United States Circuit Court in and for the District of Idaho, in the case of *The Coeur d'Alene
Mining and Concentrating Company versus the Miners' Union of Wardner et al.* filed in the office of
the clerk of the United States District Court (northern division) at Moscow, Idaho. Hereafter all
references to materials in this file will be labeled U. S. Moscow file 7. O'Brien's affidavit is 16 pages
(typewritten) in length, exclusive of exhibits.
[7] A. M. Esler, owner of the Frisco mine, asserted that the Coeur d'Alene unions were organized
by Butte union miners, in statements printed in the *Spokane Review,* December 13, 1890, p. 3, and
January 2, 1891, p. 5. However, Edward Boyce in his letter of August 18, 1936, denied that either
Butte leaders or Knights of Labor men were active in organizing the Coeur d'Alene unions.
[8] *Spokane Review,* March 11, 1891, p. 3, a report copied from the *Mullan Tribune.*

standards, the care of the sick, injured, and deceased, and the mutual improvement of the industry and of society. In actual operation the local unions in this early period of their activity were somewhat like lodges. There were frequent meetings, many officers, and a few secret ceremonials, such as the initiation of new members and the use of passwords and grips. The union constitutions and bylaws provided specific regulations for the handling of union funds; there were a treasurer, a financial secretary, a financial committee of three, and a board of five trustees in each local union.[9]

The preamble to the constitution of the union voices the objectives of that organization:

> Whereas, experience has taught us [the miners of the Coeur d'Alenes] that the dangers to which we are constantly exposed, are unfortunately, too fully verified by the serious and often fatal accidents that occur in the mines, and that Benefits in many of these cases are positively necessary; and whereas, "The Laborer is worthy of his hire," proportionate to the dangerous and laborious nature of his employment; and that it is as much to the interest of the Stockholders in mines in the Coeur d'Alenes to retain experienced labor as for the miners to receive their just recompense; and whereas, an organization, having for its objects the maintenance of the principles and the dissemination of the knowledge of "practical experience" in mining, is not only a benefit to its members, but to the community generally, therefore, that these ends may be attained, we have resolved to form an association having for its motto, "Justice to all— live and let live"— and pledge ourselves to be governed by the following Constitution and By-Laws.[10]

On New Year's day, 1891, a central union organization was set up in Wallace. The official title of the group was the Central Executive Committee of the Miners' Union of the Coeur d'Alene. It consisted of eight members, two delegates from each of the four local unions (Gem, Burke, Mullan, and Wardner), and chose its own president and secretary. At the organization meeting the constitutions and bylaws were made uniform for all the unions, were reduced to writing and signed by the eight delegates: George A. Pettibone, W. H. Luddy, P. C. Sullivan, Daniel Crowley, W. N. Dunn, J. J. Tobin, R. R. Williams, and William Powers.[11] The purpose of the central committee was to coordinate the activities of the local unions and to manage all common enterprises, such as the administration of sick benefits, and the establishment of the miners' union hospital. A year later when the strike and lockout crisis became serious, it was the central committee which directed the union policy and line of action.

The first activity of the new miners' unions, after mustering sufficient strength, was to strike for the Butte scale of wages, $3.50 per day for all men working underground, a scale which had existed in the Coeur d'Alenes, also, before 1887. In the winter of 1890-91, strikes occurred in several mines, separately and apparently independently. The Tiger at Burke was the first to feel the union attack, on December 11, 1890; the Frisco on January 1,

---

[9] Information on the early unions comes largely from O'Brien's affidavit in U. S. Moscow file 7 (see note 6 above, p. 36). Included as an exhibit is a complete copy of the constitution and by-laws of the miners' union, 13 pages (typewritten) in length.
[10] Page 1 of the constitution, U. S. Moscow file 7.
[11] These names were appended to the copy of the constitution and by-laws, p. 12, U. S. Moscow file 7.

1891; the Black Bear on May 13; the Granite on July 21; the Custer on July 22.[12] At other mines the demand for equal wages for muckers and miners was granted without recourse to the strike. By the middle of 1891, all the mines in the district except those at Wardner had agreed to the union scale of wages.[13]

Early in the new year (1891) the miners' unions began to be active upon a project dear to their hearts, a miners' union hospital. The treatment of sickness and injuries which occurred in the camps and in the mines was a much more serious problem in the 1890's than it is now. Industrial compensation laws were not then in existence, and the provisions made by the mining companies for emergency treatment were generally unsatisfactory. Most of the companies collected a "hospital due" of $1.00 per month from each man working underground. With this fund the company retained a doctor and equipped some sort of first aid infirmary. But complaints were universal that the doctors were hasty and careless and the first aid equipment inadequate.

So the union decided to care for its own sick and injured, and asked the mines and the communities to assist their efforts. The central executive committee, after wavering a few weeks between Osburn and Wallace, in April, 1891, chose its hospital site at the east end of Wallace close to the railroad junction at the mouth of Canyon Creek.[14] This was considered a central location easily reached by rail from all the camps of Canyon Creek and the Mullan area, and only twelve miles from Wardner. In emergencies, injured miners could be placed upon handcars or flatcars and taken rapidly down either canyon to the hospital by no other motive force than gravity. A spacious three story brick building with a mansard roof was planned, and the contracts let, totaling $40,000.[15] While waiting for the new building, the hospital got under way in the old American House (hotel) at Wallace on May 6, 1891, under the management of Mrs. Sarah Welch of Mullan.[16] In July, Mrs. Welch and her assistants were released and the actual operation of the hospital was entrusted to the Sisters of Providence.[17] This Roman Catholic sisterhood has remained in control of the hospital ever since, and the institution is now known as the Providence Hospital.

Funds for the building and operation of the hospital came from three sources. Contributions from citizens, mining companies, and communities gave an initial fund; then regular funds of the unions were drawn, these funds raised by $5.00 initiation fees and $1.00 per month regular dues; finally the "hospital due" of $1.00 per month from all miners and employes, including nonunion men, came directly to the hospital trustees.

To administer the hospital a special committee of five trustees was provided by the miners' union. One trustee was to be chosen by each of the four local unions; the fifth trustee was to be selected from among the ranks of

[12] *Spokane Review,* December 13, 1890, p. 3; January 2, 1891, p. 5; May 17, 1891, p. 5; July 23, 1891, p. 3; July 25, 1891, p. 5.
[13] O'Brien's affidavit.
[14] *Spokane Review,* April 15, 1891, p. 4; April 16, 1891, p. 8.
[15] *Ibid.,* June 13, 1891, p. 8.
[16] *Ibid.,* May 9, 1891, p. 2.
[17] *Ibid.,* July 19, 1891, p. 7.

the mine managers. The inclusion of a mine manager on the board of trustees was not merely a friendly gesture on the part of the union; it was an evidence of genuine cooperation in the enterprise, for many of the mining companies had contributed to the building fund, and the mine owners in general were satisfied with this solution of the sickness and injury problem.[18]

In slightly over a year between the opening of the hospital and May 25, 1892, 327 patients were cared for at the expense of the union.[19] Some of these cases were of serious injuries received in the mines, e.g., that of Con Herrington, caught in a cave-in at the Hunter mine,[20] and of Martin Quinn who fell ninety-five feet when a rope broke in the Union mine at Burke.[21] Others were of a very minor and even frivolous nature, such as that of Tom George who dislocated his wrist while wrestling one Saturday night at Mullan.[22] The miners' union hospital was undoubtedly a credit to the community and to the union, for even the Mine Owners' Association, in spite of its denunciation of everything else the union did, praised the hospital.[23]

Closely allied with the hospital service was the work of the union in providing sick benefits and burial rites for its members. The union regulation allowed a sickness or accident benefit of $10.00 per week for a maximum of ten weeks in any one year, the payments to begin one week after the incapacity occurred. In cases of extremely grave injury the benefits could be extended an additional five weeks by a special vote of the local union. Miners who were members of the Butte or Granite (Montana) unions could also participate in the benefits, after being admitted to good standing in any one of the local unions. When a miner died without means for a funeral, the union would provide a funeral and appropriate $90 for a burial benefit. If no competent relative of the deceased were at hand to conduct the funeral, the president of the local union was authorized to act in that capacity, and he was to be compensated for any work he lost in such duty at the rate of $3.50 a day from the union funds—miners' wages, no more.[24] In the first year and a half of the unions' existence they disbursed $3,875.55 in sick benefits, and paid out $2,598.45 in burial services for thirty deceased members.[25]

In each of the union camps, Miners' Union Halls were erected in 1891 and 1892. These union halls were large two or three story structures with at least one assembly room big enough to accommodate a crowd of two hundred or more. Generally they were the only halls in the mining camp capable of housing a public meeting; in Gem and Burke, at least, there were no other assembly halls. Not only were union meetings held in the union hall, but also dances and parties and public school entertainments and boxing spectacles and what not. At these functions the whole community participated, and the

---

[18] The organization of the hospital trustees described by O'Brien in his affidavit. *Spokane Review*, April 24, 1891, p. 8, and April 29, 1891, p. 5, describe meetings at Wallace to organize such a board of trustees.
[19] O'Brien's affidavit.
[20] *Spokane Review*, May 19, 1891, p. 2.
[21] *Ibid.*, September, 16, 1891, p. 2.
[22] *Ibid.*, December 3, 1891, p. 7.
[23] The mine owners' statement of March 26, 1892, which is discussed in Chapter VIII.
[24] These provisions are written in the by-laws of the union, filed with the constitution as exhibits with O'Brien's affidavit.
[25] O'Brien's affidavit.

union halls came to be centers of community life. A few reports have survived the passage of two score years to testify to the merry times in the union halls. On October 19, 1891, the Gem union gave a "first grand anniversary ball in their new hall," which a throng attended and enjoyed.[26]

The Mullan Miners' Union gave its maiden ball on November 20. A special train arrived in Mullan at 8 p.m. bearing about three hundred "well dressed women and robust miners from Wardner, Wallace, Burke, Gem and Osburn." The reporter characterized the affair as "the largest, best conducted, most orderly dance ever given in Mullan."[27]

Also at the union halls would be held political meetings, citizens' mass meetings, and all sorts of public gatherings. In the labor crisis of 1892 a great deal of confusion arose as to which were union meetings and which were citizens' meetings. And truly, there was only a fine line of distinction between the two. In a mining camp such as Burke or Gem, who were the citizens? Three-fourths of them were miners and the rest tradesmen or saloon keepers who depended upon the miners' patronage. Where would the citizens meet? In the Miners' Union Hall. Who were likely to be chairmen and leaders in a citizens' meeting? Probably the same citizens who were officers and leaders in the miners' union.

The Fourth of July, 1891, was a glorious union holiday. At the big district celebration, held at Wardner, the four local unions marched in the parade as union groups for the first time. The impression which the marching miners made upon a newspaper reporter must have been a vivid one, for his account reads:

> ... It was a grand sight to observe these magnificent looking miners march with military precision headed by the "Fighting Fourth" military band [from Fort Sherman]. . . . A more orderly or intellectual looking body of men could not be found within the bounds of the United States than these Coeur d'Alene miners.

Later in the day hard rock drilling teams representing the local unions competed in friendly rivalry. And at night the holiday dance was given under the auspices of the Wardner Miners' Union.[28] Surely, no resident of the Coeur d'Alenes could be unaware of the existence and of some of the activities of the miners' unions after July 4, 1891.

[26] *Spokane Review,* October 21, 1891, p. 8.
[27] *Ibid.,* November 22, 1891, p. 9.
[28] *Ibid.,* July 11, 1891, p. 6, a full and lyrical account of the whole day's gaudy events.

5

The Union Takes
the Bunker Hill

ONLY ONE important mine in the Coeur d'Alene district held out against the miners' union wage scale at the time of that Fourth of July celebration, 1891. That was the Bunker Hill and Sullivan at Wardner. And at the very time of the unions' dramatic parade in Wardner, a chain of events had already started which was to result in the Bunker Hill's adherence to the union scale.

The situation at Wardner was interesting. Although the hills about the town were honeycombed with tunnels and the ground piled with waste dumps, and although several important mines had been developed, such as the Last Chance, the Sierra Nevada, the Tyler, and the Stemwinder, all this development was decidedly secondary when compared with the magnitude of the Bunker Hill and Sullivan enterprise. This mine was a true "bonanza" in which the vast ore body lay in thick veins easily accessible. The location of the mine high on the hill at the head of Milo Gulch was such that the deeper deposits could be tapped by horizontal tunnels at lower levels, thus obviating the expensive procedure of vertical shafts, hoisting machinery, and continuous pumping of water.

The original locators of the Bunker Hill and Sullivan—Noah S. Kellogg (the actual discoverer), Jacob (Dutch Jake) Goetz, Harry Baer, James F. Wardner, John T. Cooper, Origin O. Peck, Phil O'Rourke, and "Con" Sullivan—realized the value of their property, but they were unable to operate so vast an enterprise on their own meager resources. In 1886, through Wardner's activity, they managed to set up a one hundred ton concentrator (the first in the district), and to make a contract with a group of Helena, Montana, mining operators who agreed to concentrate 50,000 tons of ore at $5.00 per ton. The lack of railroad transportation threatened bankruptcy for all concerned. Late in the same year, Simeon G. Reed of Portland, Oregon, bought the mine for a sum generally reported as $650,000.[1] The original owners, or at least most of them, went to Spokane, Washington, invested their fortunes in Spokane real estate, and gave that struggling town its first big boom. From the impetus of this investment, Spokane forged rapidly ahead and soon became the real metropolis of the Coeur d'Alene country, even though a hundred miles of slow travel and a state boundary lay between.

Under Simeon Reed's guidance the Bunker Hill gradually developed into a paying proposition. In 1887 the enterprise was incorporated at Portland, under the laws of Oregon, as the Bunker Hill and Sullivan Mining and Concentrating Company. In the same year Victor M. Clement, a brilliant young mining engineer with experience in Mexico and California, became manager of the mine. The narrow gauge railroad crept up the South Fork from the Mission and reached Wardner in 1887. The old concentrator was enlarged, and in 1891 a new concentrator with a daily capacity of over 400 tons of ore —twice the size of any other in the Coeur d'Alenes—was being constructed. A sensational aerial tramway carried the ore from the mine on the hillside high across town and over a ridge to the concentrator at Milo, or Wardner Junction, the site of the present city of Kellogg. About three hundred men found employment underground or in the surface works. There had been long and expensive litigation over the title to the property, but the courts had vindicated Reed's position and the mine stood ready to produce rich profits at the beginning of 1891.[2]

Simeon Reed's health was not robust, and the Coeur d'Alene climate did not improve it any. So, late in 1890, Reed disposed of his interest in the mine to a group of California and eastern capitalists headed by John Hays Hammond, already a celebrated young mining engineer of San Francisco. Some of Hammond's associates were D. O. Mills, James H. Houghteling, Edward L. Ryerson, Cyrus H. McCormick, W. H. Crocker, George Crocker, G. N. Harris, and V. M. Clement.[3] Hammond, who became president of the company in July, 1891, had its main office transferred to San Francisco where he remained in charge, making occasional visits to the mine. At Wardner, Victor M. Clement, a popular and efficient manager, continued in charge of operations. Clement had previously been associated with Hammond in Mexico. On Clement's staff were young F. W. Bradley as assistant manager, and Frank Jenkins, superintendent of the mine proper.[4] All these men, from Hammond to Jenkins, and for that matter Simeon Reed before them also, had a pride in their property, a confidence in their ability to operate it, and a contempt and bitter hostility to any interference from outside their group. They were concerned for the welfare of their employes, but in a paternalistic manner. They might be very generous to their men, but they would tolerate no dictation

---

[1] The early history of this great mine is admirably summarized in T. A. Rickard, *The Bunker Hill Enterprise* (San Francisco, Mining and Scientific Press, 1921), pp. 16-23; a clear account is also to be found in Frank R. Culbertson's article, "The Coeur d'Alene Mining District," pp. 431-435 of *An Illustrated History of the State of Idaho* (Chicago, Lewis Publishing Company, 1899), a work of composite authorship and anonymous editing.
[2] Rickard, pp. 74-76.
[3] Rickard, p. 77, for the record of these stock transactions; also John Hays Hammond. *The Autobiography of John Hays Hammond* (New York, Farrar and Rinehart, 1935, 2 vol.), I, pp. 182, 186-187.
[4] Rickard, p. 77.

from an outside group. And furthermore, the Bunker Hill was strong enough to go its way independently of its neighbor mines.

Against this citadel the miners' union laid siege in the summer of 1891, and somewhat to the surprise of the entire community emerged victorious from the conflict. The issue on which the controversy arose was the question of hospital dues. Most of the mines in the district were now withholding $1.00 per month from each employe's pay as hospital dues, and transferring the lump sum to the new miners' union hospital at Wallace. The Bunker Hill, however, continued its old practice of retaining the fund and hiring a Wardner doctor. The union miners in Wardner naturally desired to support their own hospital. Accordingly, on June 28, 1891, a written petition, signed by William Powers and J. W. Glass, union committeemen, and addressed to V. M. Clement, was presented to the company's office, requesting that the hospital dues of all employes be turned over to the miners' union hospital.[5] The petition promised that the union hospital would maintain an infirmary at Wardner to care for emergency cases.

Mr. Clement was in Portland at the time, but the petition was wired to him and he shot back a message to Bradley directing the latter to refuse the request on the grounds that not all Bunker Hill employes were union men and such a disposition of the nonunion men's hospital dues would be an injustice. Clement suggested that a vote of all the employes be taken and that the company consider the results of such a vote in determining its policy.[6]

In the middle of July a second petition was presented bearing the same request, but signed this time by a long list of employes.[7] To this petition Clement replied with a long argument against the proposition. The miners' union hospital, he said, is too far from our mine—and besides we should keep our money in our own town, Wardner. He ended, however, with an offer to put the question to a vote of the employes and a promise to abide by their decision.[8]

On August 6, the election took place. Each workman as he came on the job was presented with a ballot showing three possible votes: 1, no doctor, meaning that each man receive his full pay and the company cease providing any medical service; 2, Wardner hospital; 3, continuation of the present system, which was the hiring of a Wardner doctor by the company.[9] Union miners searched in vain for their proposition on the ballot, and then in rage at the company's trickery tore their ballots to shreds. Only two of the underground workers voted.[10] However, the unorganized mill and surface employes cast their ballots and rolled up a "majority of 93 votes" for the Wardner hospital ticket.[11] The company posted a notice in the afternoon declaring the

---

[5] This petition was printed along with several other documents in the *Spokane Review*, August 12, 1891, p. 1.

[6] Clement's reply is dated July 9, 1891. It also was printed in the *Spokane Review*, August 12, 1891, p. 1.

[7] *Ibid.*, August 12, 1891, p. 1.

[8] *Ibid.*, August 12, 1891, p. 1; also in the issue of August 9, 1891, p. 1, where it purported to be copied from the *Wardner News*.

[9] *Spokane Review*, August 12, 1891, p. 1.

[10] *Ibid.*, August 12, 1891, p. 1, in a long letter signed by Lew Roberts, president of the Wardner Miners' Union.

[11] *Spokane Review*, August 12, 1891, p. 1.

result of the election, pledging the company's support to the projected Wardner hospital, and ending with a curt statement that "all employes who do not wish $1.00 per month retained for this purpose are not only at liberty but are requested to call at the company's office for their time."[12]

The above notice further angered the union miners. The night shift of underground workers read the notice and, with the exception of four men, walked off the job.[13] A meeting gathered at the union hall, a strike was called on the Bunker Hill, and a procession of two hundred and fifty union miners marched the streets of Wardner shouting their demands. They would not go back to work until the Bunker Hill granted their request for support of the miners' union hospital, and they would not go back until the company paid $3.50 a day for all men underground.[14]

For two weeks the strike raged at Wardner. It was an effective walk-out, because not only did underground mining cease but also the concentrating mill and other surface operations had to close down for lack of ore. Feeling and excitement rose to high tension at times during the fortnight, and Sheriff Cunningham watched the situation with an anxious eye. But there was no outbreak of violence. Union president Lew Roberts led a well disciplined group, and the sympathy of the community was largely with the strikers.

The company struggled to win a victory. Manager Clement made an offer to contribute a hospital site in Milo (now Kellogg) and 50,000 feet of lumber, if the miners and citizens would furnish the rest of the equipment for the Wardner hospital.[15] The union strikers laughed the proposition to scorn. Then superintendent Jenkins attempted to operate the mine short-handed, employing what nonunion men he could get and appealing to disaffected strikers to return to work.[16] The effort failed. John Hays Hammond made a hurried trip up from San Francisco. He urged his staff to stand firm, then hastened back to California, stopping in Spokane long enough to blast the miners' union in an interview published in the *Spokane Review*.[17]

But all to no avail; the strike could not be broken. On August 21, the company capitulated and issued a statement which promised: first, to pay the hospital fees as the men desired, or to pay the wages in full; second, to pay $3.50 per day for all men underground; third, to rehire the strikers without discrimination.[18] This settlement of the strike was hailed with rejoicing by the union forces throughout the district. All the mines in the Coeur d'Alenes were now paying the union wage scale.

However, it required a little time to work out a practicable adjustment of the hospital fee problem. After several conferences between company officials and the union central executive committee, a satisfactory compact was drawn up and signed on September 24, to go into effect October first. The

---

[12] *Ibid.*, August 12, 1891, p. 1.
[13] *Ibid.*, August 14, 1891, p. 1, from a second long letter addressed "To a Generous and Justice Loving Public," by Lew Roberts.
[14] *Spokane Review*, August 9, 1891, p. 1; also the "omnibus" write-up in the issue of August 12, 1891, p. 1, already cited.
[15] *Spokane Review*, August 9, 1891, p. 1.
[16] *Ibid.*, August 14, 1891, p. 1.
[17] *Ibid.*, August 21, 1891, p. 3.
[18] *Spokane Review*, August 22, 1891, p. 1.

hospital fees from all men employed by the Bunker Hill and Sullivan were to be paid over to the miners' union hospital. In return, the central committee guaranteed to maintain a small infirmary in Wardner and have a Wardner doctor always on call in case of emergencies. The company then stood absolved from the responsibility of providing any medical or hospital services whatever.[19]

[19] *Ibid.,* September 26, 1891, p. 2, with the complete text of the agreement.

6

The Mine Owners
Organize

IN THE FACE of so broad and so successful a campaign of organization and wage strategy as was conducted by the miners' unions in 1890 and 1891, it is but natural that the mine owners should unite in defense of the privileges and profits which they enjoyed. This group of shrewd and aggressive capitalists yielded to the union as gracefully as possible when they had to yield, but resolved to yield no more. Some of the owners, such as A. M. Esler of the Frisco and John Hays Hammond of the Bunker Hill, were bad losers and expressed their indignation in the public press. The response to the miners' union's success was the organization in 1891 of a mine owners' union, the Mine Owners' Protective Association of the Coeur d'Alenes, or, as it was more generally known, simply the Mine Owners' Association, often abbreviated to M. O. A.

Exactly on what date in 1891 the association was formed remains unknown, because the group never published its minutes or its constitution—if any such formal document existed. All the members of that circle have passed from the scene; John Hays Hammond's death in January, 1936, removed the last survivor. A. M. Esler, of Helena, Montana, has been credited with being the founder of the owners' association as early as 1890, at Helena.[1] Also, many of the Coeur d'Alene mine owners, including Warren Hussey, John M. Burke, and George B. McAuley, were associated together in the Spokane Mining Exchange in 1890 and 1891.[2] Three usually reliable historians (Henderson, Shiach, and Averill), writing in 1902, date the formation of the Mine Owners' Association definitely at February 16, 1891, at Wallace, and add that it was the first such association in the United States.[3] Certainly some

---

[1] Letter from Edward Boyce, dated August 18, 1936.
[2] Something of a promotion group, organized May 20, 1890 (*Spokane Review*, May 21, 1890, p. 8).
[3] Henderson, Shiach and Averill, *An Illustrated History of North Idaho*, p. 1000. Practically all historians agree upon 1891 as the year.

organized group or committee of owners and managers met with the union representatives in April and May to set up the board of trustees for the miners' union hospital.[4] Reference to the association by name first appears in the newspapers in August, during the Bunker Hill strike.[5] And it existed for a certainty in September when the Pinkerton detective, Charles A. Siringo, was hired by the association.

Not all the mines of the Coeur d'Alenes were represented in the association. Only those which shipped ore fairly regularly to smelters outside the district could belong. This regulation cut out all mines which were merely prospects or shipped infrequently and in small quantities. Prominent mine owners, such as John M. Burke, who functioned rather as speculators or promoters than as regular producers were also barred.[6] The active members of the association were the following mines and capitalists: the Bunker Hill and Sullivan, with John Hays Hammond, Victor M. Clement, F. W. Bradley and Frank Jenkins; the Last Chance, with Charles Sweeney; the Sierra Nevada, the Stemwinder and Granite mines, all represented by George B. McAuley and Van B. De Lashmutt—the latter had been mayor of Portland, Oregon, in 1890; the Tiger, with Stephen S. Glidden and Frank R. Culbertson; the Poorman, with Patrick Clark, a much admired Montana man affectionately called "Patsy" by the Irish miners; the Helena and Frisco Company, operating the Badger and Black Bear mines and the Frisco mill, with Alfred M. Esler; the Milwaukee Mining Company, operating the Gem mine, with A. L. Gross, Amasa (Mace) B. Campbell and John A. Finch (Messrs. Campbell and Finch were also active in several smaller producing mines, such as the Union and the Standard, both close to Burke); the Custer, with C. D. Porter and Robert Porter. As to the mines in the vicinity of Mullan, the Morning and the Gold Hunter may have belonged to the association, but the former was inactive all of 1891 and part of 1892, and the latter had a very irregular record of operation in both years.

Who were the officers of the association? John Hays Hammond was reputed to be president, but he actually spent little time in the Coeur d'Alenes, and S. S. Glidden often presided at such meetings as were reported in the newspapers. John A. Finch was secretary.[7] The association met upon call of the secretary, and there seems to have been no regular meeting schedule and no regular meeting place. In the Coeur d'Alenes the Carter House at Wallace was the most frequent meeting place, while the Spokane Hotel in Spokane, Washington, was also a favorite rendezvous of the mine owners.

The avowed objectives of the association were cooperation in dealing with the railroads over freight rates, cooperation in effecting economies in the operation of mines and mills, and cooperation in dealing with the miners'

---

[4] *Spokane Review*, April 24, 1891, p. 8, tells of one such meeting in which owners and union representatives participated.

[5] *Ibid.*, August 14, 1891, in Lew Roberts' open letter "To a Generous and Justice Loving Public."

[6] *Idaho Daily Statesman* (Boise, Idaho), October 18, 1892, p. 4. These details about the owners' association were made public during the candidacy of John M. Burke for the governorship of Idaho in 1892 (See Chapter XXV).

[7] William T. Stoll, *Silver Strike* (Boston, Little, Brown and Company, 1932), p. 182. A score of references in the *Spokane Review*, in 1891 and 1892 confirm this fact. The press made no mention, however, of a definite president or a permanent chairman.

unions.[8] Within a very short time the third item of cooperation was to over-shadow both the others. To promote their policies of cooperation and to secure the best legal advice, the association early in its existence retained three lawyers: Weldon B. Heyburn, of Osburn, a mine owner in a small way himself in the Polaris mine, and acknowledged to be one of the most brilliant mining lawyers in the whole Northwest, a man destined eventually for a seat in the United States Senate; also Judge Albert Hagan, of Coeur d'Alene City, another capable lawyer with a state-wide reputation; and William T. Stoll, of Wallace, who served more or less as errand boy and handled most of the cases in the local justice courts.[9]

In September, 1891, the Mine Owners' Association took the offensive against the miners' unions by hiring a clever detective to spy upon the unions' activities and to report everything to the association. The detective was Charles A. Siringo, a Pinkerton operative from the Denver office of that agency. What the mine owners paid Siringo for his work is another un-answered mystery, but if he received his deserts it must have been a large figure. He arrived in Wallace some time in September and had a secret meeting with John A. Finch and Frank Jenkins.[10] Then he went up the canyon to Gem and secured work in the Gem mine under the name of C. Leon Allison. Only John Monahan, foreman of the Gem mine, knew his identity.[11] Two weeks after obtaining work Allison joined the Gem Miners' Union, taking the pledge of loyalty and secrecy apparently with tongue in cheek. So earnest a unionist did Allison appear that in December he was elected recording secretary of the Gem union with access to all the union records.[12] For seven critical months Siringo-Allison held this responsible position in the union, reporting all the while to the association in Wallace. In order to avoid detection he wrote out his reports in longhand, addressed them to a St. Paul, Minnesota, address, walked under cover of darkness to Wallace (over three miles) and mailed them. At St. Paul the reports were typewritten and mailed back to John A. Finch.[13] Siringo had no personal contact with his employers in that entire period. Later—in the summer of 1892—Siringo was to play a decisive role in the Coeur d'Alene labor crisis.

[8] Henderson, Shiach and Averill, p. 1000.
[9] Stoll, p. 182.
[10] Charles A. Siringo, *Riata and Spurs* (Boston, Houghton Mifflin Company, 1927), p. 158.
[11] *Ibid.*, p. 158.
[12] Siringo, *A Cowboy Detective*, p. 138.
[13] *Ibid.*, pp. 137-138.

7

The Mines Shut Down

T HE UNION MINERS' victory in the wage scale fight proved short lived. They were not long permitted to enjoy the fruits of victory. A remarkable series of accidents and litigations occurred through the late summer and fall of 1891 which interrupted mining activity and made the earning of any wages uncertain. And in the winter following, there came a shutdown of all the big mines in the district.

Wardner and Mullan were the scenes of the first sudden interruptions of mining work. The Bunker Hill and Sullivan company operated a long tramway to transport its ore from the mine to the concentrating mill. This tramline consisted of a double cable supported on high wooden trestlework towers passing directly over the town of Wardner. Along the cable buckets full of ore traveled in a continuous succession from mine to mill, returning empty or loaded with tools or supplies for the mine. One day in September the cable broke, scattering chunks of ore and fragments of the cable all over town. One bucket of ore crashed through a roof and killed a woman inside the house.[1] All work at the mine and mill was suspended until the cable could be repaired. After a few days of operation the cable broke again.[2] This time the shutdown lasted two weeks, for they had to wait for an entirely new cable to come from the East and be installed.[3] Up at Mullan the Gold Hunter mine had the same experience. Two cable breaks held up the entire workings for most of the month of November.[4]

The Wardner mines engaged in a record volume of litigation in the fall of 1891, and each suit tended to interfere with mining operations. The Last Chance and the Tyler ran into each other's workings underground, and the matter had to be taken to the United States circuit court, while all active mining was suspended in both mines.[5] The Last Chance disputed the use of

---

[1] *Spokane Review*, September 26, 1891, p. 2.
[2] *Spokane Review*, October 23, 1891, p. 7.
[3] *Ibid.*, November 3, 1891, p. 17; November 8, 1891, p. 9; both interesting accounts, revealing the magnitude of the tramway operations.
[4] *Ibid.*, November 22, 1891, p. 9; November 28, 1891, p. 5; December 2, 1891, p. 4.
[5] *Ibid.*, September 6, 1891, p. 1; October 10, 1891, p. 2; October 11, 1891, p. 10.

a water course with the Bunker Hill, and another suit resulted.[6] The Sierra Nevada also lay idle nearly all fall due to similar litigation.[7]

Some progress could be observed in the district, however. Canyon Creek worked steadily. Finch and Campbell built a big new concentrator near Wallace, and developed their Union mine near Burke into a producing property. The new concentrator operated successfully for a short time late in the fall.[8] Estimates of labor employed in 1891 in the Coeur d'Alene mines ran to 4,000 men, with a payroll of $4,000,000,[9] and the output of ore for 1891 was valued at "not less than $8,000,000."[10]

Some time in the fall of 1891—there was no public announcement of the event—the Northern Pacific and Union Pacific railroad companies raised their rates on ores transported out of the district to smelters.[11] Most of the ore was shipped to smelters at Omaha and Denver. The increase amounted to $2.00 a ton, which made the total charge on a ton of ore $16 to Omaha and $14 to Denver.[12] Freight had always been considered an expensive item in the production of the metals, and these additional rates cut $2.00 per ton off the margin of profit. The mine owners grumbled, computed their losses— Esler said it would cost the Badger one month's dividends ($20,000) a year[13]—but they paid the increased rate for awhile.

In December, however, the Mine Owners' Association took up the problem, and on about the twentieth demanded a reduction to the old rates. The owners announced that they would close their mines if the reduction were not granted by January first.[14] They would rather stop their own earnings and keep their ore reserves undepleted than work their mines out with inadequate profits. When the railroads gave a negative reply to the owners' plea, the latter, at a meeting in Spokane, set January 15 as the shutdown date.[15] On the twelfth of January the owners' association issued the definitive order closing the mines of all member companies the evening of the fifteenth.[16] That date, the fifteenth, was pay day in all the mines, and therefore a convenient day for the companies to close. A committee of four owners was also appointed to go East and reason with the railroad companies in their home offices. Messrs. Glidden, Esler, McAuley, and Clement were the committee.[17]

According to schedule, most of the big mines of the Coeur d'Alenes stood idle on the morning of January 16, 1892. Only the Sierra Nevada operated, and it by special agreement within the owners' association because it had lost so much time in litigation in the fall.[18] At the Bunker Hill and a few other big mines the concentrators continued in operation, but only until

[6] *Ibid.*, August 25, 1891, p. 7; September 3, 1891, p. 3; October 6, 1891, p. 1.
[7] *Ibid.*, December 25, 1891, p. 7.
[8] *Spokane Review*, November 26, 1891, p. 8.
[9] *Ibid.*, January 1, 1892, p. 19, from a feature article by Eugene Klein, entitled "South Fork Mines, The Greatest Silver-Lead Camp in the World."
[10] *Spokane Review*, January 6, 1892, p. 3, from the annual report (for 1891) of the Spokane Mining Exchange.
[11] *Ibid.*, December 22, 1891, p. 5, the first mention of the rate increases, in an interview given by Charles Sweeney.
[12] *Ibid.*, December 22, 1891, p. 5; Ingalls, *Lead and Zinc* in the United States, p. 165.
[13] *Spokane Review*, January 12, 1892, p. 4.
[14] *Ibid.*, December 22, 1891, p. 5.
[15] *Ibid.*, December 30, 1891, p. 5. The meeting was held the previous evening.
[16] *Ibid.*, January 13, 1892, p. 1. The order issued from Wallace.
[17] *Spokane Review*, February 3, 1892, p. 3.
[18] *Ibid.*, January 22, 1892, p. 7.

the ore bins were emptied. Small properties, not members of the association, such as the Grouse, the Argentine, and a few near Osburn, continued to mine ore as usual and to ship an occasional car load to Helena or some other smelting center. Also, at nearly all the big mines development work was undertaken and a small force of workers, preferably married men, kept at work.[19] Thus, the unemployment in the district did not approximate 100 percent by any means, yet it was serious enough. A. M. Esler estimated that 1,600 miners were cut off the payrolls,[20] while an anonymous newspaper reporter set the figure at 2,500.[21] With no immediate prospects of being rehired, and with the rigors of the Coeur d'Alene winter yet to be endured, large groups of miners and laborers left the district, scattering to Spokane, Butte, Salt Lake City, California, and other mining centers. Unmarried men and recent arrivals were the first to go. The Coeur d'Alenes settled down for a long period of depression.

Active minds, both within and without the miners' union, meditating over the stagnant situation, soon began to question whether all was exactly as it appeared on the surface. Was the railroad rate controversy the entire basis for the shutdown? Were there other motives back of the owners' action? The suspicion of a conspiracy began to arise, a possibility that the owners' association was trying to break up the labor force in the district and thus weaken the union, and then, at a favorable moment, reopen the mines at lower wages.[22] Certain of the owners had never accepted gracefully the $3.50 wage for carmen and shovelers. Van B. De Lashmutt and A. M. Esler continued, even in this January shutdown, to decry the muckers' wage scale, and in so doing lent credence to the suspicions already forming.

Late in January, George B. McAuley, De Lashmutt's associate in the Sierra Nevada and other mines, openly discussed the situation and listed three obstacles to profitable mining in the Coeur d'Alenes: low metal prices, high railroad freight rates, and high wages to labor. At least one of these factors, said McAuley, must change for the better before mining can be profitable again.[23] It did not take McAuley's auditors long to figure out which of the three factors lay most within the owners' control. Finally, early in March, an unofficial newspaper story emanating from Wardner asserted that the wage question was actually under discussion at recent Mine Owners' Association meetings, and that the association had divided sharply on the question. De Lashmutt, as was to be expected, called for lower wages; but "Patsy" Clark, "Mace" Campbell, and John A. Finch declared that they considered $3.50 not too much for men working underground.[24] And thus, a crisis in the industry caused ostensibly by high freight rates came to be expected by many to be settled by a readjustment of wages.

---
[19] *Ibid.*, January 22, 1892, p. 1.   Apparently a definite policy of the owners' association.
[20] *Ibid.*, January 12, 1892, p. 4.
[21] *Ibid.*, January 22, 1892, p. 7.
[22] Such a suspicion was voiced by an anonymous but "well known gentleman" in an interview published in the *Spokane Review*, January 20, 1892, p. 3.
[23] *Spokane Review*, January 26, 1892, p. 4.
[24] *Ibid.*, March 11, 1892, p. 5.

8

Ultimatum and Lockout

P<small>ATRICK</small> C<small>LARK</small>, of the Poorman mine, gave the first news of the settlement of the railroad rate controversy on March 15, 1892, when he talked to a newspaper reporter in Butte on his way home from the East. The railroad companies had restored the old rates, Clark announced, and the Poorman would probably be running again within 10 days. It represented a $30,000 a year victory for the Poorman, so that Clark was jubilant.[1] The majority of Coeur d'Alene residents also felt happy as the news reached them. Yet a certain apprehension lingered in their minds, and they withheld comment until the official offer to reopen the mines should come. The Mine Owners' Association gave the official word in a brief message on March 18. The railroads had conceded the old rates, announced the owners, and the mines would be reopened on April first, or sooner, if possible. Then followed the significant statement:

> ...Believing most earnestly that the advance of the wages of carmen and shovelers which was forced upon the mine owners during the past year was unreasonable and unjust, for obvious reasons, to both employers and miners, the association begs leave to announce the following scale of wages: for all miners, $3.50 per day of 10 hours; for carmen and shovelers, $3 per day of 10 hours.

The notice went on to mark a couple of exceptions to the foregoing scale. Carmen and shovelers in shaft mines would be paid $3.50 per day and so would those working in wet places in tunnel mines where gum clothing was required.[2]

The worst fears of the Coeur d'Alene community had been realized; the wage question was being thrown open in a vivid challenge to the miners' union. For three tense days people discussed the news on street corners, in saloons, in offices and stores, waiting for the reply of the central executive committee of the miners' union.

---

[1] *Spokane Review*, March 16, 1892, p. 1.
[2] *Spokane Review*, March 19, 1892, p. 8.

While this important committee is deliberating, it might be well to inspect its personnel. It was this little group of union leaders which was to direct the miners' strategy in the war the opening gun of which had just been fired. Representing the Mullan union came Thomas O'Brien, who was chosen president of the executive committee on New Year's day, 1892. O'Brien, born in 1837 in Ireland, near the town of Bantray, was already a miner in California early in the 1850's. He served in the Union army in the Civil War, and returned to mining when the war ended. He mined in Nevada, Colorado, and Montana, and came to the Coeur d'Alenes in 1889. O'Brien was an efficient miner and a lover of peace, but his faith in the justice of the miners' union cause made him a determined fighter in the crisis which lay just ahead. He was described by a *Spokane Review* correspondent as "an unpretentious, plainly dressed man, below the medium height, well built and muscular, with a rather large forehead, large brown eyes that kindle darkly when he is aroused."[3]

O'Brien's colleague from Mullan was Terrence P. Purcell, also an experienced miner, though 20 years younger than O'Brien. The delegates from Burke were Joseph F. Poynton and Patrick H. Sweeney, and the former was chosen secretary for the central committee. Poynton, though only 41 years of age, had been a miner for 20 of those years. He proved to be a capable secretary. From Gem came two younger men, Thomas Eaton, only 30 years of age, and Samuel Kellum, 38. And from Wardner, John W. Sweeney, the Wardner union president, and Quin Sullivan who had spent 18 of his 34 years in mining.[4]

On March 21, this committee's reply to the mine owners' offer was made public. It was a simple statement, short and to the point, bearing only the signature of Secretary Poynton. The miners' union, it read, could not accept the wage scale offered by the mine owners in their statement of March 18. The union, however, stood ready to return to work at the wages which prevailed before the recent shutdown.[5] Thus the gage of battle was definitely thrown down and both parties to the controversy began preparations for a long conflict. Union miners sharpened up their tools as though to go to work, but every member of the union stood firm behind the union policy. New men, drawn by the announcement of the proposed opening of the mines, drifted into the district, waiting for the actual employment to begin. The residents also waited, looking to the owners for a next move.

At a long meeting the night of March 26, in Spokane, the owners' association approved a lengthy document which was to be the explanation of their case to the public, and had it published the next morning in the *Spokane Review*.[6] The statement ran to about 8,000 words and filled six columns in the *Review*. It is unpleasant reading even today, and it must have been much

[3] *Spokane Review,* July 26, 1892, p. 1, gives a sketch of O'Brien's career, including the descriptive quotation; O'Brien's affidavit before the U. S. circuit court (U. S. Moscow file 7) also gives the facts of his life.
[4] These facts are found in corroboratory affidavits (type-written) before the U. S. circuit court (U. S. Moscow file 7), attached to O'Brien's affidavit.
[5] *Spokane Review,* March 22, 1892, p. 1, complete text.
[6] *Ibid.,* March 28, 1892, p. 5; also repeated in its entirety in Henderson, Shiach and Averill, *An Illustrated History of North Idaho,* pp. 1001-1004.

more so in 1892. The long document proved to be a tactical error, for it alienated many business and professional people who might have favored the owners' cause.[7] The first third of the statement repeats the offer of March 18, and analyzes fully the owners' case. They are opposed unalterably to the union wage scale because it pays both skilled and unskilled laborers the same. Carmen and shovelers are not skilled workers; they do not run the same risks underground as the miners; they simply are not entitled to the same pay.

The balance of the owners' statement was devoted to a denunciation of the miners' unions. There was not a word of praise for anything except the union hospital. The unions were undemocratic, being dominated by radical agitators who choked off all contrary opinion in union meetings. They were devoted to terrorism and anarchy in their policies, as, for instance, the driving of men out of the camps who refused to join the union. They had terrorized whole communities so that even independent businessmen were afraid to raise a voice in protest. The union's word was totally unreliable; and the document closed with a wager that if the union scale were continued, the miners would be demanding $4 a day within six months.

To all of the foregoing the miners' union replied on March 29 with a long document of its own, but not half so long as the owners'.[8] They answered and denied most of the charges against their organization. They took up the wage question and charged the owners with violating a covenant without consulting with one of the parties to the former agreements. Their own (the union's) wage scale was the original pay schedule in the district, so that they were actually only restoring what had formerly existed. From this the union apologists went into a defense of their equal pay system. The hazards of underground work, that is, the chances of accident or of occupational disease, were essentially the same for muckers as for miners. They denied that carmen and shovelers were unskilled; a certain degree of skill is required in any phase of mining work, and the more skilled the muckers were the better the job of mining would be done, a fact which ought to please the owners. Finally, the invention and adoption into use of automatic machine drills, whereby one machine miner can do the work of five or six hand drillers, have forced many skilled miners to take employment as muckers, and their valuable experience is an asset to the mine and should be rewarded.

While this debate was being waged in the press, miners' union members and friends were busily at work crystallizing public opinion in the district into a position sympathetic to the miners' cause. The owners' statement had antagonized many persons who had been rather unconcerned in the controversy heretofore. A series of big mass meetings were held in the towns of Wallace, Burke, Gem, Mullan, and Wardner in the week following the owners' statement.[9] Crowds of three and four hundred gathered at each meeting,

[7] *Spokane Review*, March 31, 1892, p. 6, an editorial condemns it as "too dogmatic and combative a document [with which] to begin a controversy;" *ibid.*, April 1, 1892, p. 3, quotes a prominent mining capitalist who deplored the "suspicion of trickery" which the document raised.
[8] *Spokane Review*, March 30, 1892, p. 1, prints the document in its entirety; so do Henderson, Shiach and Averill, pp. 1004-1005.
[9] Accounts of these meetings and generally the resolutions passed thereat were published in the *Spokane Review*, March 27, 1892, p. 6 (Wallace); March 30, 1892, p. 2 (Burke and Gem); March 31, 1892, p. 1 (Mullan and Wardner).

all classes of the community being represented—with the possible exception of the mine owners themselves. Some prominent businessman usually acted as chairman. Speeches on the present crisis would be delivered by union representatives and businessmen. Finally, in a burst of enthusiasm, resolutions would be presented and passed—usually unanimously—condemning the mine owners' selfish policy and pledging support to the union cause. At Mullan the enthusiasm was so great that the resolutions were passed not only unanimously but with "three cheers and a tiger."[10] The resolutions were printed in the newspapers, and they, together with a flood of letters to the press, give evidence that considerable public opinion—probably a good sized majority—existed in sympathy with the miners.

April first came and went without any mine opening. In fact, the one remaining association mine, the Sierra Nevada, closed when the new wage schedule went into effect and the union men walked out.[11] But on April 5 there appeared a significant notice from the mine owners. The earlier offer to resume work was therewith recalled; the mines would remain closed until June first; in June "certain and speedy means" would be taken to reopen the mines.[12] This was a lockout directed against the union, and it was immediately recognized as such by the union leaders.[13] Any doubt of the owners' motives was soon dispelled by the remarks of individual owners, such as Esler and McAuley, who declared that the association had resolved never to hire another member of the miners' union.[14]

Throughout late March and early April, certain well-intentioned friends of peace kept urging a conference between representatives of both sides in the hope that a solution could be evolved. The Spokane newspapers took up the idea of a conference.[15] Enough pressure was finally brought to bear upon the leaders of both sides that a conference was called and met in Wallace on April 7. It accomplished nothing.[16] John A. Finch, in speaking of the meeting later, said, "The miners had nothing to offer."[17] An unnamed Mullan miner who had been present said that T. P. Purcell had asked Finch, "Suppose we, the miners of the Coeur d'Alenes, concede your terms are you ready to resume operations?" The answer was said to have been, "No. There would have to be a full representation of the association here for me to answer that question, and all are not present."[18]

[10] *Spokane Review*, March 31, 1892, p. 1.
[11] *Ibid.*, April 2, 1892, p. 2.
[12] *Spokane Review*, April 6, 1892, p. 1, complete text.
[13] Thomas O'Brien denounced it as such in his affidavit before the U. S. circuit court (U. S. Moscow file 7).
[14] As reported in the *Spokane Review*, April 12, 1892, p. 3; May 10, 1892, p. 3; *Anaconda Standard*, April 23, 1892, p. 1; May 29, 1892, p. 8.
[15] *Spokane Review*, March 31, 1892, p. 6, an editorial.
[16] *Ibid.*, April 8, 1892, p. 1.
[17] *Spokane Review*, April 10, 1892, p. 5.
[18] *Ibid.*, April 19, 1892, p. 7.

9

The Beginning of
the Long Crisis

T HE MONTH of April, 1892, in the Coeur d'Alenes was a period of mar-
shalling resources by both sides in preparation for a long siege of industrial
warfare. A few preliminary skirmishes were fought without altering the
situation. The few men still employed about the mines in development work
were asked to quit the union or quit the job, and they quit the job. This
scene was enacted at the Standard mine, a Finch and Campbell property, late
in April.[1] At other mines, such as the Sierra Nevada, nonunion men remaining at work were individually induced by union pickets to walk off their
jobs.[2]

When the union canvassed its resources the first important item to attract
attention was the big decrease in its membership. From a possible maximum
of 2,000 members, the roll had now dwindled to 800, who were for the greater
part married men and permanent residents of the district.[3] The single men
and the drifters had gone out since the January shutdown. The membership,
by April, though diminished in number, made up a compact force determined
to win its fight.

In addition to the support of the citizens' mass meetings, as expressed
in resolutions, the union could count upon certain more tangible forces in
the community as its allies. First, the press. Adam Aulbach's *Wallace Press*
and T. K. Jerome's *Mullan Tribune* were staunch champions of the union
cause. Every week these papers ran off a fresh edition of editorial and news
material calculated to bolster up the union morale and win support to its side.
Within the county government, friendly consideration could be expected from
Sheriff Richard A. Cunningham and his chief deputy—called "undersheriff"
—Jack K. Waite. Cunningham had been the "miners' man" in the election of
1890, and he respected the votes which had elected him. If any deputizing

[1] Thomas O'Brien's affidavit (U. S. Moscow file 7), the date of this incident being given as April 22;
also *Anaconda Standard*, April 23, 1892, p. 1.
[2] As stated in affidavits of William M. Pipkin and George L. Wolf (typewritten ms.) dated May 7,
1892 (U .S. Moscow file 7).
[3] *Spokane Reveiw*, May 13, 1892, p. 1, an interview given by Tom O'Brien.

were to be done, those deputies would likely be working men.[4] Then, in three of the towns, Gem, Mullan, and Wallace, justices of the peace who were openly sympathetic to the union held court and sat in judgment over misdemeanor cases. These justices were George A. Pettibone at Gem, who had been a member of the central executive committee the year before, W. H. Frazier at Mullan, and A. E. Angel at Wallace. The justices of the peace had the power to deputize constables in any serious breach of the peace.

Outside the district, the union began to marshal the forces of organized labor in its behalf. Working through trades and labor assemblies and the labor press, and appearing in person before mass meetings, the union leaders told their story before audiences aggregating tens of thousands. Powerful committees were set up in Spokane and Portland partly to solicit relief funds and supplies and also to discourage and deflect "scab" labor from entering the district.[5]

However, the center to which the Coeur d'Alene unions looked for most help was, naturally, Butte, Montana. About April 14, a delegation of union leaders, including Tom O'Brien, Joe Poynton, and George Smith (successor to Pat H. Sweeney as Burke delegate to the central committee), arrived in Butte.[6] They appeared before the Butte Miners' Union and the Silver Bow Trades and Labor Assembly. This assembly voted them its full support and urged the individual unions to contribute to the relief fund.[7] Some of these unions took up collections; one of them, the Carpenters' Union of Butte, raised $75.[8]

The Butte Miners' Union, however, undertook the major responsibility in supporting the Coeur d'Alene miners. This big parent union, at a meeting on April 20, voted an immediate loan of $5,000 to the Coeur d'Alene unions, and then proceeded to assess itself $5 per month per member for as long as the crisis should last. The Granite Miners' Union and the other small miners' unions in Montana were advised to do the same—and "advice" from the Butte union was equivalent to a command. The membership of the Montana miners' unions was estimated at 6,000, so that the monthly relief fund to the Coeur d'Alene miners would approximate $30,000.[9] Gabriel M. Dallas, familiarly called "Gabe" Dallas, recording secretary of the Butte Miners' Union, was appointed chief liaison officer, and departed with a committee to make an inspection of the Coeur d'Alene situation at first hand.[10] Later in the month, Dallas delivered the $5,000 loan in currency to Tom O'Brien, and took a ten-year mortgage upon the union halls in the district in behalf of the Butte organization.[11]

---

[4] At least such were the charges repeatedly made by mine owners, e.g., A. B. Campbell in an affidavit before the U. S. circuit court, dated April 30, 1892 (U. S. Moscow file 7); and Messrs. Finch, Campbell, Esler, McAuley, Glidden, Clark, and Clement in a letter to Governor Willey, dated June 1, 1892, copy of which (carbon copy) is filed in U. S. Moscow file 7.
[5] *Spokane Review*, May 28, 1892, p. 5, for Spokane activity; June 28, 1892, p. 2, for Portland.
[6] *Anaconda Standard*, April 15, 1892, p. 6.
[7] *Ibid.*, April 16, 1892, p. 3.
[8] *Anaconda Standard*, April 21, 1892, p. 2.
[9] *Ibid.*, April 21, 1892, p. 2.
[10] *Ibid.*, April 23, 1892, p. 1.
[11] A copy of the mortgage was filed as an exhibit before the U. S. circuit court (U. S. Moscow file 7). The mortgage was signed by M. T. Kemmer (Gem), George M. Glover (Burke), Tom O'Brien (Mullan), and J. W. Glass (Wardner); it was witnessed by Justice of the Peace W .H. Frazier; dated April 22, 1892; and recorded April 30, 1892. The loan bore no interest.

At Wallace the union set up a central depot and warehouse for supplies. President O'Brien took charge personally of the distribution of foodstuffs and other supplies. In the camps, local committees handled the goods and distributed them to the miners' families from the union halls.[12]

On the other side of the battle line, the Mine Owners' Association was likewise active through the month of April. However, its deliberations were held behind closed doors and its decisions received no fanfare of publicity. There were frequent meetings of the association, generally in Spokane, but the proceedings of those sessions became public only through the chance remarks of individual members. The mine owners had considerable support for their cause in Wallace, Wardner, and Osburn, and even a few sympathizers in Mullan. But in regard to Gem and Burke, Patsy Clark was not far wrong when he said, "We have not a friend in the camp."[13] The *Wallace Miner* and the *Wardner Barbarian* (successor to the *Wardner News,* and edited by "Brig" Young and William Brown) gave firm adherence to the owners' position.

It became obvious, however, that the owners had only two alternatives: to make peace with the union, or import nonunion labor.[14] Toward the union there was no disposition to make concessions; indeed, several of the owners spoke more belligerently than ever. Esler said, on April 20, "We will never hire another union man."[15] In regard to the second alternative, certain difficulties appeared insoluble: armed protection would probably be necessary to guard nonunion workers; the sheriff and other peace officers of the county could not be depended upon to provide such protection; and it was a violation of the constitution and statutes of Idaho to bring an armed force into the state.[16] The owners' problem was one of winning the support of the state and federal governments; their chief resource was their wealth which should enable them to outlast the miners in a protracted contest.

---

[12] First mention of this distribution system appeared in the *Spokane Review,* May 11, 1892, p. 2; *Anaconda Standard,* May 11, 1892, p. 1.

[13] *Spokane Review,* May 7, 1892, p. 1.

[14] *Spokane Review,* April 5, 1892, p. 8, a clear analysis of the situation by a *Review* correspondent at Wardner.

[15] *Anaconda Standard,* April 23, 1892, p. 1.

[16] *Spokane Review,* May 7, 1892, p. 1, an interview given by Patrick Clark in Butte.

10

Injunctions

O<small>N THE</small> twenty-ninth of April, four men went to work in the Hidden Treasure tunnel of the Union mine in full view of the town of Burke.* This spectacle produced great excitement among the inhabitants of that camp, particularly among the union miners. An informal group congregated at the union hall to talk over this unusual development. From the group a committee of five men, not all miners, but headed by John J. Tobin, president of the Burke Miners' Union, climbed the trail to the mine with the intention of questioning the men at work, while some 50 or 60 others straggled along behind. The workmen, miners, it appeared, had been hired by Amasa B. Campbell at $3.50 a day; they were not members of the miners' union, and did not care to join the union. "You had better come down into town and tell everybody about it," advised Tobin, and the four workmen took the advice, picked up their coats, their tools, and their lunch buckets, and walked down the trail into Burke.

A citizens' meeting gathered at the union hall. About 150 men were present, three-fourths of whom were miners, and the rest townspeople, storekeepers, saloon keepers. Even a mine owner was present, namely Frank R. Culbertson, manager of the Tiger mine, who stood and watched the proceedings "just out of curiosity." John Tobin presided over the meeting and put the question, "What shall we do about the men who have come to work against the dictates of the miners' union and citizens?" The men were called upon to tell their story. Then they were given an opportunity to join the union and be supported by union relief just as the locked-out members were being supported. Two of the men agreed to join the union, but the other two, whose names were William M. Pipkin and George L. Wolf, rejected the offer and claimed their right to work for whomever they pleased, for whatever wage they pleased independent of miners' unions or any other organization.

Pipkin's speech did not please the citizens of Burke, and when the chairman's question was repeated the answer came, "Send them up the canyon!" A second opportunity to join the union was offered the two men, but they declined again. With a cry of "Burke is no place for scabs!" the

_____
* See pictorial section.

citizens in a body escorted Pipkin and Wolf to the upper edge of the town, and a small delegation accompanied the pair a couple of miles on the road toward the Montana summit and Thompson Falls. The two men had no food with them and had to cross the snowy summit before they could eat again. Down in Wallace, "Mace" Campbell learned of what had happened to his employes. He found undersheriff Jack Waite and demanded that the latter go rescue the victims. In the absence of a warrant or a written complaint or any written statement, Waite refused to make any arrests, but he went to Burke anyway and found everything quiet.[1]

This incident at Burke played directly into the mine owners' hands. Indeed, it is possible—as was later charged[2]—that those men were sent to the Union mine for the express purpose of creating an "incident" upon which legal action could be taken to break the deadlock. At any rate, Amasa B. Campbell, accompanied by lawyers W. B. Heyburn and Albert Hagan, and fortified with affidavits by Pipkin and Wolf, appeared in the United States Circuit Court for the District of Idaho, at Boise, Idaho, on May 7 and asked for an injunction against the unions.[3] The Coeur d'Alene Mining and Concentrating Company, which owned the Union mine and of which Campbell was president, was a corporation organized under the laws of the state of Washington, and was therefore legally a citizen of Washington, and could sue in the federal court. Judge James H. Beatty promptly issued an order upon the defendants asking them to appear in the court at Boise on the sixth of June to show cause why a provisional injunction should not issue. The defendants were the Miners' Union of Wardner, Idaho, the Miners' Union of Gem, Idaho, the Miners' Union of Mullan, Idaho, the Miners' Union of Burke, Idaho, the Central Miners' Union of Shoshone County, and about 120 persons individually named. The complainant corporation posted a $2,000 bond payable to the defendants as damages in case the court should rule the complaint to have been wrongfully made. That bond was furnished by Messrs. James A. Pinney and E. K. Eastman, prominent businessmen of Boise. In the meantime, that is between the date of the complaint (May 7) and the appearance of the defendants in court to show cause (June 6), a temporary restraining order was placed upon the defendants. They were restrained and enjoined from trespassing upon the complainant's properties and from interfering in any way with the mining operations of the complainant. Emphatic prohibition was made against intimidation or threats of violence upon employes of the complainant.[4]

United States Marshal Joseph Pinkham hurried north from Boise to serve the injunctions upon the unions and the individuals named as defend-

---

[1] These three opening paragraphs relating the incident at Burke are a careful synthesis of a large mass of evidence; two newspaper reports, *Spokane Review*, April 30, 1892, p. 2, and *Anaconda Standard*, April 30, 1892, p. 1; and affidavits (typewritten mss.) in U. S. Moscow file 7, by Amasa B. Campbell (April 30, 1892), William M. Pipkin, and George L. Wolf (May 7), Thomas O'Brien (May 27), John Tobin (May 25), Jack K. Waite (May 24), George A. Pettibone (May 23), William M. Pipkin, again (June 10), and Frank R. Culbertson (June 20).

[2] In O'Brien's, Tobin's, and Pettibone's affidavits, cited in note 1.

[3] *Idaho Daily Statesman*, May 11, 1892, p. 8.

[4] *Coeur d'Alene Mining and Concentrating Company versus the Miners' Union of Wardner, Idaho, et al.*, U. S. Moscow file 7. This file contains the following original documents: the affidavits of Campbell, Pipkin, and Wolf; the complete list of the defendants; the restraining order; and the bond signed by Pinney and Eastman.

ants. The original complaint of A. B. Campbell, plus the affidavits of Pipkin and Wolf, plus the restraining order of Judge Beatty made up the full copy of the injunction, and Marshal Pinkham's grip bulged with 200 copies of the long document. Now the boundaries of the state of Idaho are so inconsistent with the state's topography that Marshal Pinkham had to travel through Oregon and Washington in order to go from Boise in southern Idaho to Wallace in the northern part of the state. And although the news of Pinkham's departure reached Wallace long before that gentleman arrived, the contents of the legal papers he carried had not been made public. So a crowd of some 500 curious citizens thronged the Union Pacific station at Wallace on the eleventh of May when Pinkham arrived. The marshal smiled mysteriously and shouldered his way through the crowd to the Carter House where he conferred with his deputies, Harvey Harris, Robert M. Dryden, and W. C. Human.[5]

On the next day the service of the injunctions began. The miners' union officials determined not to resist the serving of the papers. On the contrary, the unions cooperated with the marshal by calling union meetings in all the camps, at which Pinkham or his deputies appeared and served the injunctions. At Mullan the union made a holiday of the affair and had a band at the union hall to serenade the marshal.[6] At Burke even more fun was had. Secretary Poynton of the central committee accompanied the marshal up the canyon. As Pinkham finished his business the Burke miners gave "three big cheers for Marshal Pinkham," and the marshal responded by flipping a $20 gold piece into the air and calling, "Set 'em up for the boys!"[7] Pinkham had been a miner; he came from Hailey in the Wood River mining district; and he was considered a "good scout."

Within a couple of days all the known officers and most of the prominent members of the unions had been served with copies of the injunction. Also, a few nonunion men had been enjoined, including Sheriff Cunningham, lawyer Walter Jones, and editors Adam Aulbach and T. K. Jerome.[8] The defendants were busy reading and studying the document and devising means of answering the charges. Clearly, legal advice was needed. Accordingly, Walter Jones of the Wallace law firm of Jones and Harkness was retained by the central committee.[9] At the same time, Frank Ganahl and Campbell W. Bushnell, Spokane lawyers and former residents of the Coeur d'Alenes, were also employed by the union.[10] Ganahl was said to have boasted that he could break the injunction and would do so for $5,000.[11] The union apparently heeded his boast and gave him a chance to make good.

---

[5] *Spokane Review*, May 12, 1892, p. 1. Pinney and Eastman.
[6] *Spokane Review*, May 15, 1892, p. 2.
[7] *Anaconda Standard*, May 13, 1892, p. 1.
[8] *Ibid.*, May 14, 1892, p. 1.
[9] *Ibid.*, May 14, 1892, p. 1.
[10] *Ibid.*, May 14, 1892, p. 1.
[11] *Anaconda Standard*, May 14, 1892, p. 1.

11

Armed Guards
and "Scabs"

O N THE fourteenth of May the union miners of the Coeur d'Alene came
to realize the full meaning of the federal injunction, and thereupon all the
holiday and festive events associated with the long document ceased. The
suspicion that the owners would attempt to operate the mines with nonunion
labor had long been entertained.[1] On the morning of the fourteenth, a dispatch from Missoula, Montana, notified the people of the Coeur d'Alenes
that a trainload of such miners under the protection of armed guards was
just leaving westbound over the Coeur d'Alene cutoff. "Joe" Warren was reported to be in command of over 50 guards, escorting somewhat less than
100 "scabs" into the district.

At Wallace the stir of new excitement penetrated all corners of the town.
A certain John Graham made a complaint before Justice A. E. Angel, charging Joel Warren and 54 other persons unknown by name with bringing an
armed force into the state of Idaho to suppress local disorder. Judge Angel
promptly issued a warrant for the arrest of Joel Warren et al. and placed it
in Sheriff Cunningham's hands.[2] Joel Warren was well known in the Northwest, a prominent detective who had been chief of police in Spokane in 1890.
A large and boisterous crowd gathered at the Northern Pacific station awaiting the arrival of the train. Sheriff Cunningham rode a horse across the station platform, brandishing the warrant in his hand and forcing the crowd
back from the tracks.[3]

With a roar and a whistle the train approached down the valley of the
South Fork. Then, greatly to the chagrin of the waiting multitude, at the
junction at the east end of town the train took the switch without stopping

---

[1] Such a conclusion could be deduced from the owners' lock-out statement, April 5, 1892; also from
remarks by Patrick Clark in *Spokane Review*, May 7, 1892, p. 1, and a sextet of owners (Clark, Campbell, Clement, Culbertson, Esler, and McAuley), in *ibid.*, May 13, 1892, p. 1.
[2] The original complaint and the original warrant, along with other documents are filed at the Shoshone County court house, Wallace, Idaho. The District Court, First Judicial District, in and for Shoshone
County, Idaho, *The State of Idaho versus Joel Warren.* Hereafter the contents of this file will be cited as
Idaho Wallace file 92.
[3] Charles A. Siringo, *Riata and Spurs*, pp. 160-161, for this picturesque detail.

and roared up Canyon Creek toward Burke at a speed of 25 miles per hour. J. G. Boyd, Northern Pacific agent, had thrown the switch himself.[4]

Without a stop the train ran to Burke and came to a halt at the trail leading to the Union mine. There the guards and nonunion miners disembarked. It was easy to distinguish guards from miners, for the former carried rifles and wore blue ribbons on their hats. Up the trail the group marched, Joe Warren and a man later identified as Charles Sweeney, owner of the Last Chance mine, leading the way. At the company boarding house the group halted. The miners were moved quickly into the tunnel; the guards loafed in the boardinghouse, their rifles hidden from view; and deputy United States marshal Harvey Harris stationed himself at the entrance to the company's property with a supply of injunction papers to serve on anyone who came up the trail.

Late in the afternoon Sheriff Cunningham arrived on horseback, still flourishing his warrant. No one else was permitted to pass the deputy marshal. Cunningham arrested Joe Warren, but none of the guards, since he found no one armed and could not tell guards from miners. Down the trail went the sheriff and his prisoner, down into Burke where they were surrounded by a shouting mob of indignant union miners. Shouting was the extent of the mob's action, however, for the men heeded the exhortation of both sheriff and union officers not to commit any violence. Warren was taken to Wallace, arraigned before Judge Angel, and released immediately upon $2,000 bond, provided by Charles Sweeney.[5] Ten days later he was tried before Judge Angel and bound over to the district court, since his alleged offense was a felony. Once again he was released on bond, this time in the amount of $2,500, and signed by George B. McAuley and Frank R. Culbertson.[6]

Little by little the details of the owners' coup became known. Joe Warren, who claimed Idaho citizenship and a residence in Kootenai County,[7] went to the Palouse wheat farming district of northern Idaho, as soon as the injunction had been granted at Boise. There in the Idaho farming towns of Moscow, Genessee, and Lewiston he rounded up a force of 54 guards. All were Idaho citizens; all were offered employment at $3.00 a day in the name of the Mine Owners' Association; and many of them claimed that Warren promised them that they would be deputized as deputy United States marshals.[8] The little force gathered at Pullman, Washington, May 12, and traveled by special railroad car via Spokane to Rathdrum, Idaho, county seat of Kootenai County, where they spent the night. Charles Sweeney joined the group at Rathdrum, and on the thirteenth the whole party moved east to Helena, Montana, over the Northern Pacific. They met two carloads of

---

[4] Siringo, *A Cowboy Detective,* p. 502.
[5] *Spokane Review,* May 15, 1892, p. 1; *Anaconda Standard,* May 15, 1892, p. 1; for rather full accounts of the day's events.
[6] *Anaconda Standard,* May 24, 1892, p. 1; also the documents in Idaho Wallace file 92, such as the transcript (ms.) of proceedings in the Justice court, bail bond, etc.
[7] Affidavit of Joel Warren before the U. S. circuit court, June 16, 1892 (typewritten), U. S. Moscow file 7.
[8] William B. Forsyth and E. D. McCarty, members of Warren's force, made such claims in affidavits before the U. S. circuit court, dated June 2, 1892. Warren and Charles Sweeney in their affidavits before the same court, June 16 and June 15, respectively, denied making any such promise. U .S. Moscow file 7.

miners at Helena—the nonunion men had been routed via Helena in order to avoid possible interference at Butte.

At Missoula, on the morning of the fourteenth, a special train was made up for the final lap of the trip into the Coeur d'Alenes. There were two coaches of miners, 74 in all, mostly recent immigrants from Finland, Poland, Austria, and Sweden, who had been recruited in the iron and copper districts of northern Michigan by a certain employment agent called Captain Vivian Prince, who was with the party himself. At each end of the miners' coaches stood guards with rifles in their hands. The rest of the guards occupied a separate coach where Warren and Sweeney were in charge and were distributing additional rifles, rounds of ammunition, and blue ribbons for their hats. The train stopped at Mullan because a derail switch had been opened, and while the train crew closed the switch under the protection of rifles, the miners and the guards were treated to a chorus of choice epithets from a rowdy mob of union members and sympathizers who swarmed on both sides of the track.[9]

Throughout the rest of May and June and the first week of July the nonunion miners continued to enter the district and to secure employment in the mines. They came generally in small groups without the dramatic circumstances of the first trainload. However, John Hays Hammond tells in his autobiography of an exciting ride from Tekoa to Wardner with a train of nonunion miners he had recruited in California to work in the Bunker Hill.[10] The railroad stations were always crowded with union men at train times so that the "scab" miners had to run a gauntlet of persuasion and abuse before they reached the protection of mine boarding houses. Union pickets hung close to the mining companies' property lines and harangued or taunted the workers at every opportunity.

Thus, half a dozen of the association mines operated in May and June and July: the Union, the Gem, the Badger (Frisco), the Granite, the Bunker Hill, the Last Chance, the Sierra Nevada. However, they ran shorthanded and they shipped but little ore in comparison with their normal output. Furthermore, such operation was expensive because of the cost of maintaining armed guards and also because of the frequent desertions from the mining crews to the union camp. Mine owners' estimates had 300 nonunion men at work in the association mines by June 1.[11], 500 by June 15, [12] and 800 by July 1. [13] The owners felt victory coming within their grasp.

---

[9] In addition to affidavits already cited, there was an affidavit by Jacob Grilz, one of the nonunion miners on the train, before the U. S. circuit court, dated May 18, 1892, U. S. Moscow file 7; also statements to the press by participants in the affair; Jacob Grilz and John Drenig, nonunion miners, *Spokane Review*, May 17, 1892, p. 1; Joseph Pulaski, nonunion miner, *ibid.*, May 18, 1892, p. 1; and Charles Sweeney, *ibid.*, May 19, 1892, p. 1.

[10] John Hays Hammond, *Autobiography*, I, pp. 190-191. Hammond gave an interview dealing wtih this incident to the *Spokane Review*, May 27, 1892, p. 1, which dates the expedition to Wardner as of May 21. The incident reads more thrillingly in the autobiography, however, written about forty years later.

[11] *Spokane Review*, May 28, 1892, p. 1; May 31, 1892, p. 2.

[12] *Ibid.*, June 14, 1892, p. 2, statement and tabulation by John A. Finch.

[13] *Ibid.*, July 1, 1892, p. 7.

Enter the Governor

ABOUT A WEEK after the arrival of the "scab" train, another sensation burst upon the harried community. From Boise, Idaho, in the newspapers of May 22, an alarming report told of the holdup of a Northern Pacific train at Mullan the night before. Armed men had stopped the train and had forbidden the crew to proceed.[1] A telegram from G. W. Dickenson, assistant general superintendent of the railroad, at Tacoma, Washington, addressed to Governor Norman B. Willey, complained of the outrage at Mullan and demanded military protection of the railroad's property by the state.[2] This Boise report created a furor in the Coeur d'Alene district, because no news of any such event had been received from local sources.

The good people of Mullan felt particularly outraged at the tidings from Boise. Half a dozen leading citizens, including Justice W. H. Frazier, wrote a hot telegram to the governor, denying that the alleged occurrence ever took place.[3] Besides, said they, there is no Northern Pacific train through Mullan in the night. Sheriff Cunningham also gave a statement denying the whole incident.[4] Down at Boise, Governor Willey wired Superintendent Dickenson that the matter would be investigated and that steps would be taken to protect the property and keep the road open.[5] Dickenson, however, became impatient and sent a second message to the governor asking immediate action.[6]

Probably the governor of Idaho had kept himself fairly well informed of recent developments in Shoshone County. He at least knew of the injunction secured by the Coeur d'Alene Mining and Concentrating Company in the circuit court, and he probably had read of the importation of nonunion men.

---

[1] *Spokane Review,* May 22, 1892, p. 1; *Idaho Daily Statesman,* May 22, 1892, p. 5.
[2] Dickenson's telegram, dated May 21, published in *Idaho Daily Statesman,* May 22, 1892, p. 5, and *Spokane Review,* May 25, 1892, p. 1, did not charge that an armed force had stopped a train, although the newspaper reports cited in note 1 did so state. Dickenson said merely that "parties at Mullan are boarding our trains and interfering with our passengers, and preventing our train crews from the proper performance of their duties."
[3] *Spokane Review,* May 24, 1892, p. 2.
[4] *Ibid.,* May 24, 1892, p. 2.
[5] *Idaho Daily Statesman,* May 22, 1892, p. 5; *Spokane Review,* May 25, p. 1. Complete text of Willey's message in both papers.
[6] *Idaho Daily Statesman,* May 24, 1892, p. 5, complete text not given.

However, this telegram of Dickenson's was the first direct plea to the governor to take a hand in the labor crisis. On the twenty-second of May Willey determined to go north and investigate the situation himself. So, after dispatching a brief telegram to Senator Shoup, in Washington, D .C.,[7] Governor Willey took the morning train for Spokane on May 23. Accompanying the governor on this trip was James F. Curtis, of Boise, who held the position of inspector general in the Idaho National Guard[8]—a man destined to play an important role in the Coeur d'Alene drama before two months were gone.

At Spokane on the twenty-fourth the governor was met and entertained by prominent mine owners. He sat in a box at a theatrical performance that evening with Mr. and Mrs. S. S. Glidden.[9] This association was not remarkable, because Willey had been, and, in fact, still was, something of a mine owner himself in the Warren district of the Salmon River country. After another day in Spokane, the governor proceeded to Wallace, arriving on the afternoon train on the twenty-sixth.

Wallace gave Governor Willey a rousing welcome. A big crowd lined the Union Pacific platform and cheered the governor's arrival. A band played, and after the governor had been installed at the Fuller House, the band continued its serenade there.[10] Willey and Curtis remained four days in the district, alternating between Wallace and Wardner. The governor conferred at length with county officials, with prominent mine owners, and also with the officers and attorneys of the miners' unions. Mullan, Gem, and Burke decorated their streets and made elaborate plans to entertain Governor Willey, but they were doomed to chagrin and disappointment; the governor went no farther east than Wallace. Mullan felt particularly grieved that the governor did not come to view the scenes of the alleged violence which had been the cause of his trip in the first place.[11]

On the thirtieth, Willey was back in Spokane, en route to Boise. All along the journey he had spoken with great discretion of the labor situation, favoring neither one side nor the other. At Spokane he announced himself as satisfied with the situation. He rejoiced that no violence had occurred and he felt hopeful that everything would work out all right. The governor apparently considered the controversy simply a dispute over wages, and one which would eventually be settled by compromise.[12]

Before leaving the Coeur d'Alenes, Governor Willey apparently asked some of the leading mine owners to make a summary of their case in writing. Under date of June 1, 1892, such a letter was written and signed by John A.

---

[7] This brief message, not important in itself, forms the first item in a series of 84 telegrams and letters dealing with the Coeur d'Alene labor crisis sent and received by the Idaho delegation in Congress. Items in this file will be cited as *Congressional Dispatches*. This same telegram also forms the first item in another collection of documents, the telegrams and messages sent by Governor Willey, 101 in number, and hereafter to be referred to as the *Willey Collection*.
[8] The Idaho National Guard, though it had been created by an act of the state legislature on March 14, 1891, had not yet completed its organization. No regimental colonel had yet been chosen, and Inspector General J. F. Curtis shared with Adjutant General E. J. Curtis the highest offices in the organization.
[9] *Spokane Review*, May 25, 1892, p. 1.
[10] *Spokane Review*, May 28, 1892, p. 1.
[11] *Ibid.*, June 3, 1892, p. 2.
[12] *Ibid.*, May 31, 1892, p. 2; similar remarks to Boise reporters, as printed in the *Idaho Daily Statesman*, June 5, 1892, p. 8.

Finch, V. M. Clement, George B. McAuley, A. M. Esler, S. S. Glidden, A. B. Campbell, and Patrick Clark. This letter ran to six pages and summarized the charges of the owners against the union.[13] It was probably this letter which served as the basis for Governor Willey's proclamation of June 4, which commenced with the phrase, "Whereas, it has come to the knowledge of the executive of this state by the affidavits and petitions of reputable citizens and property owners of the county of Shoshone . . . ."

The governor's proclamation, dated June 4, went on to charge the existence of unlawful association of men conspiring to disturb the peace of the county, and it called upon such unlawful assemblage to disband. It also urged a strict obedience to the law, and it threatened to invoke martial law in case violence broke out.[14]

A storm of disapproval and dissatisfaction swept the district upon the publication of the governor's proclamation. The owners were mildly dissatisfied because it did not denounce the miners' union by name and because it did not actually declare martial law. Union leaders and members felt that they had been unjustly attacked, although a few hair-splitters took the proclamation and interpreted the "unlawful association of men" to mean the Mine Owners' Association. Mass meetings in Mullan, Wallace, Burke, and Gem denounced the proclamation and passed fiery resolutions condemning the governor for taking a partisan view of the crisis.[15] Mullan, Burke, and Gem reiterated their disappointment that the governor had not made a thorough investigation of the Coeur d'Alenes—in other words that he had not come in person to Mullan, Burke, and Gem.

Governor Willey took the trouble to answer the letters and resolutions of the Mullan and Burke citizens. In a letter dated June 10, he advised the men of Mullan to consider one statement in the proclamation seriously and personally, namely, the admonition to all citizens to obey the law and preserve the peace. If they did so, all would be well; but if violence flared, then "a declaration of martial law and a file of soldiers will speedily follow it." The governor's letter to Burke citizens, dated June 13, carried a similar message.[16]

What actually happened at Mullan on May 21? A careful sifting of all the evidence indicates that nothing of any gravity occurred. Citizens of Mullan—union miners and sympathizers—had adopted the practice of running through the passenger coaches of Northern Pacific trains as they stood at the Mullan station en route from Missoula to Wallace. These citizens would quickly look over the passengers and try to spot any probable nonunion miners coming into the district. They would send word ahead to Wallace by

[13] Included (carbon copy) as an exhibit with the affidavit of Campbell, McAuley, Sweeney, and Clement, dated June 16, 1892, before the U. S. circuit court, U. S. Moscow file 7.

[14] The original copy of Governor Willey's proclamation lies in the governor's vault in the state capitol, Boise, Idaho. Another perfect copy with original signatures, seals, etc. is filed with the mine owners' affidavit (cited in note 13 above), U. S. Moscow file 7. Copies were printed in the newspapers, *Idaho Daily Statesman,* June 5, 1892, p. 8; *Spokane Review,* June 5, 1892, p. 1.

[15] *Spokane Review,* June 8, 1892, p. 2, Mullan; June 9, 1892, p. 5, Gem and Burke; June 11, 1892, p. 8, Wallace.

[16] Both letters (carbon copies) are preserved in the correspondence files in the governor's vault, state capitol, Boise, Idaho. Hereafter, all letters from these files will be referred to simply as *Governor's.* The Mullan letter is addressed to W. H. Fraser, M. T. Wright, A. W. Steele and 184 other citizens. The Burke letter is addressed to George M. Glover. The letter to the Mullan citizens was printed in the *Idaho Daily Statesman,* June 11, 1892, p. 5; and *Spokane Review,* June 11, 1892, p. 8.

telephone or telegraph so that union pickets would be sure to be posted. These volunteer traffic inspectors undoubtedly caused the train crews inconvenience, and delayed their departures for Wallace.[17] A report on these incidents evidently was sent to Superintendent Dickenson and he wired Governor Willey. The holdup story apparently originated with the political news reporter on the *Idaho Daily Statesman* who first wrote up the incident after reading the Dickenson telegram. His story was copied in the *Spokane Review.*

Nevertheless, despite the flimsy basis of this railroad sensation, the situation at Mullan was recognized to be full of hazards. Some of the Mullan citizens who were boarding Northern Pacific trains and searching for guards and "scabs" were believed to be deputy sheriffs or deputy constables. On the other hand, the armed guards were believed by many to be deputy United States marshals. "What would happen," asked an *Anaconda Standard* correspondent, "if a deputy sheriff tried to arrest a deputy marshal?" This same newspaper man went to great length to convince his readers that the crowds at the Mullan railroad station were perfectly orderly, sober, law-respecting citizens, but his question remained unanswered to plague the worried minds of the Coeur d'Alene residents.[18]

What results followed Governor Willey's visit to the Coeur d'Alenes? There were no immediate results beyond the proclamation and the public reaction thereto. However, in the long run, a benefit accrued to the mine owners. They had had a chance to meet and talk to the governor personally; they had occupied the majority of his time at Wallace, Wardner, and Spokane. Their policy from thenceforth was to put constantly increasing pressure upon the governor to convince him that violence was imminent and that martial law was the only solution. The master technician in this campaign of pressure was Weldon B. Heyburn, chief attorney for the Mine Owners' Association.

Therefore, it is extremely interesting to observe the role played by the state and federal governments in the Coeur d'Alene struggle from this point on. Little by little, the state government and the state's representatives at Washington, D. C., were won over to the support of the mine owners' cause, until finally, in the July crisis, the entire machinery of the state power plus the military arm of the federal government were exerted in the owners' behalf. Selig Perlman, distinguished historian of American labor, comments upon the role of the government, thus:

> Beginning with a violent clash between miners and mine owners in the silver region of Coeur d'Alene, Idaho, in the early 90's, the mining States of the West became the scene of many labor struggles which were more like civil wars than like ordinary labor strikes.
>
> A most important contributing cause was a struggle, bolder than had been encountered elsewhere in the United States, for control of the government in the interest of economic class. This was partly due to the absence of a neutral

---

[17] This is the explanation by union apologists as published in *Anaconda Standard*, May 23, 1892, p. 1, and *Spokane Review*, May 27, 1892, p. 1. The same view was advanced by Inspector General J. F. Curtis in an interview upon his return to Boise, *Idaho Daily Statesman*, June 2, 1892, p. 8.

[18] *Anaconda Standard*, May 29, 1892, p. 8, a brilliant feature article entitled "The Big Strike," signed C.H.E.

middle class, farmers or others, who might have been able to keep matters within bounds.[19]

And in a more recent work, Perlman, in collaboration with Philip Taft, concludes:

> . . . We have seen government virtually giving up every pretense of acting as an impartial arbiter, and serving instead as the controlled agent and even avowed spokesman of one or the other of the contending parties, more frequently of the employers.[20]

[19] Selig Perlman, *A History of Trade Unionism in the United States* (New York, The Macmillan Company, 1922), p. 213.
[20] Selig Perlman and Philip Taft, *Labor Movements, 1896-1932* (vol. IV, *History of Labor in the United States*) (New York, The Macmillan Company, 1935), p. 189.

13

Union and Community in Crisis

MAY AND JUNE, 1892, were a period of vital activity and high nervous tension in the Coeur d'Alenes. The entire community was stirred to its profoundest depths by the economic conflict which rapidly approached its crisis. The tactics of the mine owners have already been revealed—lockout, injunctions, operation with "scab" labor, and pressure upon the governor. In the same period the miners' union activities were just as significant. And the position of the business group in the district was also of first importance.

"Peaceful persuasion" was the union's answer to the owners' importation of labor.[1] The various activities which came under the heading of peaceful persuasion would probably be classified as picketing in more modern terminology. Union members and sympathizers met all trains entering the district. They swarmed around the suspected "scabs" as the latter stepped out of the cars. The union men would try to isolate the new arrivals, that is break up any group, surround the individuals, and start talking to them. As the nonunion workman struggled away from the station toward a mining office or boarding house the union pickets stayed with him and continued their harangue, all of which was directed toward persuading him from going to work and to winning him over to the union point of view. When unsuccessful in converting the newcomer at the time of his arrival, the process of peaceful persuasion followed the workman to his job. Pickets posted themselves close to the mining properties at Gem and Wardner, whence they talked and argued with all workers who passed within earshot.[2]

Not all of this picketing was as peaceful as the phrase would suggest. Occasionally arguments arose, scuffles occurred, the pickets "ganged up" on

---

[1] *Anaconda Standard,* May 13, 1892, p. 1, a statement of the union's policy.
[2] Detailed accounts of picketing procedures are found in the bill in equity of A. M. Esler (typewritten), dated May 26, 1892, and the affidavits of C. G. LeBlond, E. H. Blood, and Jeremiah Finnan, nonunion miners (typewritten), all dated May 24, 1892, and all presented before the U. S. circuit court in the case of *The Helena and Frisco Mining Company versus The Miners' Union of Wardner, Idaho, et al.,* U. S. Moscow file 9.

persistent nonunion men, the epithets "scab" and "son-of-a-bitch" rang out above more ethical language.[3] However, no serious injury was done to any man and no general brawls occurred; cooler heads among the union leaders always intervened in time.

The union picketing achieved considerable success. Many of the "scabs" were induced to quit their jobs or to abandon their efforts to seek jobs. Of the 74 miners brought in to the Union mine on the first train in May, about 30 quit the mine, went down into Burke, and joined the miners' union forces there.[4] Estimates varied as to the success of peaceful persuasion, but it is probable that at least 50 percent of the men who came into the district seeking work were taken into camp by the union.[5]

Union relief was most important to the men and their families whose income—never very large—had been cut off for five or six months. The central depot at Wallace and the local committees in the camps worked efficiently, so that no one suffered from hunger or exposure. Supplies to the value of $400 were distributed every day.[6] The men who had been induced to quit jobs and to join the union were provided with the same relief as those who had been locked out from the first. Many of the new "converts" were given jobs alongside old time union men cutting wood at Mullan. Tom O'Brien and Jack Lucy possessed wood ranches in that vicinity and they had obtained a $10,000 order for firewood. This wood was cut by strictly union labor at $3.00 per day. Over a hundred men worked pretty steadily on that project.[7] From time to time freight cars loaded with supplies for union relief would arrive from Spokane or Butte, and each arrival became the occasion for a celebration.[8]

Union morale, in the face of discouraging obstacles, was maintained at a fairly high level by such celebrations. There were also frequent meetings at union headquarters and often in the open street. Speeches were made by such orators as Gabe Dallas, Tom O'Brien, C. W. Bushnell, Terrence Purcell, John Sweeney, Fred Dean. The speakers rallied their auditors to the continued support of the union cause, always prophesied the eventful victory of the union, and always cautioned against a resort to violence, which, they said, would play the union into the hands of its enemies. When James Perry, a Mullan miner, died at the miners' union hospital on April 18, his funeral procession through Mullan out to the cemetery enlisted every union member who could be mustered from the entire district. The march became a demonstration of union solidarity.[9]

Publications also tended to bolster up union morale. A handbill addressed

---

[3] An example of minor violence was the case of William Linney, nonunion Bunker Hill miner, assaulted in Wardner on June 3, as reported in the *Idaho Daily Statesman*, June 4, 1892, p. 1, and in his own affidavit (typewritten), dated June 6, 1892, and filed in U. S. Moscow file 7.

[4] *Spokane Review*, May 25, 1892, p. 2, deputy sheriff Jack Waite obtained the luggage of 28 deserters upon a writ of replevin.

[5] Governor Willey estimated a majority was won over to the union side, in his remarks upon returning to Boise, *Idaho Daily Statesman*, June 5, 1892, p. 8. *Spokane Review*, May 24, 1892, p. 2, Burke dispatch says most of the men coming to Burke go over to the union; *ibid.*, June 3, 1892, p. 2, Wardner dispatch says about half go over to the union.

[6] *Anaconda Standard*, May 29, 1892, p. 8, an interview with union officials.

[7] *Anaconda Standard*, May 16, 1892, p. 1; *Spokane Review*, June 3, 1892, p. 2.

[8] *Anaconda Standard*, May 11, 1892, p. 1; May 18, 1892, p. 1; *Spokane Review*, June 9, 1892, p. 5; June 10, 1892, p. 8; July 1, 1892, p. 3.

[9] *Spokane Review*, April 27, 1892, p. 7.

to all miners and mining laborers asking them to remain outside the district until the present fight was over was composed by the central executive committee on May 19, was extensively printed, and circulated all over the Northwest.[10] The local press continued to give hearty support to the union cause. Spokane and Butte newspapers brought encouragement almost daily in the reports of sympathetic meetings and the publication of favorable resolutions and letters from neighboring communities. "The miners have almost the undivided sympathy of Southern Idaho," read a Boise dispatch, for an example.[11]

Encouraging news and florid resolutions were not the only support which the union received from outside the district. Money and provisions poured in from Butte and Spokane. Miners' unions' from as far away as Eureka, Utah, sent contributions—Eureka's was $500.[12] The work of the Spokane labor committee was particularly effective. This committee under the leadership of John Roche, T. H. Burns, and Olaf Lund collected money from trade unionists and other sympathizers, gathered foodstuffs from farmers through the Farmers' Alliance, purchased other supplies, loaded and shipped half a dozen freight cars of goods to Wallace, each car bearing a bright painted banner reading, "From the workingmen of Spokane to their brothers in the Coeur d'Alenes."[13] The Spokane committee also patrolled the railroad stations and yards on the lookout for probable "scabs" whom they tried to dissuade from going to the Coeur d'Alenes—and often succeeded in their attempts, too.[14] They reprinted the notice of the central committee and gave it still further circulation.[15] And they held mass meetings at which union leaders such as Gabe Dallas and Fred Dean appeared and spoke for the union cause.[16]

Within the district, the strain of the long continued crisis was felt sharply in May and June. All classes of society were involved in the ruinous struggle. The small group of mine owners, managers, foremen, and minor executives whose interests were bound together in the operation of the mines were boldly struggling by expensive methods to run their mines and crush the union opposition. The union miners, on their side, were existing from day to day upon the charity of their sympathizers and were fighting a determined and desperate battle. In between lay the business class which was rapidly going bankrupt from the heavy losses of trade. Even early in May, business houses began closing in Burke, Gem, Wardner, Mullan, and Wallace, and their proprietors began leaving the district.[17] Since the middle of January there had been no payroll in the larger mines, and the loss of wages to the laboring group was estimated at over $1,000,000 by the first of June.[18]

[10] Copies of the original bill were presented as exhibits before the U. S. circuit court and are on file in U. S. Moscow file 7.
[11] *Anaconda Standard*, May 17, 1892, p. 6.
[12] *Ibid.*, May 18, 1892, p. 1.
[13] *Spokane Review*, June 9, 1892, p. 5.
[14] *Anaconda Standard*, May 29, 1892, p. 1, lists three successful forays upon the nonunion ranks.
[15] Copies of the Spokane handbills are also on file in U. S. Moscow file 7.
[16] *Spokane Review*, May 28, 1892, p. 5; this account gives also the complete personnel of the Spokane organization.
[17] *Anaconda Standard*, May 11, 1892, p. 7.
[18] *Ibid.*, May 29, 1892, p. 8, estimate of F. R. Culbertson; Thomas O'Brien estimated the payroll loss at $200,000 per month, in his affidavit, U. S. Moscow file 7.

Faced with bankruptcy, the businessmen of the Coeur d'Alenes were forced to throw their sympathy to one side or the other and to work to bring a speedy victory to the favored side.

The sympathy of the business community was divided about equally. One Wallace merchant declared his belief that the owners had made a fair offer and that the men ought to accept it, or at least cease to obstruct other men from accepting.[19] Another Wallace merchant thought that both sides had made mistakes. The 50 cent wage difference ought to be arbitrated or settled at once; the community had already paid enough in losses.[20] A Mullan businessman, on the other hand, expressed a strongly partisan viewpoint—that the owners, not content with running their mines, want to run stores, boarding houses, saloons and all sorts of businesses so that they can "make all there is in this country." The miners' union is fighting the battle of the small businessman, and as for himself he would "shoulder a gun in their defense, if necessary."[21] In Burke eight saloons had closed and only one remained in business.[22] At Mullan a store had closed and a sign hung across the front of the building announcing to all who read, "Closed by order of the Mine Owners' Association."[23]

The communities reacted to the tension under which they lived. A whole series of minor incidents reveal the intensity of the strain upon individuals and groups as the weeks and months wore on. Editor Adam Aulbach received a copy of the injunction on May 12,[24] and, believing that he had been served with the paper in consideration of his prounion stand, he censored his issue of the *Wallace Press* which appeared May 14. The *Press'* front page was a blank except for one line in huge letters, "The Press Gagged!"[25] Sheriff Cunningham, about May 15, in the interest of public order, went about the district closing some saloons and appealing to the saloon keepers to put their whiskey out of sight. At Mullan the sheriff got into an argument with Justice W. H. Frazier. Hot words led to actual fighting, and Frazier gave the sheriff a bloody nose, an event which was accredited as the first bloodshed in the crisis.[26]

More serious was the arrival at Wallace by express on May 11 of three cases of Winchester rifles and a case of ammunition addressed to Thomas O'Brien, president of the miners' union. O'Brien insisted that the rifles were the purchases of individual men for their own defense, and not an arming of the union as a whole, yet a bad and lasting impression was created by the facts.[27]

Late in May, about the time of the Mullan railroad scare, some 50 constables were deputized by Justice W. H. Frazier of Mullan, which seemed a large number of peace officers in a situation where everyone was denying that

[19] *Spokane Review*, June 9, 1892, p. 5, letter from a Wallace business man, signed G.A.B.
[20] *Ibid.*, June 2, 1892, p. 2, letter from Wallace, signed Merchant.
[21] *Spokane Review*, May 12, 1892, p. 2, Mullan dispatch, unsigned.
[22] *Ibid.*, May 25, 1892, p. 2.
[23] *Ibid.*, June 3, 1892, p. 2.
[24] *Anaconda Standard*, May 14, 1892, p. 1.
[25] *Ibid.*, May 14, 1892, p. 1; *Idaho Daily Statesman*, May 17, 1892, pp. 4, 5.
[26] *Spokane Review*, May 18, 1892, p. 2.
[27] *Ibid.*, May 12, 1891, p. 1; May 14, 1891, p. 1; also the mine owners' letter to Governor Willey, June 1, 1892, U. S. Moscow file 7.

anything unlawful had happened.[28] United States Marshal Joe Pinkham arrived in the district on the first of June with a second batch of injunction papers, and he seemed grieved that the miners did not cooperate with him so helpfully as before. Pinkham had to earn his fee every time he served a copy in June.[29] Union members kept an eagle eye upon the men serving as guards at the various mines, and whenever one of the guards ventured into town he would be promptly arrested, haled before Justice Pettibone at Gem or Justice Angel at Wallace, charged with carrying concealed deadly weapons, placed under $200 bond, and eventually tried and fined $50, which the mining company would have to pay.[30]

Once in a rare while in May or June the opposing forces in the conflict came together in the open. On the seventh of June, Frank R. Culbertson, manager of the Tiger mine, engaged in a discussion with John J. Tobin and about a hundred union miners on the main (and only) street of Burke. The discussion was warm, but entirely in good humor.[31] A few days later at Mullan, George B. McAuley and Terrence P. Purcell met before a crowd of miners and exchanged views for over an hour. McAuley admitted, so goes the newspaper report, that he personally had no objection to paying $3.50 a day to any man working underground, but he would insist on dealing with the men individually and not with a union.[32] In general, however, there were no serious attempts to bring the two sides to a common understanding after Governor Willey's unsuccessful effort. It was quite clear that the 50 cent wage difference was no longer the main issue. After all, there were probably not over 500 muckers employed in the mines, so that the sum in question would amount to only $250 a day for the whole district.[33] The issue of May and June was whether the miners' union should continue to exist as a wage bargaining agency.[34]

Early in June the union unexpectedly won a limited victory. The Tiger and Poorman mines at Burke opened at the union wage scale on the eleventh of June. S. S. Glidden of the Tiger and Patrick Clark of the Poorman signed an agreement with Tom O'Brien and Joseph Poynton to resume work at $3.50 per day to all men underground. The mines would hire without questioning as to union membership, but would give the preference to their former employes. They would also "fire" without dictation from any organization.[35] When the news spread through the district the union men celebrated this first turn of the tide of events in their favor. Bands played in Mullan and

---

[28] As charged by mine owners in letter to Willey, June 1, 1892, U. S. Moscow file 7.

[29] *Spokane Review*, June 2, 1892, p. 2; June 4, 1892, p. 5; June 5, 1892, p. 1. These were injunctions granted by Judge Beatty upon application of the Bunker Hill and Sullivan and the Helena and Frisco companies.

[30] *Anaconda Standard*, May 31, 1892, p. 1; *Spokane Review*, June 1, 1892, p. 2; *ibid.*, June 4, 1892, p. 5. Also, the mine owners complained to Governor Willey of these prosecutions in their letter of June 1, 1892, U. S. Moscow file 7.

[31] *Spokane Review*, June 10, 1892, p. 8.

[32] *Spokane Review*, June 12, 1892, p. 1.

[33] *Anaconda Standard*, May 29, 1892, p. 8, as told to a *Standard* reporter by owners McAuley, Culbertson, and Porter.

[34] This point of view was expressed by spokesman of both sides: G. M. Dallas in the *Anaconda Standard*, April 23, 1892, p. 1; A. M. Esler in *Spokane Review*, May 10, 1892, p. 3; G. B. McAuley in *Anaconda Standard*, May 18, 1892, p. 1.

[35] *Spokane Review*, June 12, 1891. p. 1, with complete text of the agreement.

Wallace, cheering miners paraded the streets, and dynamite was exploded on the hilltops above both towns.[36]

The Tiger and Poorman capitulation was not so grand a victory as it seems at first glance. In the mine owners' original offer, back on March 18, both the Tiger and the Poorman were permitted to pay $3.50 to muckers, since both mines were shaft mines. It is probable that Glidden and Clark observed how their fellow mine owners were operating, even though under difficulties, and decided that they had everything to gain by opening their own mines, especially since their wage scale coincided with the union demand. Charles Sweeney shrugged his shoulders and commented, "Yes, the Tiger and Poorman have thrown up the sponge." But the rest of the owners remained firm in their fight.[37] The union men went back to work gradually in the Burke mines, and full crews were working by July 1.[38]

[36] *Ibid.,* June 12, 1892, p. 1; June 14, 1892, p. 2.
[37] *Ibid.,* June 14, 1892, p. 2.
[38] *Ibid.,* July 1, 1892, p. 7.

14

On the Eve

So much happened in the Coeur d'Alene district in the first six months of 1892, and the situation had changed so often in that time, that a brief view of conditions as they existed on July first should aid in making intelligible what followed that date. Within the district itself the two parties to the dispute were holding to their policies with determination and apparently well disciplined ranks. Probably close to a thousand nonunion miners and muckers were at work in the mines of the owners' association and were protected to a greater or less degree by armed guards. Two large mines were employing perhaps 300 union miners at Burke. Throughout the district, particularly in the Mullan and Osburn areas, a great deal of constructive mining work was being done on smaller properties independent of the owners' association and paying the union wage scale.[1] Within the camps and towns of the South Fork the people were holding their breath in apprehension of some new sensation which might set off an outbreak of violence.

At Boise, in the United States Circuit Court for the District of Idaho, the injunction cases had become active. On May 28, two additional injunctions had issued from Judge Beatty in behalf of the Helena and Frisco Mining Company, a corporation of Montana, and the Bunker Hill and Sullivan Mining and Concentrating Company, a corporation of Oregon. These new injunctions resembled closely the earlier one issued in behalf of the Coeur d'Alene Mining and Concentrating Company.[2] The answers and affidavits of the union miners, defendants in the first injunction, had been filed with the court early in June.[3] Then the complainant had taken two weeks in which to file rebuttals. By June 28, the papers were all in Judge Beatty's hands and the arguments began. For three days the attorneys argued,[4] Heyburn and Hagan for the complainants and Ganahl and Bushnell for the defendants. At this time James H. Hawley, a prominent Boise lawyer, became associated

---

[1] Accounts of this productive mining appeared in *Spokane Review,* March 31, 1892, p. 1; May 7, 1892, p. 7; June 7, 1892, p. 5; June 17, 1892, p. 7.
[2] *Spokane Review,* June 2, 1892, p. 2. The documents in these cases are on file at Moscow, Idaho: *The Bunker Hill and Sullivan Mining and Concentrating Company versus The Miners' Union of Wardner, Idaho, et al.* in U. S. Moscow file 8; *The Helena and Frisco Mining Company versus the Miners' Union of Wardner, Idaho, et al.* in U. S. Moscow file 9.
[3] *Spokane Review,* June 7, 1892, p. 5; June 8, 1892, p. 2; *Idaho Daily Statesman,* June 8, 1892, p. 8.
[4] *Spokane Review,* June 29, 1892, p. 1; June 30, 1892, p. 1; July 1, 1892, p. 7, for accounts of the hearing.

with Ganahl and Bushnell in the unions' defense.[5] On the first of July Beatty
took the case under advisement and promised to render his decision soon. The
newspapers freely predicted that Beatty would continue the injunction, since
he allowed the temporary restraining order to remain in force while he deliberated.[6]

On July 11, the judge continued the injunction in an order which stated
the individualistic capitalistic philosophy of the mine owners much more
clearly than any of them had been able to do. After reviewing the facts as
presented by both sides, Judge Beatty declared:

> Whatever enthusiasts may hope for, in this country every owner of property
> may work it as he will, by whom he pleases, at such wages, and upon such terms
> as he can make; and every laborer may work or not, as he sees fit, for whom,
> and at such wages as, he pleases; and neither can dictate to the other how he
> shall use his own, whether of property, time, or skill. Any other system cannot
> be tolerated.[7]

Over at the state capitol, Governor Willey had spent an exhausting
month since his return from the Coeur d'Alenes the first of June. He had
been bombarded with letters, telegrams, resolutions, appeals from both sides
in rather obvious attempts to win his sympathy. Each new event in the district brought a new pile of messages. Willey probably realized the gravity
of the situation, but he was reluctant to take any decisive action. He also
knew that, if violence did break out and he were obliged to deliver on his
threat to declare martial law, the state's military resources would be hopelessly inadequate. Accordingly, on June 25, the governor wrote to President
Benjamin Harrison, explaining the critical situation and asking that four
companies of federal troops be moved into the district to help prevent an outbreak of violence.[8] The President, after a conference with the Idaho Congressional delegation in Washington, replied on the fourth of July, declining the
governor's request for troops, and pointing out the legal procedure in case of
an outbreak of violence.[9]

In the meantime, Willey had written to all the Idaho National Guard
units warning them of a possible call to arms and inquiring into the strength
each company could muster.[10] The replies to the governor must have been discouraging, for he came to the conclusion that he could count on less than 200
state troops.[11]

An incident occurred at Boise on July 5 which embarrassed the governor. On that date the *Idaho Daily Statesman* published a telegram from Senator Shoup to Governor Willey, dated July 2. Willey had refused to give the
message to the paper, believing that its publication would be a mistake. By
some means, the *Statesman* obtained a copy of the telegram and printed it

---

[5] *Idaho Daily Statesman,* June 29, 1892, p. 8.
[6] *Spokane Review,* July 1, 1892, p. 7.
[7] *Idaho Daily Statesman,* July 12, 1892, p. 1, complete text of Judge Beatty's order printed in three columns of fine print. It also appears in *The Federal Reporter,* LI (St. Paul, Minn., West Publishing Company, 1892), pp. 260-268.
[8] Carbon copy in *Governor's;* also *Congressional Dispatches,* pp. 3-4.
[9] Original in *Governor's.*
[10] *Idaho Daily Statesman,* June 25, 1892, p. 8.
[11] In his letter to President Harrison, June 25, Willey referred to the guard as "without effective organization and discipline." In his telegram of July 11, Willey told the president that "the immediate
available military force of the Idaho National Guard numbers but 196 men."

along with an editorial which condemned the governor's Coeur d'Alene policy as ineffective and bungling.[12] Shoup's message merely stated that the federal government was reluctant to promise troops in case of a violent outbreak, and urged Willey to work through the state and county civil authorities until every resource of preserving the peace had been exhausted. The governor felt that such a publication might give encouragement to hotheads among the union membership who perhaps wanted violence.[13]

Inspector General James F. Curtis left Boise for Wallace on July 2, informally commissioned to represent the governor at the scene of action.[14] Curtis' first duty upon his arrival was to inspect Company A, second regiment, of the Idaho National Guard at Wallace. This company had had a shaky existence for over a year. In April of 1892, it had changed commanders in an attempt to build up its membership and morale; Captain W. E. Hood had replaced Captain Thomas A. Linn.[15] Now it was hopelessly divided upon the labor controversy. The officers and enlisted men were resigning daily, declaring that they would not bear arms against the miners' union in the district.[16] On Saturday night, July 9, ten stands of guns were stolen from the armory. Captain Hood suddenly left town and could not be found.[17] General Curtis received the remaining arms and stored them in the Hussey bank building.[18] On July 11, in the excitement of the actual hostilities, Curtis tried to muster the company. Less than 20 men responded.[19] In a telegram to Governor Willey, Curtis recommended that the Wallace company be disbanded on the technical ground that it had fallen below the minimum authorized strength.[20]

The Fourth of July, 1892, fell upon a Monday. The National holiday, it seems, was to be celebrated with all the gaiety possible, in spite of the depressing situation in the district. For one day a truce was called in the warfare, and all classes celebrated 1,200 strong at Mullan. But not quite all classes celebrated after all, for the nonunion miners were held to their boarding houses lest their presence at the holiday festivities should create disorder. With this single exception, the whole community relaxed its tension and enjoyed a jolly holiday. Justice Angel read the Declaration of Independence and Alexander E. Mayhew delivered the oration of the day. The races were lively, with Wallace contestants winning most of them. A team from the Gem Miners' Union won the drilling contest amid the hearty applause of the throng. Fireworks flashed from Knob Hill, and the grand ball was as vivacious and colorful as ever that night.[21]

---

[12] *Idaho Daily Statesman*, July 5, 1892, p. 4, editorial entitled "Straightened Out."
[13] An exchange of telegrams on July 3, regarding this question: Shoup to *Statesman*, Willey to Shoup, *Statesman* to Shoup, in *Congressional Dispatches*, p. 6; and letter dated July 5, Willey to Shoup, *ibid.*, pp. 7-8; this letter (carbon copy) also in *Governor's*.
[14] *Idaho Daily Statesman*, July 3, 1892, p. 4.
[15] Letter, Willey to Capt. T. A. Linn, April 12, 1892, in *Governor's*, recommends the change.
[16] *Anaconda Standard*, May 13, 1892, p. 1; May 20, 1892, p. 1, news dispatches from Wallace telling of the company's disintegration.
[17] George Edgar French, 1st Lieut. U.S.A., "The Coeur d'Alene Riots of 1892," in *Overland Monthly*, XXVI, July, 1895, p. 36.
[18] French, p. 36.
[19] *Congressional Dispatches*, p. 11, in which Willey quotes Curtis' message in a telegram to Senator Shoup, July 11, 1892, 5 p.m.
[20] French, p. 36.
[21] *Spokane Review*, July 7, 1892, p. 7.

The Coeur d'Alene
Mining War of 1892   a pictorial review

MINERS, MINE OWNERS, and the community cooperated in building a hospital in Wallace in 1891. It was one of the first projects of the miners' union. Centrally located in the Coeur d'Alene mining district and operated by the Sisters of Providence, it was supported originally by union dues and payroll deductions (see page 20). Above, Providence Hospital as it appeared at the time of the mining conflict and below, as it appears today, 70 years later.

Photos taken 1906 and 1960.

BURKE, IDAHO, in the 1890's. Four nonunion men went to work in the Hidden Treasure tunnel of the Union mine near here on April 29, 1892, provoking first incident of Coeur d'Alene war.

AT MULLAN miners caused rumors of "holdups" when they searched incoming trains for nonunion laborers to warn union people at Wallace of their impending arrival. Local citizens later blew up tracks to stall federal troops from Missoula who came to quell the union uprising. Photo taken about 1890.

GEM, IDAHO, as it appeared in 1902. A typical canyon camp of the 1890's, Gem had its single street, double row of stores and houses, railroad, and flumes crowded into one narrow valley. In July 1892, Charles A. Siringo, undercover Pinkerton detective, escaped from the miners by cutting a hole in the floor of a house in Gem and crawling under the board walk—while searchers tramped overhead (see page 67).

FIRING BEGAN at the Frisco mill (the mill on the right in above photo) at 5 a.m., July 11, 1892. Inaccurate fire by both sides brought no serious casualties. Then, down the railway in rear of the Frisco mill, union men sent an ore car loaded with dynamite in an attempt to blast the "scabs" out of the canyon. The bomb exploded too soon causing only minor damage in rear of mill (see page 65). Mill on left is Black Bear.

NEXT ATTEMPT did not fail. Union men reached the upper end of the penstock—tube at left behind mill used to bring down water—and sent down the pipe a charge of dynamite sufficient to reduce the 4-story structure to a pile of splinters (opposite page). Explosion took the life of one nonunion man, who was killed by falling timbers. Rest of defenders surrendered and Frisco mill was for the time in union hands.

FRISCO MILL AFTER EXPLOSION, JULY 11, 1892

AT GEM, rifle fire began an hour later on July 11 than at the Frisco mill. Barricaded behind cordwood in the Gem mill (above), guards and nonunion men exchanged fire with union attackers who hid behind trees and buildings. Two nonunion and three union men were killed, others wounded. Mine officials negotiated surrender; defenders joined those from the Frisco as prisoners in Gem union hall (left). ◀

WARDNER, in upper part of Milo Gulch, as it appeared about 1890. A bucket of ore falling from an aerial tramway and killing a woman in a house in Wardner had helped cause a crisis in September 1891 (see page 31). ▶

MILO GULCH—present site of Kellogg, Idaho. Union forces headed for the Bunker Hill and Sullivan property in Milo Gulch on the evening of July 11. Finding the mine heavily guarded, the miners surrounded the ore concentrator and took ten guards prisoner—without firing a shot. Company officials saw they could not hold out and capitulated. This was high water mark of the union's conquest (see pages 68-69).

ON JULY 14, 1892, state and federal troops entered Wallace (below) to place the Coeur d'Alene country under martial law. Union did not resist; hundreds were taken into custody. Evidence was gathered for trials to come.

MILO GULCH

GENERAL STORE

WALLACE, IDAHO. JULY 1892

THE CLUB

IDAHO NATIONAL GUARD and federal troops set up bivouac in Wallace (above and below). Since no prison in the district could hold all union men taken into custody, two cottages and a large warehouse served as a temporary jail in Wallace to hold for trial prisoners taken at Gem, Burke, Mullan, and Wallace. The thrifty Idaho governor withdrew state troops and turned prisoners over to federal authorities as soon as he conveniently could, to save the state expense.
Photos by Barnard Studio, Wallace, Idaho.

15

What Happened
at Gem and Why

Incidents of the utmost importance occurred in the week of July 4 to 10 which changed the entire picture. On the morning of July 11, just a week after the Mullan celebration, rifles were spitting death in Canyon Creek, and the Gem Miners' Union, far from receiving the plaudits of the district for its fast drilling team, was involved in a bloody feud which brought condemnation and ruin. Many explanations have been written to tell why the outbreak occurred at Gem, but all have been incomplete and all more or less unsatisfactory. Yet this problem is the key to the understanding of the whole Coeur d'Alene story.

Certain it is that a large number of armed men congregated in the town of Gem Saturday night, July 9.[1] Presumably they—or at least many of them—were union miners. On Sunday the tenth, the number of armed loiterers at Gem increased. The union hall, the stores, and the saloons were crowded with them. They tramped the board sidewalks with a sinister tread. Wives and children of miners living at Gem moved either up the canyon to Burke or down to Wallace.[2]

At the same time, and presumably in response to the same events, reinforcements were hurried to the nonunion mines adjacent to the camp—the Gem and the Frisco. On Saturday, a barricade of cordwood was piled up around the Gem mine and mill, and this barricade stood not over 300 feet from the center of the town itself.[3] On Sunday, A. M. Esler sent up two cases of rifles to the Frisco mill.[4] Armed guards were posted at both mines, and no nonunion men were permitted to leave the properties. Two of them who slipped down into town for a drink in a saloon were badly beaten and

---

[1] *Spokane Review,* July 12, 1892, p. 2; Charles A. Siringo, *Riata and Spurs,* pp. 164-165.
[2] *Spokane Review,* July 12, 1892, p. 2; Siringo, *A Cowboy Detective,* p. 154; *Idaho Daily Statesman,* August 7, 1892, p. 8, in the report of Siringo's testimony in the contempt trial at Boise.
[3] *Idaho Daily Statesman,* August 10, 1892, p. 8, testimony of John McGowan and J. F. Moffatt in the contempt trial at Boise.
[4] *Spokane Review,* July 12, 1892, pp. 1, 2.

had to be rescued by guards.[5] The situation at Gem was virtually a state of siege.

It should be recalled that the crisis in the Coeur d'Alenes had been long and severe—almost six months had elapsed since the January shutdown, and over three months since the April lockout. During all that time constant friction and irritation had created a reservoir of bad feeling. Both sides were armed—hired guards at the mines and individually armed miners in the union. The fingers of both sides were literally on the trigger.

In addition, there was undoubtedly a group of hotheads within the union ranks, a minority, and probably a small minority, but a difficult group to control. For example a terrorist group claiming to number 17, wrote a threatening letter to Campbell and Finch early in April. This little gang announced that the miners' union was too slow and conservative for it.[6] Certainly a number of union miners were impatient with the union policy—the hiring of lawyers, the dependence upon peaceful picketing, etc. As the mining operations with nonunion men were extended, and as these discontented union members saw their jobs and livelihoods being lost before their very eyes, a desperate desire for effective retaliation seized some of them, predisposing them to favor violence when a serious issue should present itself. Furthermore, the reports from Boise as to the probable outcome of the injunction suit were discouraging. It was felt that the union had failed to dissolve the injunction, and this disappointment tended to make even those unionists who had relied entirely upon peaceful and lawful methods a little more sympathetic toward a violent solution of the problem.

Certain events of the first week in July added highly inflammable fuel to the mass already awaiting the torch. The publication in the Boise *Statesman* on July 5 of Senator Shoup's telegram to Governor Willey, which implied that federal military aid would be unlikely in an emergency, may have encouraged the hotheads to more daring exploits by lulling them into a false security.[7] Much more significant, however, was the news which swept and electrified the entire nation on July 7. The preceding day (July 6), the locked-out steel workers at Homestead, Pennsylvania, had given battle to two barge-loads of Pinkerton detectives coming up the Monongahela River from Pittsburgh as strikebreakers. After a day of fighting, three of the Pinkertons lay dead, a dozen were wounded, and the remaining force had surrendered to the workers.[8] Here was the example of apparently successful "direct action" by an organized labor force. The disastrous consequences at Homestead, namely, martial law and the eventual loss of the strike, could not be foreseen by the Coeur d'Alene miners.

With these facts and conditions in mind, it might be well to consider

---

[5] *Ibid.*, July 12, 1892, pp. 1, 2; Siringo, *Riata and Spurs*, pp. 164-167; *Idaho Daily Statesman*, August 7, 1892, p. 8, testimony of Siringo in the contempt trial at Boise. Siringo named Perry Barker as the "scab" beaten on Saturday night and E. W. Putnam as the one beaten on Sunday.

[6] The original handwritten note, dated April 4, 1892, is included as an exhibit with A. B. Campbell's affidavit before the U. S. circuit court, April 30, 1892, U. S. Moscow file 7.

[7] *Spokane Review*, July 7, 1892, p. 5, a Mullan dispatch reports general satisfaction over the rebuff to Governor Willey.

[8] Samuel Yellen, *American Labor Struggles* (New York, Harcourt, Brace and Company, 1936), p. 86.

for a moment the two most frequently quoted theories which attempt to explain the outbreak of violence at Gem. The simplest explanation, and the least satisfactory, was given by Charles A. Siringo, the Pinkerton detective employed by the mine owners while serving as recording secretary of the Gem Miners' Union. According to Siringo, the union leaders were "a vicious and heartless gang of anarchists. Many of them had been rocked in the cradle of anarchy at Butte City, Montana, while others were escaped outlaws and toughs from other states." These leaders coldly plotted a violent uprising and set the date in advance as July 11.[9] Siringo's explanation has been repeated by William Stoll,[10] Mary Hallock Foote,[11] and others to whom it appeared reasonable.

The second theory goes considerably beyond Siringo. It acknowledges other factors beside anarchism. It recognizes the critical situation in the Coeur d'Alenes and seeks to find some overt incident which brought on the fighting of July 11. The beating of the nonunion miners in the saloon brawls at Gem on Saturday and Sunday nights (July 9 and 10) seems to explain why firing opened on a large scale the following morning. This theory is the one advanced by the contemporary newspapers in their efforts to satisfy their readers' curiosity as to the origins of the battle, and it has been repeated by most of the historians who have followed the newspapers as their chief source, e.g., Nelson W. Durham,[12] and George W. Fuller.[13] Yet in reality, this explanation does not satisfy entirely. Occasional beatings had been administered to nonunion men earlier in the crisis without precipitating bloodshed.[14] And besides, if the union assailants were victorious, as they were at Gem on July 9 and 10, why should the union muster its armed force and—as was generally alleged—begin the battle?

Some more fundamental reason must have existed for the violent events of July 11. Judge Fremont Wood, in an interview given at Boise, Idaho, in the summer of 1936, suggested what is probably the true explanation. Judge Wood, one of the few surviving participants in the events of 1892 (he was then United States Attorney for the district of Idaho), declared that the disclosure of Charles A. Siringo's identity as a mine owners' spy was what caused the union uprising.[15] That disclosure occurred on Saturday, July 9.[16]

Let the reader here consider the full import of Judge Wood's suggestion. Remember again the long strain of the crisis and the bitter feeling it had created. Add the exciting effect of the news of the Homestead "massacre." Then climax it all with the revelation that C. Leon Allison, recording secretary of the Gem Miners' Union, was a spy. In the face of such a sickening and confidence-shaking revelation, the fury of the union miners burst all bounds. Not Tom O'Brien, not Gabe Dallas, not even shrewd, eloquent

---

[9] Siringo, *A Cowboy Detective*, pp. 139-140.
[10] His book, *Silver Strike* (Boston, Little Brown and Company, 1932), 273 pp.
[11] Her novel, *Coeur d'Alene* (Boston, Houghton Mifflin Company, 1894), 240 pp.
[12] *History of the City of Spokane and the Spokane Country, Washington* (Chicago, The S. J. Clarke Publishing Company, 1912), 3 vol.
[13] *The Inland Empire of the Pacific Northwest, a History* (Denver, H. G. Lindermann, 1928), 3 vol.; *A History of the Pacific Northwest* (New York, Alfred A. Knopf, 1931), 383 pp.
[14] For example, the case of William Linney, Wardner. See Chapter XIII, note 3.
[15] The interview was given by Fremont Wood to the writer at Boise, Idaho, July 14, 1936.
[16] Siringo, *Riata and Spurs*, p. 164.

Peter Breen, recently arrived from Butte, could check the frenzied demand for revenge. It was not until the night of Saturday the ninth—after Siringo's identity had been made public—that armed men began to gather in Gem. The assaults upon the luckless nonunion men were not the cause of the battle; they were merely the first minor skirmishes. Saturday night and all day Sunday the armed forces of the union patrolled Gem, facing the enemy at the Gem and Frisco mines, planning to repay with vigorous, decisive, violent action the black treachery of Siringo.

16

The Battle at Gem

About 5 a.m. on Monday, July 11, fighting began at the Frisco mine and mill above the town of Gem. There was a long exchange of rifle fire between union miners in the hills above the mine and armed forces within the barricade. Who fired the very first shot will probably never be known. Indeed, sworn testimony in three long trials before judges and juries failed to establish conclusively which side began the battle.

The early firing at the Frisco was distinguished by inaccurate marksmanship; nobody was killed or seriously wounded. Along about 7:30 a.m. an ore car went whizzing down the incline toward the mill. Just before reaching the mill, the car blew up. It had been loaded with dynamite. Even in this exploit but little damage was done. The car, the track and a corner of the ore bin were demolished. For over an hour all was quiet, although men could be seen moving through the timber on the hillside. Then, with a terrific roar and a detonation which shook the whole countryside, the Frisco mill was blown up, leaving a heap of debris where a four-story wooden structure had been.* A charge of dynamite had been sent down the penstock into the mill where it had exploded. The nonunion crew of the mine and mill surrendered after the blast. They marched out under a white flag; their arms were taken by the union guards, and the men themselves were held prisoners at the Gem Miners' Union Hall.[1]

The Frisco mill which was blown up was called the "old mill" and it was not in use at the time. One worker, Archie T. McDonald by name, was killed by falling timbers at the time of the explosion. The obvious reason for the attack upon the Frisco was to drive the nonunion men out of the canyon. The reason for the destructive ferocity of the attack lay in the special and deep-seated antipathy of the union men toward A. M. Esler, manager and chief owner of the Frisco. For several months Esler had seldom opened his mouth in public except to denounce and vilify the union. One particular utterance,

---

* See photo section.
[1]. *Spokane Review*, July 12, 1892, pp. 1 and 2; also detailed accounts of the Frisco affair by survivors, W. W. Wood, *Spokane Review*, July 13, 1892, p. 2, and F .E. Clarke, *ibid.*, July 15, 1892, p. 2. Also the testimony of witnesses in the contempt trial at Boise, particularly John Kneebone, *Idaho Daily Statesman*, August 5, 1892, p. 8. Also a series of 13 affidavits, transcripts of testimony of survivors, given July 15 and 16, 1892, and filed as exhibits before the U. S. circuit court, U. S. Moscow file 9.

at Spokane, on May 8, had aroused bitter enmity. On that occasion Esler had called the union men "liars," "flannel-mouths," and "Mollie Maguires" all in one paragraph.[2] It is probable that many union miners felt a degree of satisfaction in seeing Esler's mill blown up.

Fighting began at the Gem mine and mill about 6 a.m. A sharpshooter in the town of Gem—or was it a stray wild shot from the men at the mine?—killed Ivory Bean, a Thiel detective who had come in with Joe Warren's original force, as he walked between the boarding house and the mill. The firing was more intense and more deadly at the Gem than it had been at the Frisco. In spite of the protection afforded by the barricade, another nonunion man was killed in the battle, namely John Stanlick. The whole business district of Gem was raked by a continuous fire from the mine barricade, and Bill Daxon's saloon, which had been a popular hangout for unionists, was riddled with bullet holes. The union forces fought from the shelter of buildings, trees, and rocks, but three of their men fell dead during the fight: James Hennessey, Gus Carlson, and Charles Cummings. Half a dozen were wounded.

The Gem mine was cut off from communication with the town or with Wallace or Burke. The men inside the barricade heard the explosions at the Frisco, but could only guess what was happening up the canyon. An order to surrender came from the union side. Superintendent John Monahan refused to surrender until ordered by the company officials. Accordingly, a truce was called while the terms of surrender were discussed, written, and signed by A. L. Gross, a representative of the company. Charles Bonner, a citizen of Gem, and Peter Breen, spokesman for the union. Under these terms the men surrendered, their arms were handed over to a joint committee, they were guaranteed a safe conduct to Wallace, and the company was assured protection to its property.[3] Once again, the chief motive of the attack was to clear the canyon of nonunion men. In addition, the Gem's barricade was considered a menace to the town, standing as it did only 300 feet from the main (and only) street. Also, the hated villain of the drama, detective Siringo, had taken refuge in the Gem mill.

At the Gem Miners' Union Hall, the prisoners, numbering about 150, and their armed union guards, awaited a special train which would carry them to Wallace. The dead and wounded and the surrendered arms were also sent down the canyon on the same train. But on the way down a union party, headed by Tom Heney of Mullan, intercepted the car and appropriated the guns. At Wallace, the nonunion men were given 24 hours in which to draw their pay and leave the country. They were fed and housed that night at the expense of the owners—only two of whom, however, Gross and DeLashmutt, were left in Wallace.[4]

[2] *Spokane Review,* May 10, 1892, p. 3.
[3] *Spokane Review,* July 12, 1892, pp. 1 and 2; also testimony of Charles A. Siringo in the contempt trial at Boise, *Idaho Daily Statesman,* August 7, 1892, p. 8; also testimony of Frank L. Higgins in the Leasure murder trial at Rathdrum, Idaho, *Spokane Review,* December 3, 1892, p. 2; the original handwritten copy of the terms of surrender of the Gem mine is included as an exhibit before the U .S. circuit court in the case of *The United States versus Peter Breen et al,* in U. S. Moscow file 1.
[4] *Spokane Review,* July 12, 1892, pp. 1 and 2; also testimony of W. C. Human and A. L. Gross in the contempt trial at Boise, *Idaho Daily Statesman,* August 7, 1892, p. 8.

A close scrutiny of the prisoners at the union hall failed to reveal the face and figure of Siringo. Where had he gone? Where indeed! The man's actions in the last three days had displayed a personal courage and an iron nerve which call forth admiration, regardless of what one thinks of the ethical side of his relations with the union. His identity had been suspected by Gabe Dallas of the Butte miners' union, and the positive identification of Siringo as a Pinkerton detective had been verified on Saturday the ninth by a certain "Black Jack" Griffin of Mullan.[5] Late on Saturday night, after his exposure as a detective and in the face of a hostile community, Siringo took the beaten nonunion man to Wallace on a hand car and summoned Dr. W. S. Sims to attend him.[6] Then, on Sunday, he returned openly to Gem on the morning train, sitting in the same coach with Justice Pettibone, and carrying his rifle in his hands and his Colt revolver strapped around his waist.[7] The coolness of the man's daring acts seemed to have hypnotized his enemies, who watched him with a cat-like intensity but never made a move to lay hands upon him. Siringo slipped away to the Gem mine where he spent Sunday night, but he returned to his room in Gem early Monday morning, and he was there when Ivory Bean fell.[8]

As the fight in Gem grew more intense, Siringo's situation became more untenable, so that he had to make a "get-away," if possible. It was possible, but almost miraculous. Descending through a hole sawed in the floor, he passed under the house, crawled half a block in the narrow space under the board sidewalk—while people walked overhead—ran to the creek under a saloon building, waded the stream, and climbed to the Gem barricade with no more protection than clumps of willows.[9] When the Gem surrendered, Siringo preferred to take his chances in the hills rather than in the union hall. He and a like-minded companion named Frank Stark escaped into the timber above the mine. Later, toward evening, they descended from the hills near Wallace, crossed through the town in the dark, and hid in the hills of the Placer Creek section. From a high viewpoint the two fugitives were able to watch developments until the arrival of federal troops.[10]

---

[5] Siringo, *Riata and Spurs*, pp. 162-165.
[6] *Ibid.*, p. 166.
[7] *Ibid.*, p. 167.
[8] *Ibid.*, pp. 167-169.
[9] Charles A. Siringo, *Riata and Spurs*, pp. 169-174.
[10] *Ibid.*, pp. 175-180.

17

Wardner and Wallace
Under Union Guards

T HE FIGHTING began and ended at Gem. The Union's conquest of the rest of the district was bloodless, achieved without firing another gun, but always backed by the threat of further violence in case resistance were offered. Violence did not appear to have been part of the union leaders' policy. But once the struggle had been begun it was carried through to its logical conclusion by those leaders who evidently tried to make the best of a bad cause.[1] Tom O'Brien, Campbell W. Bushnell, Gabe Dallas, and Peter Breen—to mention only the four most active leaders—worked tirelessly in the brief period of union domination to prevent any further bloodshed or destruction of property. For example, Bushnell and Breen rode the entire night of July 12, covering all the camps of the district and pleading for orderly control.[2]

Next to Gem, Wardner experienced the most exciting events in the labor war. Flushed with victory after expelling the nonunion miners from Canyon Creek, and burning with a desire to settle accounts with the citadel of the mine owners' anti-union activity, namely the Bunker Hill and Sullivan company, a large force of union miners went down to Wardner the evening of July 11.* Perhaps 400 armed men rode flat cars and handcars down the valley. At Wardner this force was augmented by perhaps another 100 men of the Wardner union. After a brief consultation, the men scattered out into the hills and were lost to view in the timber and the darkness.

This time there was no random shooting to begin hostilities. Shrewder heads were now directing the attack. Finding the Bunker Hill and Sullivan mine barricaded and heavily guarded, the union forces abandoned the idea of storming it. However, they found the big concentrator at the railroad junction practically abandoned; only 10 men were in the entire works. Quickly sur-

---

[1] *Spokane Review*, July 13, 1892, p. 2, in what purports to be an official union statement, though unsigned and not attributed to any individual leader.
[2] *Spokane Review*, July 14, 1892, p. 8.
* See photo section.

rounding the concentrator, the unionists took the crew prisoners without firing a shot. The same tactics were employed at the Last Chance and Sierra Nevada concentrators.[3]

In the morning of Tuesday the twelfth, a committee of armed union leaders composed of Tom O'Brien, Fred Dean, Ed Boyce, Thomas Heney, and George M. Glover called upon the mine owners in Wardner. They found V. M. Clement, Charles Sweeney, George B. McAuley, Frank Jenkins, and F. Rockwood Moore. After explaining that the concentrators had been captured, the union leaders demanded the discharge of all nonunion workmen and their departure from the district within 48 hours. The refusal of the demand meant the destruction of the concentrators. With very little hesitation the owners agreed to pay off their nonunion employes and urge them to leave the district within the specified time.[4]

An interesting question has arisen from this Wardner incident. Was the Bunker Hill and Sullivan concentrator loaded with dynamite by the union forces so that it could be destroyed easily in case the owners refused to come to terms? The newspaper accounts tell of such a maneuver,[5] and in the contempt trial at Boise, a month later, the foreman of the concentrator, Robert Shain, testified that 4,000 pounds of dynamite were carried into the mill.[6] Yet Edward Boyce, one of the union committee who confronted the Wardner mine owners with the union's ultimatum, declared that no dynamite was ever placed in the concentrator.[7] "No reason existed for the miners to do so," said Boyce. "If they had wished to destroy the concentrator, a match would have served the purpose better than dynamite." The whole dynamite story, according to Boyce, was an invention of the press for the purpose of discrediting the union and its cause.[8]

In the morning of the thirteenth, a Union Pacific train carried the majority of the Wardner miners to Tekoa, whence they could proceed to Spokane or Pendleton. Union guards at the station and those still on duty at the Bunker Hill concentrator and a crowd of several hundred people cheered derisively as the train pulled slowly by. Within an hour the union leaders turned the property back to its owners, the mill and its valuable machinery unharmed. The union guards had taken some food from the boarding house kitchen for the night shift, and they promised to pay for it as soon as the company rendered them a bill.[9]

At Wallace there was no resistance to the union's action. Sheriff Cunningham was powerless; he could not raise a posse, though he tried to do so.[10] Inspector General Curtis was likewise helpless; he could not muster his company of national guards.[11] For all practical purposes the union headquarters

   [3] *Spokane Review*, July 13, 1892, p. 1; July 14, 1892, p. 1.
   [4] The details of this conference were revealed in testimony in the contempt trial at Boise, *Idaho Daily Statesman*, August 13, 1892, p. 8.
   [5] *Spokane Review*, July 13, 1892, p. 1; July 14, 1892, p. 1.
   [6] *Idaho Daily Statesman*, August 13, 1892, p. 8.
   [7] Letter, Edward Boyce to the writer, August 18, 1936.
   [8] Letter, Edward Boyce to the writer, August 18, 1936. John Hays Hammond in his autobiography makes no mention of dynamite in the mill. However, Hammond was not in Wardner during the union occupancy.
   [9] *Spokane Review*, July 14, 1892, p. 1.
   [10] *Ibid.*, July 13, 1892, p. 2.
   [11] *Spokane Review*, July 13, 1892, p. 2.

replaced the town hall. Union guards patrolled the town for three days and nights, maintaining a reasonable degree of order.

On the twelfth, the nonunion men from the Gem and the Frisco were hurried out of town on the westbound Northern Pacific narrow gauge train.[12] On the thirteenth occurred the funeral of the three union miners killed in the Gem battle; Hennessey, Carlson, and Cummings. All the union men in the district, except those actually on guard duty, marched in the procession from Wallace to the Miners' Union Cemetery. O'Brien and other leaders spoke and urged the men to return to their homes and prepare to go to work the next day.[13]

O'Brien's advice, though excellent, proved too difficult to be followed exactly. Wallace was filled that night with a boisterous crowd celebrating the union's victory. The hated "scabs" were all gone. The mine owners were beaten and humiliated. In their glee the celebrants imbibed freely of liquor and some became disorderly. Citizens who had been outspoken in their opposition to the union were "serenaded;" they were told to "shut up or pack up." Certain inebriated unionists when warned that state and federal troops were on the way to the district rashly offered to engage the army in battle.[14]

At Mullan the days passed somewhat less eventfully. There were no nonunion men at work there. The Mullan union men, though they had no work of expulsion to do in their own town, were active in engagements and demonstrations elsewhere in the district. Late in the night of the twelfth, two explosions startled the citizens of Mullan. Someone had blown up a small bridge and a short section of railroad grade on the Northern Pacific line, the effect of which was to tie up traffic on the Coeur d'Alene cut-off and delay the entrance of federal troops from Fort Missoula, Montana.[15] But on the thirteenth, when Wallace was entertaining a wildly celebrating crowd, Mullan reported, "All is as quiet here as an inland town in the Palouse country at cow-milking time."[16]

---

[12] *Ibid.*, July 13, 1892, p. 2.
[13] *Ibid.*, July 14, 1892, p. 1.
[14] *Spokane Review*, July 15, 1892, p. 1.
[15] *Ibid.*, July 14, 1892, p. 8.
[16] *Ibid.*, July 14, 1892, p. 8.

18

The "Massacre"
at the Mission

O<small>N THE MORNING</small> of July 14, the *Spokane Review* shocked and horrified its readers with four full columns of harrowing details of an incident which came to be known as the Mission "massacre."[1] In addition to the news space, the *Review* in its editorial columns published a flaming denunciation of the miners' union under the title "Savagery Succeeds Lawlessness." "The instincts of civilization have been thrown to the winds, and all that is vile in human nature has been brought to the surface."[2]

What were the facts of the outrage at the Mission? This much is certain. The nonunion miners from the Gem and Frisco mines, numbering 132 men with a few women and children, after being paid off at Wallace on the twelfth, went west on the Northern Pacific narrow gauge train that afternoon. They arrived at the old Mission without incident.[3] There, at a tiny settlement made up chiefly of a hotel and a few saloons, they had to wait for the steamer "Georgia Oakes," which would carry them down the river and down the lake to Coeur d'Alene City whence they could entrain again for Spokane. This evening the wait was unusually long, because the steamer was engaged in moving United States troops up the lake from Fort Sherman to Harrison.[4]

Suddenly, from out of the dusk came a group of eight or a dozen men riding horseback down the track, yelling and shooting guns. They swooped down upon the little group of deported miners and scattered the latter in all directions. Some fled into the woods of Fourth of July canyon, others took refuge in the river or in the brushy ground beside the river. The riders came on, cursing and firing their guns. Whenever they overtook a fugitive they robbed him. Eventually, along about 11 p.m., the steamer arrived and took aboard the women and children and what few men were near the landing.[5]

---

[1] *Spokane Review*, July 14, 1892, p. 1, col. 1-4.
[2] *Ibid.*, July 14, 1892, p. 6.
[3] *Ibid.*, July 13, 1892, p. 2.
[4] *Spokane Review*, July 13, 1892, p. 2.
[5] *Ibid.*, July 14, 1892, p. 1.

All day long on the thirteenth, and the fourteenth too, the victims of this brutal attack straggled into Spokane. There they were fed and housed at the mine owners' expense. Each man and woman as soon as he felt able, went to the Spokane Hotel and told his story to W. B. Heyburn, who recorded it as evidence in case of future legal action.[6] These tales told to Heyburn were the basis both for the original atrocity stories published in the *Review* and for subsequent stories.[7] There were narrow escapes by swimming the river or by pretending to be shot and lying inert on the meadow grass. The universal testimony was of being robbed of all their valuable possessions—money and watches particularly. The fugitives also testified of seeing a number of men killed or wounded, but, with one exception, no positive identification of the dead or injured could be made. John Monahan, superintendent of the Gem mine, was reported killed, and the headlines in the *Review* carried the sad tidings, but on the fourteenth, Monahan appeared in Spokane hale and hearty, and thus made the headlines a second time, although his return to life was not so exciting in print as his alleged demise.[8]

In the face of such tragic reports, it is natural that investigation should have been made of the Mission "massacre." The first such investigation was made by a party of five men from Wardner and Wallace, headed by Peter Porter. These men, on the thirteenth and fourteenth, rode through the Fourth of July canyon and searched carefully along both sides of the road. They found no dead bodies, no wounded men. Thirty-eight men had passed safely through the canyon the night of the attack, they reported.[9] After the United States Army troops occupied the Coeur d'Alene district, three separate searching parties were sent into the canyon in response to persistent suspicions that the bodies of dead men were concealed in the forest. None of the military parties found any bodies or any traces of human slaughter or burial.[10] Someone brought forward a ghastly theory, namely that the bodies of the dead were taken to the river bank; there the abdomens were cut open and the corpses heaved into the river where they sank never to rise to the surface. The river bed was dragged in the vicinity of the Mission, but no bodies, mutilated or otherwise, were found.[11]

When the results of all these investigations are sifted, the facts of the Mission "massacre" appear much less alarming than the original reports in the *Spokane Review*. The whole affair was deplorable, and no possible justification can be found for it. A gang of desperadoes whose identity remains unknown attacked the defenseless group at the Mission. Their sole purpose seemed to be that of robbery, in which they were successful. But nobody was

---

[6] Thirteen transcripts of such testimony were compiled as affidavits and placed before the U. S. circuit court as exhibits in the contempt trial at Boise, August 8, 1892, U .S. Moscow file 9.
[7] E.g. *Spokane Review*, July 15, 1892, p. 1, col. 1; p. 2, col. 1-3.
[8] The death headline in the issue of July 14, the return to life in that of July 15.
[9] *Spokane Review*, July 15, 1892, p. 2.
[10] *Ibid.*, July 17, 1892, p. 1, the search conducted by Lt. Helmick from Fort Sherman; *ibid.*, July 19, 1892, p. 1, search conducted by Capt. Thompson from Fort Sherman; *ibid.*, July 21, 1892, p. 1, search conducted by Lt. McQuiston and Lt. Smith. Also Col. Wm. P. Carlin's review of the investigations in his report, dated July 26, 1892, and published in *War Department Messages and Documents, 1892*, vol. I, pp. 110-112.
[11] *Spokane Review*, July 19, 1892, p. 1, the theory was advanced by Judge Advocate General George Parsons of the Idaho National Guard; repeated by Charles A. Siringo in *A Cowboy Detective*, pp. 181-182.

killed and apparently nobody was wounded, although several of the victims suffered from exposure and shock.

The importance of the Mission incident lies in the publicity it received and the public reaction to the reports. The atrocity stories in the *Review* were copied all through the Northwest. Editorial comment universally condemned the perpetrators of the crime. Since the victims were the deported nonunion men, the supposition was easily created that the attack was just another part of the union campaign against the "scabs." The mine owners' lawyers, W. B. Heyburn, and the *Spokane Review,* which was inclined to favor the owners' side in the controversy, both charged the responsibility for the attack to the union.[12] And the whole public reaction to the incident was undoubtedly damaging to the union cause. Statements by union leaders denying the responsibility and deploring the event, and the negative reports of the investigating groups never received anything like the publicity of the original horror stories.

---

[12] *Spokane Review,* July 14, 1892, p. 6.

19

State and Federal
Government Intervene

Dᴜʀɪɴɢ those hectic July days (eleventh, twelfth, and thirteenth) one must not suppose that the state and federal authorities were sitting idly by while the miners' union swept the Coeur d'Alenes of nonunion labor. Indeed, Boise and Washington, D. C., and certain western army posts saw plenty of activity in those same days. Yet the state government was taken somewhat by surprise by the outbreak at Gem on Monday morning. Governor Willey had been reassured that all was quiet in the district.[1] And Inspector General Curtis had felt so confident of the situation that he left Wallace Sunday afternoon, July 10, bound for Boise.[2]

As soon as the fighting commenced at Gem, startling telegrams began to pour in upon Governor Willey. Gross, DeLashmutt, Finch, and Esler at Wallace; Clement and McAuley at Wardner; Glidden, Campbell, and Heyburn at Spokane; Hammond at San Francisco; all wired their hastily gathered versions of the affair, and called for immediate assistance.[3] Willey was undoubtedly alarmed, but he wanted more reliable information before acting. He located General Curtis by wire at Tekoa and sent him back to Wallace on a special train.[4] After Curtis returned to the scene, he communicated with Governor Willey every half hour. One of the first messages to reach the governor was a request from John A. Finch to borrow the state arms (the remaining rifles of the expiring national guard company) for the defense of his property, the Gem mine.[5] Willey wired back to Curtis, granting the authority to lend the arms to the mine owners,[6] but it is almost a certainty that those rifles were not made available in time to be used in the fighting that morning.

---

[1] As he (Willey) indicated in a letter to President Harrison, July 8, 1892, filed in *Governor's*.
[2] *Spokane Review,* July 12, 1892, p. 2.
[3] One such message, Finch to Willey, is repeated in *Congressional Dispatches,* p. 9; the *Willey Collection,* nos. 7 and 9, give the governor's replies to Clement and Hammond; *Spokane Review,* July 12, 1892, p. 2, says that 16 telegrams were sent by mine owners in Spokane to Willey on the eleventh without eliciting a reply; *Idaho Daily Statesman,* July 12, 1892, p. 8, mentions receipt of messages from Heyburn, Finch, and Clement, no texts, however.
[4] *Idaho Daily Statesman,* July 12, 1892, p. 8. Curtis at Tekoa at 9 a.m. on the eleventh.
[5] *Ibid.,* July 12, 1892, p. 8.
[6] *Willey Collection,* no. 6, a Western Union blank, written in ink, signed.

74

Although he had little faith in its success, the governor tried to halt the lawlessness by an exercise of the state authority in Shoshone County. Willey wired Sheriff Cunningham, "You must stop that riot at all hazards."[7] The fighting at Gem was almost over before that message came through. Sheriff Cunningham did what he could, which was little indeed. He tried to summon a posse comitatus; he issued subpoenas upon some 300 men known to favor the mine owners' side in the controversy, but not a man responded.[8] Late in the afternoon the county officers gave up the attempt. General Curtis, Sheriff Cunningham, Prosecuting Attorney Charles W. O'Neil, and County Commissioners George T. Crane and John L. Livers united in a message to the governor announcing their incapacity to control the situation and calling for state and federal troops.[9] Subsequently, Sheriff Cunningham followed the crowds, going wherever the excitement and the possibility of violence were greatest, and confining his activities to counseling moderation and maintaining a semblance of order, in company with Bushnell, Breen, and other union leaders.

As the day wore on, excitement ran high in Washington, D .C. The Idaho Congressional delegation was deluged by the same sort of messages from Wallace, Wardner, and Spokane.[10] W. B. Heyburn kept the telegraph lines busy and proved himself a master alarmist in the brief form of the telegram, magnifying the casualties and coloring his messages with picturesque and forceful language. Senators George L. Shoup and Fred T. Dubois and Congressman Willis Sweet held a continuous conference all day long and most of the night trying to arrange matters to obtain federal aid.[11] Yet no call came from Governor Willey. Without a direct request from the governor declaring that the state authority had been exercised and found insufficient, neither the President nor the War Department could or would act.

Governor Willey was still too busy exercising the state authority to communicate with the national capital. He called six companies of the Idaho National Guard into active service and ordered them to entrain early the following morning for Shoshone County.[12] There were three companies from southern Idaho: Company A, Boise; Company B, Hailey; Company F, Weiser; and three from northern Idaho, all from Latah County: Company K, Moscow; Company L, Genessee; Company M, Vollmer. Other companies, such as the one at Grangeville, in Idaho County, which were much closer to the scene of the disturbance than the southern companies, could not be called into service because they had no railroad facilities. The southern companies were to leave on the regular westbound Union Pacific (Oregon Short Line) train on the twelfth.[13] A special train would carry them north from Pendleton, Oregon. At Colfax, Washington, the three northern companies would join

[7] *Ibid.*, no. 2, executive stationery, typewritten, unsigned.
[8] *Spokane Review*, July 13, 1892, p. 2.
[9] *Willey Collection*, no. 13, typewritten (carbon) on executive stationery, marked *copy*, unsigned, used perhaps as an exhibit with Willey's message to the president, no. 12.
[10] Three of these messages of July 11 are included in the *Congressional Dispatches*, p. 9, Esler and Finch; p. 11, Heyburn; p. 12a, McAuley.
[11] *Spokane Review*, July 13, 1892, p. 2, Washington dispatch; also *Congressional Dispatches*, p. 14.
[12] *Idaho Daily Statesman*, July 12, 1892, p. 8; *Willey Collection*, no. 3, telegram, Willey to Curtis.
[13] *Idaho Daily Statesman*, July 13, 1892, p. 8, for departure of Company A, Boise; July 14, 1892, p. 1, for progress of southern Idaho companies as far as Pendleton.

the train. The entire force was to proceed and place itself under the command of Inspector General Curtis.[14]

This duty done, Governor Willey called in Attorney General George H. Roberts and together they composed the appeal to the President. The message began: "This morning riot and bloodshed by the striking miners of the Coeur d'Alene District commenced." It summarized the day's violence, announced that the state legislature was not in session and could not be convened promptly, that the civil authority of county and state was inadequate, and that the available Idaho National Guard force was 196 men. The appeal concluded: "I therefore request that a sufficient force be detailed from Fort Sherman or elsewhere to act in concert with State authorities in maintaining public order."[15] Late at night, in fact just before midnight, and while the union miners were closing in on the Bunker Hill and Sullivan concentrator at Wardner Junction, this important message was flashed eastward to the capital.

President Harrison was summering at Saratoga, New York, and Secretary of War S. B. Elkins was also outside the capital. By telegram they agreed to send a military force in response to Governor Willey's plea.[16] This decision came early in the morning of the twelfth. Major General J. M. Schofield, commanding the Army, was entrusted with the actual military movements. The orders issued from General Schofield's headquarters in Washington, D. C., and went direct to Brigadier General Thomas H. Ruger, commanding the Department of the Columbia, at San Francisco, and to Brigadier General Wesley Merritt, commanding the Department of Dakota, at St. Paul, Minnesota. Schofield's messages also went to Governor Willey, to Colonel William P. Carlin, commanding Fort Sherman on Coeur d'Alene Lake, and to the commander of Fort Missoula, Montana. General Ruger from San Francisco also directed Colonel Carlin, and maintained communication with Governor Willey throughout the duration of the troop movements.[17]

The orders to Colonel Carlin were to take all the available troops from Fort Sherman and proceed to Wardner as quickly as possible, there to cooperate with Inspector General James F. Curtis and Idaho state forces.[18] Although Carlin's orders reached him late in the afternoon on the twelfth, he had been anticipating them. All day the usually placid army post on the lake buzzed with activity as four companies of the Fourth United States Infantry prepared to go into action. The colonel and his force with a large quantity of field equipment embarked on the Northern Pacific steamer "Georgia Oakes" about 5:30 p.m.[19] Two hours later they were at the town of Harrison at the

---

[14] *Spokane Review,* July 12, 1892, p. 2, copy of telegram from E. J. Curtis (Adjutant General) at Boise to J. F. Curtis (Inspector General) at Wallace, dated July 11, headed General Order 14.
[15] The best copy of this telegram is found in the *Willey Collection,* no. 12, on executive stationery, typewritten and signed. Another authentic copy, signed, is filed in *Governor's;* also included in *Congressional Dispatches,* p. 16; and printed in *Idaho Daily Statesman,* July 12, 1892, p. 8; *Spokane Review,* July 13, 1892, p. 2; *New York Herald,* July 13, 1892, p. 1.
[16] Harrison's telegram to Elkins was printed in *New York Herald,* July 13, 1892, p. 1; *Spokane Review,* July 13, 1892, p. 2.
[17] The military orders are best followed in the *War Department Messages and Documents, 1892,* I, pp. 106-112, Ruger and Carlin; pp. 118-119, Merritt. Governor Willey's communications with Schofield, Ruger, and Carlin are included (in part) in *Willey Collection,* nos. 23, 37, 38, 40, 41, all of July 12, 1892. *Idaho Daily Statesman,* July 13, 1892, p. 8, prints Schofield's original message to Willey. *Spokane Review,* July 13, 1892, p. 2, Washington dispatch, outlines the War Department's activities on July 12.
[18] A copy of the message, Schofield to Carlin, July 12, 1892, in *Congressional Dispatches,* p. 19.
[19] Carlin's report, *War Department Messages and Documents, 1892,* I, p. 110.

mouth of the Coeur d'Alene River. Prudently, Carlin decided not to proceed up the river in the darkness, fearing a possible ambush and realizing that his 168 men could not cope with a large force well armed and disciplined, as the rioters were reported to be. So, while the unfortunate nonunion men were waiting for the "Georgia Oakes" at the Mission, and were being robbed and harried into the forest while they waited, Colonel Carlin and his four companies unloaded their field equipment from the same "Georgia Oakes" and made camp at Harrison.[20]

At Fort Missoula, Montana, a similar scene was being enacted that day. Under orders from General Merritt, three companies of the Twenty-fifth United States Infantry (colored), under Captain W. I. Sanborn, were sent forward to the Coeur d'Alenes, there to report to Colonel Carlin and the authorized officer.[21] This force left Missoula on a Northern Pacific special train over the cutoff some time in the night of the twelfth. The Missoula companies arrived at Mullan about 6:30 a.m. on the thirteenth, the first troops to enter the Coeur d'Alene district. At Mullan their progress was halted, however, by the gaps in the track caused by the explosions the night before. The soldiers picnicked along the railroad all morning, but did not move far from their train, since they were getting a frosty reception from the citizens of Mullan. About noon Captain Sanborn received orders from Colonel Carlin to return to Missoula and to join him (Carlin) as soon as possible by way of Sandpoint and Coeur d'Alene City.[22] On the return trip to Missoula that afternoon of the thirteenth, the train carrying the troops had as a passenger, Peter Breen, of the Silver Bow Trades and Labor Assembly, on his way back to Butte.[23] Colonel Carlin was later severely criticized for sending the Missoula companies back, after they had already entered the district,[24] but he defended his action in his report to General Ruger, saying that he believed "it of the utmost importance that the United States troops should not meet with a defeat or even a check."[25]

On the morning of the thirteenth, Colonel Carlin moved up the Coeur d'Alene river valley over the Union Pacific line to Cataldo, a point just above and across the river from the old Mission. There he was joined by the six companies of the Idaho National Guard, 192 strong. At Harrison, the night before, Inspector General Curtis had joined the force and had assumed the joint command with Colonel Carlin.[26] Curtis' military rank was actually that of colonel, earned in the Civil War where he commanded a regiment in California. Previous to the war he had been chief of police in San Francisco.[27] Curtis did not presume to give military orders to Carlin, but since he represented the state authority and since the federal troops were sent specifically to assist the state in restoring and preserving order, the command was vested

---

[20] Carlin's report, *War Department Messages and Documents, 1892*, I, p. 110.
[21] General Merritt's report, *ibid.*, 1892, I, p. 118.
[22] *Ibid.*, I, p. 118; *Spokane Review*, July 14, 1892, p. 8.
[23] *Spokane Review*, July 14, 1892, p. 8.
[24] By W. B. Heyburn in telegrams to Senator Dubois, July 13 and 14, *Congressional Dispatches*, pp. 23, 28, 29.
[25] Carlin, I, p. 111.
[26] *Ibid.*, I, p. 110.
[27] A sketch biography of J. F. Curtis appeared in *Spokane Review*, October 15, 1892, p. 5.

in Curtis. Throughout the four months of the military occupation, Carlin and Curtis worked together in commendable harmony.

Colonel Carlin was still unwilling to advance into the heart of the Coeur d'Alenes without a larger force. So he established a camp at Cataldo on the thirteenth, and waited for reinforcements which arrived during the next 24 hours from Fort Spokane, Washington. Still other troops were on the way from Fort Keogh and Fort Missoula, Montana, and Vancouver Barracks, Washington.[28] Another reason prompted Carlin to remain a day at Cataldo. The nonunion men at Wardner had not yet been sent out of town; the Bunker Hill concentrator still remained in the control of the union guards. Manager Clement feared that a hasty advance of the troops to Wardner might result in the destruction of the mill, a possible massacre of the nonunion men, and a pitched battle in the valley. Accordingly, Clement wired to Carlin, to Governor Willey, and to W. B. Heyburn to delay the advance of the troops until the men could be sent out safely.[29] At Spokane Heyburn denounced this message as bogus—a union forgery—and he wired Carlin, Wiley, and the Idaho delegation in Washington to disregard the alleged message from Clement and push on to Wardner.[30] In spite of the frenzied efforts of Heyburn to speed the military advance, Colonel Carlin and General Curtis, in close proximity to the scene, determined that Clement's message was not only genuine but also excellent advice.[31] In the evening of the thirteenth the trainload of nonunion miners passed Cataldo on its way to Tekoa. Sheriff Cunningham had accompanied the train down from Wardner to the Shoshone County line —just east of Cataldo—and he dropped off for a conference with the military commanders before returning to Wallace.[32]

Late in the same day, Wednesday the thirteenth, Governor Willey at Boise issued a proclamation which laid Shoshone County under martial law.[33] A copy was at once telegraphed to General Curtis at Cataldo, with instructions that he publish and post it conspicuously throughout the county.[34] This proclamation did not actually use the phrase "martial law." It declared the county to be in "a state of insurrection and rebellion."[35] Subsequent orders from the governor to General Curtis provided the authority for the suppression of the rebellion and the exercise of the powers of martial law.[36] Other state appointees, commissioned by the governor and en route to the scene of action, were A. J. Pinkham, Secretary of State (not to be confused with Joseph Pinkham, United States Marshal), as Quartermaster General; George M. Parsons of Hailey as Judge Advocate General; and Dr. S. E. Bibbex of

[28] Carlin, I, p. 110.
[29] *Ibid.*, I, p. 110, for the message to Carlin; *Idaho Daily Statesman*, July 13, 1892, p. 8, for a copy of Clement's message to Willey.
[30] *Congressional Dispatches*, pp. 21, 26-27, Heyburn to Dubois; *Idaho Daily Statesman*, July 13, 1892, p. 8, Heyburn to Willey; *Willey's Collection*, no. 31, gives Willey's acknowledgment of Heyburn's message.
[31] Carlin, I, p. 110.
[32] *Idaho Daily Statesman*, July 14, 1892, p. 1.
[33] Issued upon application from C. W. O'Neil, Prosecuting Attorney, and H. S. Gregory, Probate Judge, of Shoshone County. Their message printed in *Idaho Daily Statesman*, July 14, 1892, p. 8.
[34] *Willey Collection*, no. 51, Western Union blank, handwritten, signed in pencil; also *Idaho Daily Statesman*, July 14, 1892, p. 8.
[35] A perfect copy of the proclamation with signatures and seals in *Governor's*, and attached to it is a pencil draft of the same paper. Also *Willey Collection*, no. 44; and *Idaho Daily Statesman*, July 14, 1892, p. 8.
[36] A full discussion of these orders in the following chapter.

Grangeville as Surgeon General. These appointees, attached to the national guard organization, were to constitute General Curtis' staff.[37]

In the morning of July 14, the military camp at Cataldo was leveled to the ground, packed, and loaded aboard a special Union Pacific train. The combined state and federal military forces, numbering now about 800 men, also boarded the train and the start was made for the Coeur d'Alenes. Slowly, very slowly, the train crept up the valley. A flat car loaded with a company of soldiers was pushed ahead of the engine. At every bridge on the way the train would stop, and the men from the flat car would inspect the bridge thoroughly before the train crossed it. Rumors had drifted down the valley that rioters had planted dynamite under the bridges in order to blow them up as the troops advanced. But no explosions occurred and no dynamite was found. About 9:30 a.m. the troop train reached Wardner. By 12:30 p.m. it had reached Wallace.* All appeared quiet in the Coeur d'Alenes.[38]

At every camp or town in the district a garrison was stationed. Colonel Carlin made his headquarters at Wardner, and kept a large force there under his direct command. General Curtis held his headquarters at Wallace where half a dozen companies were also encamped. At Osburn, Wardner Junction, Gem, Burke, and Mullan smaller units were located. Idaho National Guard companies were brigaded along with army companies.[39] Toward the close of the day (still the fourteenth), the Fort Missoula companies came into Wardner from the west;[40] still later six companies from Vancouver Barracks arrived;[41] and on the morning of the fifteenth five companies from Fort Koegh, Montana, reached Mullan over the Northern Pacific. The troops in the district numbered close to 1,500.[42]

[37] Pinkham accompanied the Boise National Guard company, *Idaho Daily Statesman*, July 13, 1892, p. 8; Bibbex and Parsons were ordered to the field in telegrams, dated July 11 and 12 respectively, *Willey Collection*, nos. 11 and 17 respectively.
* See photo section.
[38] Carlin, I, p. 111; Lt. George Edgar French, *The Coeur d'Alene Riots of 1892*, p. 39; *Spokane Review*, July 15, 1892, p. 1.
[39] Distribution of the troops described in *Spokane Review*, July 15, 1892, p. 1; French, p. 39; Carlin, I, pp. 111-112.
[40] *Spokane Review*, July 15, 1892, p. 8; Carlin, I, p. 111; French, p. 39.
[41] *Idaho Daily Statesman*, July 15, 1892, p. 1; Carlin, I, p. 111; French, p. 38.
[42] *Spokane Review*, July 16, 1892, p. 2; Carlin, I, p. 112; French, p. 39.

20

Martial Law

For four months the Coeur d'Alene country, in fact all of Shoshone County, was governed under martial law. At the base of the military regime lay Governor Willey's proclamation of July 13, 1892, which declared the county to be in a state of insurrection and rebellion.[1] Upon this proclamation was built a structure of government in the form of executive orders, first, from the governor at Boise to his representative in the field, Inspector General James F. Curtis; and second, from Curtis to his subordinates and to the public at large.

The first order to General Curtis accompanied the governor's proclamation, and was simply a general order to "take full charge of all operations in the field."[2] Later the same day (July 13) a communicatioon went forward to Curtis specifying his powers and duties. He was to protect human life and property in Shoshone County; protect the right of every man to labor freely for any employer without interference; and protect the railroad and the telegraph. He was to arrest and keep safely all persons known to have been engaged in acts destructive to life and property. He was to meet force with force in order to reestablish law, order, and domestic tranquillity in the county. Details in carrying out these orders were left to General Curtis' own best discretion.[3] On the morning of the fourteenth, Governor Willey sent a postscript authorizing General Curtis and his troops to shoot anyone caught in the act of dynamiting a railroad bridge or mining property.[4] Finally, on the fifteenth, Curtis was appointed Provost Marshal of Shoshone County with the power to choose his own deputies.[5]

Clothed with this broad authority, General Curtis proceeded at once to execute his orders. Upon his return to the district with the state and federal troops on the fourteenth, he had the governor's proclamation printed and posted in all the camps and towns. However, his agents would no sooner post

---

[1] Already discussed; see Chapter XIX, note 35.
[2] *Idaho Daily Statesman,* July 14, 1892, p. 8; also in *Willey Collection,* no. 51, Western Union blank, handwritten in pencil, signed.
[3] *Idaho Daily Statesman,* July 14, 1892, p. 8; *Spokane Review,* July 14, 1892, p. 8. This important order not included in the *Willey Collection.*
[4] *Willey Collection,* no. 56, executive stationery, typewritten (carbon), signed in pencil; *Idaho Daily Statesman,* July 15, 1892, p. 8; *Spokane Review,* July 15, 1892, p. 2; French, *The Coeur d'Alene Riots of 1892,* p. 40.
[5] *Idaho Daily Statesman,* July 16, 1892, p. 8; *Spokane Review,* July 16, 1892, p. 2. Not included in the *Willey Collection.* For an interesting discussion of this whole procedure of instituting martial law, see the Report of the Committee on Military Affairs, *Coeur d'Alene Labor Troubles,* 56th Cong., 1st sess., H. Doc. 1999 (Washington, Government Printing Office, 1900), pp. 62-64.

a copy and turn away than people would crowd around it, read it with mount-ing indignation, then tear it down and make confetti of it. Curtis had to post a second series of copies and station a guard at each copy in order to keep the proclamation intact before the public.[6]

On the fifteenth, the martial rule began in earnest. An order was issued over Curtis' signature calling upon all officers and members of the miners' union of the Coeur d'Alenes to surrender themselves and their arms to the commanding officer in each locality.[7] Not a union miner ever surrendered either himself or a firearm; the order proved a waste of paper. Another order went to the Northern Pacific and Union Pacific railroads, directing them to carry no passengers within or out of the district without military passes.[8] This order remaining in force for two days (July 15 and 16) was intended to prevent the escape of rioters from the district by rail. A third order made a significant change in the personnel of the county government. Sheriff Richard A. Cunningham was summarily removed from office by order of General Curtis, and Dr. W. S. Sims, the county coroner, became acting sheriff.[9] Sims' appointment became permanent on August 1, by another order signed by Curtis.[10] Undoubtedly Cunningham proved reluctant to act and difficult to control under the new regime. Sims was an energetic man who had been active in support of the mine owners' point of view in the long crisis. He would be an ideal sheriff to conduct arrests of union leaders.[11] As soon as the new ma-chinery could be put into motion, the arrests of union leaders and members began—that very day, the fifteenth, in fact.

Late on the fifteenth came a document from Washington, D. C., intended to strengthen the state's position in the troubled district. It was a proclama-tion from President Harrison, calling upon all persons who had participated in acts of violence in Shoshone County to disperse and retire to their homes.[12] The President's proclamation was posted on the sixteenth,[13] but its admonition appeared several days too late to have any effect upon the situation—if, indeed, it would ever have been effective.

In the long period of martial law which began theoretically July 13, and actually on the fourteenth, it is interesting to observe the exact role of the military forces. They were, first and foremost, to assist in making arrests. The actual arrests were supposed to be made by civil officers, such as the sheriff and his deputies and the United States marshal and his deputies. The soldiers were to accompany the civil officers, protect them in making the arrests, and take into custody the arrested men.[14] Actually, there was much

[6] *Spokane Review*, July 15, 1892, p. 1; *Idaho Daily Statesman*, July 15, 1892, p. 8; French, p. 41.
[7] *Spokane Review*, July 16, 1892, p. 2; *Idaho Daily Statesman*, July 16, 1892, p. 1; French, p. 40.
[8] *Spokane Review*, July 16, 1892, p. 1; *Idaho Daily Statesman*, July 16, 1892, p. 8; French, p. 41.
[9] *Spokane Review*, July 17, 1892, p. 1; *Idaho Daily Statesman*, July 17, 1892, p. 5; French, p. 41. French alone gives the text of Curtis' order, dated July 15, 1892, and headed Special Order no. 3.
[10] Headed General Order no. 5, dated August 1, 1892, and printed in *Spokane Review*, August 2, 1892, p. 2. Three of Cunningham's bondsmen withdrew from his bond on August 1, and the county commissioners declared the office vacant, as reported in the *Idaho Daily Statesman*, August 3, 1892, p. 1.
[11] Judge Fremont Wood in an interview at Boise, Idaho, July 14, 1936, said that Cunningham was not corrupt nor particularly incompetent. The change was made in order to utilize Sims who was eager to coöperate with both the military authorities and the mine owners.
[12] Richardson, *Messages and Papers of the Presidents*, IX, pp. 288-289; *Spokane Review*, July 17, 1892, p. 1; *Idaho Daily Statesman*, July 17, 1892, p. 1.
[13] French, p. 41.
[14] *Idaho Daily Statesman*, July 15, 1892, p. 1, a statement by General Schofield outlining the duties of the troops. Colonel Carlin reported this procedure followed in arrests made at Wardner, his report, *War Department Messages and Documents, 1892*, I, p. 112.

confusion in the making of arrests. Governor Willey, in his anxiety lest the rioters escape, telegraphed Curtis on July 15, authorizing the latter to "arrest and hold till further orders such principal offenders as may be pointed out to you without process."[15] It is probable that the soldiers made many arrests with no civil officer present.[16]

Then came the military duty of guarding the prisoners, which turned out to be a long and arduous task. The latter half of July, all of August, and even a few days of September saw the soldiers monotonously guarding day and night a varying sized group of unwilling and uncooperative prisoners. An additional duty for the troops lay in the protection of the mines when they reopened with nonunion labor.[17] This service saved the mining companies the expense of hiring armed guards, which would otherwise have been a necessity.

The military force, at its maximum strength of about 1,500 men from July 15 to 22, gradually was cut in size. There was no need for so large a force, particularly since no actual fighting occurred and since no disposition to resist arrest appeared. The position of the Idaho National Guard was especially unsatisfactory, and it was the first unit of Curtis' force to be dispersed.

The Idaho National Guard had been in existence only a little over a year, since it was created by the first legislature of Idaho in an act passed March 15, 1891.[18] It had never received adequate funds nor adequate equipment. Most of the infantry companies were carrying cavalry carbines. Even the organization was still incomplete in 1892; there was no regimental colonel, who would have been the normal commanding officer.[19] Nevertheless, the six companies of the guard responded admirably to the governor's call. The guardsmen left their civilian occupations and endured considerable hardship in the field. Quartermaster General A. J. Pinkham struggled heroically to provide proper equipment, but he did not secure enough tents for his men until after they had been caught in one heavy summer rainstorm in the Coeur d'Alenes.[20] Although inexperienced in military service, the state troops bore their share of the martial duties and received a warm compliment from Colonel Carlin.[21]

Governor Willey became anxious to bring the guard home. After all, they were not professional soldiers. Their civilian duties called them, and their individual requests for special discharges were beginning to pile up. Furthermore—and Governor Willey was always conscious of this item—the expense was mounting day by day. The state treasury had no funds for such an emer-

[15] *Willey Collection,* no. 58, Western Union blank, handwritten in pencil, signed.
[16] *Spokane Review,* July 28, 1892, p. 3, statements delivered and resolutions passed at a mass meeting in Spokane, July 27.
[17] French, p. 40, tells of a strong guard posted at the Bunker Hill and Sullivan to protect the nonunion miners. Also *Spokane Review,* July 16, 1892, p. 1. According to *ibid.,* July 24, 1892, p. 8, the garrison was still being maintained at the mine.
[18] *General Laws of the State of Idaho Passed at the First Session of the State Legislature* (Boise, Statesman Printing Company, 1891), pp. 217-226.
[19] Conditions revealed in Adjutant General E. J. Curtis' report to Governor Willey, *Idaho Daily Statesman,* June 24, 1892, p. 5.
[20] *Idaho Daily Statesman,* July 21, 1892, p. 8.
[21] Carlin, I, p. 112; also quoted in *Spokane Review,* September 28, 1892, p. 2.

gency.[22] So the guard came home after only two weeks' service. Willey's order to Curtis requesting their release was given on July 24;[23] two days later most of the boys were at home. Company A of Boise, on its return trip, served as guard for the 25 prisoners sent to Boise for trial in the federal court. Guards and prisoners arrived in Boise on July 25, the former to receive a rousing ovation from the citizens of the capital city.[24] One company, Company K, of Moscow, remained on duty in the Coeur d'Alenes until August 9, merely for the sake of keeping a state force in the field.[25] The governor thanked each of the six companies for their service, in a friendly personal letter.[26] However, the guardsmen had to wait until the next session of the legislature—until March, 1893, in fact—for the pay for their service.[27]

Federal troops likewise withdrew from the Coeur d'Alenes from time to time. July 27 saw the Fort Keogh and Fort Missoula battalions leave for their Montana posts.[28] On September 14, the Vancouver troops left the district.[29] A force of Fort Spokane and Fort Sherman soldiers went out on September 21.[30] A garrison of four companies of the Fourth United States Infantry, two companies from Fort Spokane and two from Fort Sherman, remained in the Coeur d'Alenes until November 15. On that date the "Georgia Oakes" carried the last unit of the army of occupation to its lakeside post.[31]

The rigors of martial law in the Coeur d'Alenes were also gradually diminished. The restriction upon railroad travel was soon lifted.[32] Then, before the end of July, the civil courts began to function again.[33] However, in August a sudden flurry of apprehension caused General Curtis to tighten up his regime. The Tiger and Poorman mines at Burke were closed down by Curtis' order and saloons were closed all over the district.[34] Not a few critics, however, saw in these moves only a further persecution of the miners' union, many of whose members had remained at work in these two friendly mines throughout all the disturbance.[35] Early in October General Curtis took a leave of absence. He had been nominated by the Republican party for Secretary of State, and he wanted to take a swing around the Idaho circle. In his absence Captain John G. Ballance of the regular army took his place as representative of the governor and head of the military government.[36] Captain Ballance had been assigned previously to assist Judge Advocate General Parsons in the

[22] *Willey Collection*, no. 72, Willey to Secretary of War, July 22, 1892; *ibid.*, no. 74, Willey to J. F. Curtis, July 22; *ibid.*, no. 75, Willey to General Ruger, July 23.
[23] *Willey Collection*, no. 77, letterpress copy, handwritten, signed; *Idaho Daily Statesman*, July 26, 1892, p. 1.
[24] *Idaho Daily Statesman*, July 27, 1892, p. 8.
[25] *Spokane Review*, August 10, 1892, p. 1.
[26] The letters dated July 25, 1892, and signed by Willey and Adjutant General E. J. Curtis, *Idaho Daily Statesman*, July 27, 1892, p. 1, for a copy of the letter sent to the Boise company.
[27] *Idaho Daily Statesman*, March 5, 1893, p. 5, for the report of the appropriation; *ibid.*, March 16, 1893, for the issuance of the treasury warrants.
[28] *War Department Messages and Documents*, 1892, I, p. 108, General Ruger; *ibid.*, I, pp. 118-119, General Merritt.
[29] *Idaho Daily Statesman*, September 15, 1892, p. 8.
[30] *Spokane Review*, September 22, 1892, p. 6.
[31] *Ibid.*, November 16, 1892, p. 8.
[32] It was in force for two days only, July 15 and 16.
[33] By an order dated July 22, 1892, signed by Curtis, and addressed to District Judge James [should be Julius] Hollemann. *Spokane Review*, July 23, 1892, p. 1.
[34] *Spokane Review*, August 19, 1892, p. 8; August 20, 1892, p. 5; *Idaho Daily Statesman*, August 23, 1892, p. 1; French, p. 44, gives the text of the orders to the Tiger and Poorman mines, dated August 16, 1892, and headed Special Order no. 53.
[35] *Idaho Daily Statesman*, August 23, 1892, p. 1; *Spokane Review*, September 2, 1892, p. 2.
[36] *Willey Collection*, no. 97, Willey to Ballance, October 7, 1892, Western Union blank, typewritten, signed in ink.

legal work connected with the release of prisoners, and had thus become associated with the state's staff.[37] In October there also occurred another change
of sheriff in Shoshone County. This time it was the county commissioners
who chose S. P. Donnelly to replace Dr. Sims who had resigned—a change
of procedure which shows the relaxation of the military rule.[38]

Governor Willey, reluctant to undertake military intervention in the first
place, soon became eager to end martial law. As early as July 28, he suggested
withdrawing the troops and restoring the civil government.[39] Again in August, September, and October, the governor repeated the suggestion.[40] Each
time, however, his proposal encountered vigorous objections from the mine
owners and their sympathizers who announced that a withdrawal of the troops
would result in a renewal of hostilities in the district. Their nonunion operations still required military protection.[41] Each time General Curtis sided with
the mine owners, and their combined voice induced Willey to continue the
military rule month after month. Finally, when Willey became convinced that
the fears of the mine owners were groundless, that is, in the middle of November, he issued his proclamation ending martial law. The message to Curtis
which contained the proclamation was dated November 15. The date on the
proclamation upon which martial law should end was left blank. General
Curtis filled in the blank with November 19.[42]

A curious sidelight of the subject of martial law in the Coeur d'Alenes
revealed the militant temper of one group of the population. Late in July the
substantial business folk of the district (61 residents of Wallace and an unknown number from Wardner), headed by prominent mine owners, drew up
and signed a petition begging President Harrison to establish a permanent
military post within the district. Fort Sherman was too far away, they argued,
in case there should be a repetition of the present emergency.[43] Even earlier,
the Idaho senators had been approached on this proposition by the Pinkhams.[44] The movement, which got away to a brilliant start, soon found itself
heading in three directions, as the advocates of Wallace, Wardner, and Osburn began to clamor for the location of the proposed post. [45] On July 27,
Governor Willey wrote to President Harrison and recommended the establishment of such a post, but in Willey's letter there is a singular lack of enthusiasm for the project.[46] Harrison's reply was entirely unsympathetic, and
the movement collapsed.[47]

[37] *Idaho Daily Statesman,* July 24, 1892, p. 1, for first mention of Ballance; also *Willey Collection,*
no. 87, Willey to Curtis, July 27, 1892, Western Union blank, handwritten in ink, signed.
[38] *Spokane Review,* October 13, 1892, p. 1; *Willey Collection,* no. 98, Willey to Ballance, October 12,
1892, and *ibid.,* no. 99, Willey to John L. Livers, October 14, 1892.
[39] *Willey Collection,* no. 88, Willey to Curtis, dated July 28, Western Union blank, handwritten in
ink, signed. Also letters from Willey to Curtis and Willey to George B. McAuley, both dated July 28,
1892, filed in *Governor's.*
[40] *Willey Collection,* no. 94, Willey to V .M. Clement, dated August 5, 1892; *ibid.,* no. 95, Willey to
Curtis, September 8, 1892; letter, Willey to Clement, dated September 6, 1892, in *Governor's;* letter,
Willey to John A. Finch, dated October 27, 1892, in *Governor's.*
[41] *Spokane Review,* July 29, 1892, p. 2; July 30, 1892, p. 1; September 7, 1892, p. 2; October 3,
1892, p. 8; *Idaho Daily Statesman,* September 13, 1892, p. 8.
[42] The original proclamation is filed in *Governor's.* Copies were printed in Spokane Review, November 19, 1892, p. 2; *Idaho Daily Statesman,* November 19, 1892, p. 1.
[43] *Spokane Review,* August 3, 1892, p. 2, for a belated general report of the petition.
[44] *Congressional Dispatches,* pp. 32-33, four messages dated July 19, 1892, in which Senators Shoup
and Dubois inform the Pinkhams that such an application must come from the governor.
[45] *Idaho Daily Statesman,* July 23, 1892, p. 1.
[46] The letter is filed in *Governor's.*
[47] Harrison's letter, dated August 2, 1892, was printed in *Idaho Daily Statesman,* August 9, 1892,
p. 1.

21

Arrested and Held Prisoners

ARRESTS of union leaders, members, and sympathizers began on July 15 and continued at a feverish rate for several days. Over a hundred prisoners were taken in Wardner on that first day of arrests, and a similar number at Wallace.[1] Newly appointed Sheriff Sims led in person a file of soldiers up and down the streets and alleys of Wallace, pointing out his victims.[2] The sheriff's attendant upon this and other arresting expeditions was none other than Charles A. Siringo, the Pinkerton detective, who had dropped out of the hills into Wallace as soon as the troops entered the district.[3] O'Brien, Poynton, and Eaton of the central executive committee were taken immediately at Wallace; also Dean, Heney, Tobin, and other prominent union leaders,[4] none of whom offered any resistance to arrest. At Burke, 76 miners—over half the day shift at the Tiger and Poorman mines—were taken prisoners as they stepped out of their shafts for their noon lunch on the sixteenth. The men were hustled away to Wallace without opportunity to change from their heavy underground working clothes.[5] Within a week, Justices George A. Pettibone of Gem and W. H. Frazier of Mullan, and Postmaster G. W. Marsh of Mullan were also held prisoners.[6]

Few arrests were made at Mullan, largely because the Mullan miners got away into the hills and over the state line into Montana before the officers and soldiers came after them.[7] On the nineteenth, after hearing that a gang of desperate rioters had a rendezvous in the hills above Mullan, Colonel Carlin and Lieutenant Colonel Page took two companies of soldiers and went up the

[1] *Spokane Review*, July 16, 1892, p. 2; French, *The Coeur d'Alene Riots of 1892*, p. 40; Carlin, in his report, *War Department Messages and Documents*, 1892, I, p. 112.
[2] *Spokane Review*, July 16, 1892, p. 2.
[3] Siringo, *A Cowboy Detective*, pp. 177-178.
[4] *Spokane Review*, July 16, 1892, p. 2.
[5] *Spokane Review*, July 17, 1892, p. 2.
[6] *Ibid.*, July 17, 1892, p. 2; July 21, 1892, p. 1.
[7] *Ibid.*, July 17, 1892, p. 2; *Congressional Dispatches*, p. 32, Clement to Shoup, July 19, 1892, Clement says "All of Mullan escaped to the mountains."

Northern Pacific line to investigate and capture. The party came to the Montana summit without finding a trace of the gang. Pausing a moment at Lookout station on the railroad, Carlin dispatched a telegram to Governor Joseph K. Toole of Montana, asking permission to cross the state line in pursuit of fugitives from Idaho. Without waiting for an answer, Carlin and his party pushed on to Saltese, Montana, in the St. Regis valley. Still no trace of the desperate rioters.[8] Returning to Wallace in the evening, Carlin found a sharp telegram awaiting him from Governor Toole, who announced that he would honor any requisition from the governor of Idaho for the return of a fugitive, but he would not permit indiscriminate pursuit over the state line.[9] Probably a large number of union miners obtained safety in flight to Montana.

Later, Governor Willey sent requisition papers to Governor Toole for the arrest of Peter Breen, Gabriel M. Dallas, and John W. Sweeney.[10] Dallas and Sweeney were never apprehended. Breen, however, was arrested in Butte on August 2, and was brought back to Wallace where Sheriff Sims took custody of him as a state prisoner, on a charge of murder.[11] Peter Breen was an important figure in Montana. He had served the state as a delegate to the constitutional convention in 1889 and had been elected to the first state legislature in 1890. In labor circles he had long been prominent, particularly in the Knights of Labor, for whom he had served as master workman. In 1892 Breen was an officer (statistician) of the Silver Bow Trades and Labor Assembly, and a member of the Butte Miners' Union.[12]

The total number of arrests made in the Coeur d'Alene district was somewhere near 600, though the largest number of prisoners held at any one time was about 350, in the period of July 16 to 20.[13] With the exception of those who fled to Montana, all the union leaders, practically all of the union membership, and a considerable number of union sympathizers were taken prisoners. Most of these prisoners were confined under military guard; a few of the so-called dangerous men were held by Sheriff Sims in a temporary county lockup at Wallace. Among this latter group were Peter Breen, George A. Pettibone, Barney Reilley, and Webb Leasure.[14]

There were no prisons in the Coeur d'Alenes large enough to accommodate such an army of captives. The county jail was a tiny affair and situated at Murray, some 20 miles from the scenes of the arrests. Wardner and Wallace both had town jails which were even smaller than the county lockup at Murray. With the tremendous influx of prisoners some arrangements had to be made. In Wallace, two cottages and a large wooden storehouse were used to confine the prisoners arrested at Wallace, Gem, Burke, and Mullan.* Around these buildings high fences were built, which permitted the prisoners

---

[8] *Spokane Review*, July 20, 1892, p. 1; *Idaho Daily Statesman*, July 20, 1892, p. 1; Carlin, I, p. 112.
[9] *Spokane Review*, July 21, 1892, p. 1; July 22, 1892, p. 2, a dispatch from Helena, Montana, which gives the texts of Carlin's and Toole's messages.
[10] *Spokane Review*, July 23, 1892, p. 1; *Willey Collection*, no. 65, Willey to Curtis, July 18, 1892, regarding requisition procedure; *ibid.*, no. 66, Willey to Toole, July 18, 1892, asking coöperation.
[11] *Spokane Review*, August 3, 1892, p. 1; August 5, 1892, p. 1.
[12] Facts about Breen gathered in interviews with his surviving relatives and associates in Butte: Timothy Nolan, June 3, 1936; Joseph V. Flaherty, June 4, 1936; George O'Malley, June 4, 1936.
[13] *Spokane Review*, July 17, 1892, p. 2; July 20, 1892, p. 1; July 21, 1892, p. 1; French, p. 42.
[14] *Spokane Review*, August 24, 1892, p. 1.
* See photo section.

to exercise and made the guard duty easier.[15] In Wardner a big warehouse by the Union Pacific railroad track served as a prison for those arrested at Wardner, Osburn, and Murray. A stockade 14 feet high surrounded the warehouse and made it secure.[16] These were but inadequate makeshift, yet they had to serve, for nothing better could be found. Sanitary arrangements had to be constructed, and at first these too were inadequate.[17] Quartermaster General A. J. Pinkham found it impossible to provide beds and bedding for all; even the feeding of the prisoners proved to be a difficult job for Pinkham.[18]

Complaints, long and loud, went up from the prisoners and their friends. Eventually these complaints reached influential persons at Boise and Washington, D. C. Investigations were ordered by Governor Willey and the Department of Justice.[19] The reports of the investigating committees showed that by the middle of August conditions in the military prisons had materially improved,[20] but they disclosed bad conditions still existing in the county cells under Sheriff Sims. George Pettibone complained of being kept four weeks in solitary confinement. Peter Breen made a succinct statement of his discontent:

> . . . I have been shut up in a small cell without ventilation and with little light except what comes through the bars. No friends have been permitted to see me. We could not get permission to have a barber shave us. The soldier barbers are not permitted to work among us. Each one was obliged to eat alone. That is all I have to say.[21]

Sheriff Sims admitted that he did not allow the prisoners to talk because they had talked too loudly, and he would not permit them to see visitors because that would require an additional deputy.[22]

How to dispose of so many prisoners presented a difficult problem to the state and federal authorities. To hold 300 or 400 men in prison awaiting trial would be a terribly expensive policy, considering the ordinary slowness of the courts. To turn them loose, they feared, would be to invite a repetition of the violent scenes of July 11 and 12. Judge Advocate General Parsons and a small staff of assistants began on the twentieth examining the cases of prisoners, and when they found no cause for further detention such prisoners were released.[23] However, the releases were so few that they no more than equalled the number of new arrests. On the twenty-first, a parole system was devised whereby the majority of the prisoners could go free upon signing a parole. To the surprise of the officers, very few prisoners signed the parole, and those few were not members of the miners' union. The union members uniformly rejected the offer of parole, because of certain terms in the pledge which they were required to sign:

[15] French, p. 41; *Spokane Review*, July 24, 1892, p. 1.
[16] French, p. 41; *Spokane Review*, July 17, 1892, p. 1.
[17] *Spokane Review*, July 21, 1892, p. 1.
[18] French, p. 42.
[19] *Spokane Review*, August 21, 1892, p. 1; August 23, 1892, p. 2; French, p. 45.
[20] *Idaho Daily Statesman*, August 23, 1892, p. 1; *Spokane Review*, August 24, 1892, p. 1, report of F. B. Crossthwaite of the Department of Justice; French, pp. 45-46, report of committee of officers appointed by Carlin at Curtis' request.
[21] *Spokane Review*, August 24, 1892, p. 1.
[22] *Ibid.*, August 24, 1892, p. 1.
[23] French, p. 43; *Idaho Daily Statesman*, July 21, 1892, p. 1.

... I will not attend a meeting of any society that counsels such interference [with persons engaged in mining]; ... I will not attend any unlawful assemblage of persons, or give aid or counsel to them in any way; ... I will respect and obey the proclamations of the governor of the state of Idaho and of the president of the United States.[24]

About this time—late in July—came worried messages from Governor Willey to Curtis and Pinkham. The prisoners must be disposed of at once. The governor's thrifty nature was alarmed by the mounting totals of state expenses.[25] So, on July 29, all the prisoners at Wallace were transferred from state to federal supervision.[26] The Wardner prisoners were likewise transferred on August 10.[27] Judge Charles Hoffman, United States Commissioner, at Coeur d'Alene City, came to Wallace on July 28. Charles A. Siringo appeared before Hoffman and swore out three complaints, charging violations of federal statutes and injunctions by some 500 persons. On the basis of these complaints, warrants for the arrest of the 500 named persons were issued.[28] On these warrants, the state prisoners became federal prisoners, and the expense of their housing and food was lifted from the state's tender shoulders and placed squarely upon the broad back of Uncle Sam.

Under the energetic administration of Commissioner Hoffman, Special Investigator Frank B. Crossthwaite from the Department of Justice, and United States Attorney Fremont Wood, the prisoners' cases began to receive attention. About 200 prisoners were taken over by the federal authorities.[29] Many were released on bonds ranging from $300 to $5,000.[30] Certain others were sent to Boise or Coeur d'Alene City for trial. The number of prisoners would have decreased greatly had it not been for new arrests under the federal warrants, and additional arrests in August when General Curtis was cleaning out the Tiger and Poorman mines again. On September 3, there were still well over a hundred prisoners being guarded by United States troops. On that date all prisoners not scheduled for trial—135 in all—were released upon their own recognizance, even though all of them were under indictment by a federal grand jury.[31]

How did the union miners spend their days or weeks in the military prisons? It was a monotonous existence, of course. Yet there was considerable gaiety too inside those stockades and fences. The men were jolly and full of good spirits at first. The arrest and the confinement were novelties. They sang songs to an accordion accompaniment; they told jokes; they greeted each newcomer by his nickname, slapping him on the back and making him welcome.[32] John Tobin, of the Burke union, had served in the British army

    [24] *Spokane Review*, July 22, 1892, p. 1; *Idaho Daily Statesman*, July 22, 1892, p. 1, both papers print the text of the parole. *Spokane Review*, July 29, 1892, p. 2; July 31, 1892, p. 3; August 3, 1892, p. 2, for comment on the small number paroled.
    [25] *Willey Collection*, no. 88, Willey to Curtis, July 28, 1892, Western Union Blank, handwritten in ink, signed; *ibid.*, no. 89, Willey to Pinkham, July 28, 1892, Western Union blank, handwritten in ink, signed.
    [26] *Spokane Review*, July 30, 1892, p. 1; French, p. 43.
    [27] *Spokane Review*, August 11, 1892, p. 1; French, p. 43.
    [28] The complaints and the warrents, all dated July 29, 1892, are on file in the U. S. Moscow file 1.
    [29] *Spokane Review*, July 30, 1892, p. 1; August 11, 1892, p. 1.
    [30] *Spokane Review*, August 2, 1892, p. 2; August 9, 1892, p. 2; August 10, 1892, p. 1; August 11, 1892, p. 1.
    [31] *Ibid.*, September 6, 1892, p. 2; French, p. 47.
    [32] *Spokane Review*, July 24, 1892, p. 1.

and he organized a guard mount squad from his fellow prisoners at Wallace to give a little competition to the troops. The men in the formation carried wooden guns and Tobin flourished a wooden sabre. On cool summer evenings the martial performance inside the prison fence was a colorful one. Tobin was proud of his men's precision, and when the squad occasionally faltered, he would chastise them with this devastating rebuke: "I am disgusted with yees; ye don't drill any better than the Idaho militia."[33] An example of the good humor prevailing at the Wardner prison was given one day in August when the mail was being distributed. A corporal was calling off the names from a bundle of letters and papers. After calling a few prisoners' names, he sang out "George B. McAuley." The roar of laughter which went up was audible a mile away.[34]

There were some unpleasant pictures, too, in the prison camps. When the midsummer heat came on late in July and August, the gay spirits of the prisoners wilted. They lay inert upon the ground on the shady side of the buildings or stockades through the heat of the day—"a sweltering mass of humanity," as a Spokane reporter wrote it.[35] Personal feuds sprang up among the prisoners. On August 1, Barney Reilley pulled a knife and stabbed M. J. Donnelly painfully in the arm and in the abdomen before the soldiers could separate them.[36] The constant presence of the soldiers became annoying to the prisoners after a time. And once, when Charles A. Siringo went into the prison yard to identify a certain prisoner, the anger of the captive miners flared up into a near riot. Siringo's presence was like a red flag before a corral of angry bulls. Only the cocked pistol in Siringo's hand and the ready rifles in the soldiers' hands preserved peace.[37]

The sympathetic attention and kind favors of wives, relatives, and friends in the community helped to make the miners' stay in the prison pens tolerable. Every day visitors came with fruit, books, pastries, newspapers, and little luxuries for the men. A box of chewing gum one day made the whole group happy, and gifts of tobacco were particularly welcome.[38] The crowning event of the prison season probably was a banquet spread for the prisoners by about 40 ladies of Wallace on Tuesday night, July 19. Fresh strawberries and cream, sandwiches, pies, ice cream, and cake were served in both of the Wallace guard houses that night. G. W. Marsh, postmaster at Mullan, acted as toastmaster at guardhouse no. 2, and he proposed a vote of thanks to the Wallace ladies in a speech full of gratitude and chivalry.[39]

[33] French, pp. 46-47.
[34] *Spokane Review*, August 3, 1892, p. 2.
[35] *Ibid.*, August 2, 1892, p. 2.
[36] The whole incident is vividly told in the transcript of proceedings agianst Reilley in the Justice court, filed in the case of *The State of Idaho versus Bernard Reilly* in the District Court, First Judicial District, in and for Shoshone County, Idaho. Idaho Wallace file 91.
[37] Siringo, *A Cowboy Detective*, pp. 179-180; John Hays Hammond, *Autobiography*, I, p. 195.
[38] *Spokane Review*, July 21, 1892, p. 2.
[39] *Spokane Review*, July 21, 1892, p. 2.

22

Community Life
Under Martial Law

MARTIAL LAW during the four months of its existence brought new factors into the community life of the Coeur d'Alene district. The first of these was the military population, the troops. Varying in number from almost 1,500 men in the middle of July to about 200 in October and November, the blue-clad army men made a colorful new element in the Coeur d'Alene communities. The life of the army camps was an interesting one.

Most of the soldiers were quartered at Wallace and Wardner. The men lived in small tents set up on vacant land. Practically all the valley bottom land in both these towns had been occupied even in 1892, so that the soldiers camped on rough, uneven ground which generally precluded the neat regular rows of tents of a model camp. One old veteran declared that the Coeur d'Alene camps resembled the small short-time encampments of the Civil War, with the tents set irregularly on the rough ground and with fires burning at intervals throughout the camp.[1] There was but little shade available and the camps were hot and dusty through the midsummer season. At Wardner military drills and parades were held on the baseball diamond where the men went through their maneuvers enveloped in a cloud of dust.[2]

The relations of the soldiers to the civilian population in the district were harmonious and friendly in general. There were no brawls and very few cases of drunkenness.[3] Not until after the bulk of the arrests had been made, however, did discipline relax to the point of permitting social contacts with the townspeople.[4] Then there occurred a series of social events in which both elements of the population participated. The ladies of Wallace who had spread a feast for the union prisoners, when they learned that the army fare did not compare any too favorably with prison food, promptly spread a sim-

---

[1] *Spokane Review,* August 25, 1892, p. 8.
[2] *Spokane Review,* September 2, 1892, p. 2.
[3] Colonel Carlin in his report, *War Department Messages and Documents,* 1892, I, p. 112, compliments the troops on their good conduct record; repeated in *Spokane Review,* September 28, 1892, p. 2.
[4] *Spokane Review,* July 24, 1892, p. 2, tells of the formal relations of troops and citizens early in the occupation.

ilar festive board for the soldiers.[5] Prominent citizens of Wallace entertained the officers with a banquet early in August, at which Colonel Carlin and General Curtis and other officers responded to elaborate toasts.[6] The ladies of Wardner invited their military men to a dance.[7] The soldiers responded with public entertainments at the camps, in which band music and amateur dramatics were featured.[8] One Sunday evening in July (the twenty-fourth), a religious service was held in the Wardner camp, and a quartet of singers from the Negro companies sang gospel hymns far into the night.[9] Baseball games between army teams and town teams occurred and were hotly contested affairs. When the Wallace team nosed out the picked nine from the Fort Keogh companies by a score of 12 to 11, it was an epic struggle indeed.[10] In August and September the troops performed a valuable service to Wallace and Wardner when they made sanitary cleanups in both those towns. Noxious odors were eliminated so that the towns "smelled sweet in the sunshine."[11]

Within the camps the soldiers found many devices for whiling away the long summer days and evenings when they were not on active guard duty. The men stationed at Burke went huckleberry picking in the hills in August and had delicious pies afterwards.[12] Some hunted; some fished; many sat and sang around bonfires in the evenings.[13] One soldier shot a bear within a mile of the Wardner camp, and he and his comrades skinned the carcass.[14] Those troopers who were stationed at the Bunker Hill mine and mill took to riding empty buckets on the tramway. Nearly all the men collected ore specimens, and some did a little amateur prospecting on the side.[15]

A few records tell of remarkable feats of ingenuity by the soldiers. Two men in the Wardner camp spent a whole day in the midsummer hot season building a bower of evergreen branches to shade their tent. When the work was done, observers found the tent not only shaded, but also decorated with skull and crossbones and bearing signs which read "Bill Jones' Sweat Hotel; Proprietor late of Arizona," "Free Dance," "Guests will meet with prompt service when their demands are enforced with a six-shooter."[16] Three other men worked two days constructing a miniature model of the Bunker Hill tunnel, tramway, and concentrator. After it had been on display a short time, "strikers" came rioting and blew up the tunnel, destroyed the tramway, and burned the mill. Then "troops" came in, dispersed the "strikers" and put them to work cutting wood for the cook fire. Thus the Coeur d'Alene labor war was reenacted in miniature by some of the actual participants.[17]

Payday was eagerly awaited in the camps, and there was a good deal of

[5] *Ibid.*, July 24, 1892, p. 1, dates this event as July 21.
[6] *Ibid.*, August 7, 1892, p. 8, dates this gathering as August 6; *Idaho Daily Statesman*, August 11, 1892, p. 5, prints Curtis' response to a toast to Governor Willey.
[7] *Spokane Review*, August 30, 1892, p. 5, the dance occurred on August 27.
[8] *Ibid.*, August 25, 1892, p. 8, tells of one such entertainment given on August 23.
[9] *Ibid.*, July 29, 1892, p. 2.
[10] *Ibid.*, July 26, 1892, p. 1, game played on Sunday, July 24.
[11] French, *The Coeur d'Alene Riots of 1892*, p. 45; also *Idaho Daily Statesman*, September 8, 1892, p. 4, quoting a report in the *Wardner Barbarian*.
[12] *Spokane Review*, August 5, 1892, p. 2.
[13] *Ibid.*, July 29, 1892, p. 2.
[14] *Ibid.*, August 6, 1892, p. 8.
[15] *Ibid.*, July 24, 1892, p. 8.
[16] *Ibid.*, August 6, 1892, p. 8.
[17] *Spokane Review*, August 25, 1892, p. 8.

dissatisfaction when the paymaster came late.[18] With money in their pockets the soldiers could cut a larger figure in town. It was shortly after one such payday that the only recorded clash between soldiers and civilians occurred. At Wardner on the night of September first a group of soldiers fought with a certain ex-deputy sheriff called Pete Clancy. Pete drew a gun on the boys, whereupon they promptly beat him up, took his gun, and carried it away.[19]

Perhaps the mere presence of the troops in the district was responsible for a military spirit which flourished in the Coeur d'Alenes that summer. More probably the interest in military affairs was due to the desire and even the anxiety of lovers of "law and order"—the mine owners and their sympathizers—to keep the upper hand in the struggle for power in the community. The agitation for a permanent army post in the Coeur d'Alenes has already been discussed; as have also the successful efforts of this same group to extend the duration of martial law.[20] On September 7 they succeeded in reorganizing the Wallace company of the Idaho National Guard. The circumstances of this reorganization were unusual. Whereas other companies throughout the state had waited long for rather poor equipment, Company A, Second Regiment, was immediately and handsomely equipped, by means of a $5,000 donation from the Mine Owners' Association.[21] In addition, a shipment of supplies ordered by Company K, of Moscow, arrived in Wallace and was handed over to the new company, much to the Moscow men's disgust.[22] Sheriff Sims became captain of the new Wallace company, and the 52 enlisted members were described as "a company of picked men,"[23] "the most substantial business men in Wallace,"[24] "the most prominent and influential young men in the county."[25]

In the period preceding the Wallace militia company's reorganization, its place in the community was taken by a group of veterans at Murray, the Canby Post No. 11 of the Grand Army of the Republic. Through their post commander the Murray veterans offered their services to the governor in the local crisis and requested arms and equipment.[26] Governor Willey granted their request to the extent of "20 stand of arms with equipment and 2,000 rounds of ammunition."[27] The members of the Canby Post were credited with ten arrests in the vicinity of Murray.[28]

On the economic side, the production of lead and silver was resumed on a large scale, with nonunion labor in the mines and military protection for both mines and laborers. The 300 nonunion miners who were sent out of Wardner on the thirteenth, were brought back on the fifteenth, escorted by a company of infantry.[29] The Bunker Hill and Sullivan, the Gem, the Morning,

---

[18] *Ibid.*, August 18, 1892, p. 2. *Ibid.*, August 27, 1892, p. 2, and September 14, 1892, p. 7, tell of paydays in camp.
[19] *Ibid.*, September 2, 1892, p. 2.
[20] See Chapter XX.
[21] *Idaho Daily Statesman*, September 10, 1892, p. 8.
[22] As revealed in a letter from Governor Willey to Captain J. H. McCallie of the Moscow company, October 7, 1892, in *Governor's*.
[23] *Idaho Daily Statesman*, September 10, 1892, p. 8.
[24] *Spokane Review*, September 9, 1892, p. 7.
[25] French, p. 48.
[26] French, p. 47 .
[27] A special order, dated August 11, 1892, signed, and filed in *Governor's*; not included in the *Willey Collection*.
[28] *Idaho Daily Statesman*, July 17, 1892, p. 1.
[29] *Spokane Review*, July 16, 1892, p. 1; French, p. 40.

the Sierra Nevada, the Granite, the Custer, and the Union mines, all resumed operations soon after the entrance of the troops. The Tiger and the Poorman operated with their old crews, subject to occasional interruptions as arrests and military regulations interfered. The Frisco had a special job of removing the debris of the explosion and rebuilding the mill. The wage scale offered by the mines was the same as that announced in the March ultimatum, $3.50 per day for miners; $3.00 per day for carmen and shovelers.[30] One concession was made by the owners. In a statement signed by V. M. Clement, George B. McAuley, and Charles Sweeney, and dated July 16, the owners granted their employes the rights to live and trade wherever they pleased, thus marking the end of the boarding house monopoly and weakening the company store monopoly—and, at the same time, realizing one of the miners' unions' objectives.[31]

Exact employment figures are not available, but 10 days after martial law was proclaimed, the owners reported themselves swamped with applications for work.[32] By October first, employment was back to normal.[33] By the end of November, new employment and production records were being reported.[34] For over a month of the martial law period union men worked steadily in the Tiger and Poorman mines at Burke. Then, on August 17, General Curtis closed these mines[35] and held them idle until September first, when they were reopened with a majority of nonunion men.[36] Curtis' complaint was that the union men congregated in the mines and conspired against the peace and public order of the district.[37]

Gradually the ban upon union miners was lifted. At first only those known to have taken no part in the violent scenes were hired. They worked alongside the nonunion men and received the same pay.[38] In December, when A. M. Esler acquired the Argentine mine and started extensive development work, he hired a number of prominent union men. When questioned about this reversal of his labor policy, Esler is said to have replied that he was ready and willing to bury the hatchet, and that he would hire anybody except those directly responsible or engaged in blowing up the Frisco mill.[39] A similar sentiment seemed to prevail throughout the district as the winter advanced. Union men were hired pretty generally. Even the *Wallace Miner* displayed a tendency to cease its antiunion campaign and to bury the antipathies of the past. "Let us have peace," repeated the *Miner*. "Our modes of earning a livelihood differ, but all are absolutely dependent upon the mining industry. Therefore all have a common interest in the successful operation of the mines."[40]

When the troops entered the district and arrested the union leaders, they disrupted the working of the union relief system. Immediately the destitute

[30] *Spokane Review*, July 17, 1892, p. 2.
[31] *Ibid.*, July 17, 1892, p. 2; July 23, 1892, p. 1, for the full text of the owners' statement; French, p. 41.
[32] *Spokane Review*, July 24, 1892, p. 1.
[33] *Ibid.*, October 3, 1892, p. 2.
[34] *Ibid.*, November 27, 1892, p. 8; November 28, 1892, p. 3.
[35] *Ibid.*, August 19, 1892, p. 8.
[36] French, p. 44.
[37] *Idaho Daily Statesman*, August 24, 1892, p. 4.
[38] *Spokane Review*, October 3, 1892, p. 2.
[39] *Ibid.*, December 19, 1892, p. 3.
[40] *Ibid.*, November 22, 1892, p. 6 .

families of the arrested miners applied to General Curtis for subsistence. Curtis turned them over to Quartermaster General A. J. Pinkham, as if that harried officer had not enough on his hands with prisoners and national guardsmen to provide for.[41] Pinkham telegraphed Governor Willey asking what to do in the situation, and the governor replied advising him to care for the destitute until the county commissioners were able to do so.[42] It proved to be easier to restore the union relief service than to work through the county, however. So Quartermaster General Pinkham, on July 21, in cooperation with union miners' wives and sympathetic citizens and military officers, set the relief machinery in motion again.[43] This was an easy solution to the subsistence problem, particularly since supplies were still coming in for the union from Butte and Spokane.[44]

Prounion sympathy ceased to be expressed openly in the Coeur d'Alenes after July 14, particularly during the period of the mass arrests. Union members and their friends who remained at large quietly accepted or endured the imposition of martial law. Adam Aulbach of the *Wallace Press,* disgusted at the outcome of the labor struggle in which he had been a prominent gladiator, sold out his interest in the *Press* and retired to Murray, on the North Side, where he still had his *Coeur d'Alene Sun.*[45] T. K. Jerome of the *Mullan Tribune,* labor's other spokesman, also quietly folded his tent and stole away.[46] The miners' union itself ceased to exist openly, unless the assembled prisoners in the military guard houses could be called the union. The union halls were closed and locked.[47]

The antiunion faction rode in the saddle, triumphant but apprehensive. They appropriated for themselves the title "lovers of law and order." The activities of this faction along military lines have already been discussed. They realized that the military force was all that kept them in power, at least in the first month of martial law. To strengthen still further their position, they set up defensive civilian organizations in all the Coeur d'Alene towns. These were known as "Law and Order Leagues."[48] The membership of these leagues was reported to number about 800, a figure which included nearly all the mine owners, most of the business and professional men in the district, and nearly all the employers of labor and the moulders of public opinion.[49] The league members paid dues[50] and pledged themselves to obedience to the law and assistance to officers of the law in maintaining public order.[51]

[41] French, p. 42; *Idaho Daily Statesman,* July 20, 1892, p. 5.
[42] *Willey Collection,* no. 68, Willey to A. J. Pinkham, July 19, 1892, Western Union blank, handwritten in ink, signed.
[43] *Spokane Review,* July 22, 1892, p. 2; *Idaho Daily Statesman,* July 22, 1892, p. 1; both papers print the text of the order.
[44] *Spokane Review,* July 21, 1892, p. 2.
[45] *Idaho Daily Statesman,* July 21, 1892, p. 1.
[46] *Ibid.,* July 22, 1892, p. 1.
[47] *Spokane Review,* July 26, 1892, p. 1.
[48] *Ibid.,* July 26, 1892, p. 1, for first mention of the leagues.
[49] As set forth in an affidavit of October 11, 1892, in support of a motion for change of venue in the case of *The State of Idaho versus Peter Breen et al.* The affidavit (typewritten) is signed by Breen, Leasure, and six others, filed in Idaho Wallace file 93.
[50] Henry Howes of Wallace testified in the Leasure murder trial that he had paid $2.00 dues to the Wallace League, *Spokane Review,* December 10, 1892, p. 8.
[51] The objectives of the leagues were explained by their founders, Wm. H. Clagett and W. W. Woods, in an affidavit of October 12, 1892, before the district court in the case of *The State of Idaho versus Bernard Reilly,* Idaho Wallace file 91.

William H. Clagett and W. W. Woods, distinguished pioneer citizens of the district, were the founders of these societies. Nevertheless, in spite of their illustrious founders and their noble objectives, the leagues quickly fell into questionable repute. The members began to search for evidence which would lead to arrest and conviction of participants in the recent uprising.[52] Union sympathizers characterized the leagues as adjuncts and tools of the Mine Owners' Association who did the owners' dirty work for them.[53] Even Governor Willey feared that it was only a vigilance committee under a deceptive name.[54] The "law and order" people were particularly worried because, although hundreds of union members were arrested, less than a score of rifles were ever found by arresting and searching parties. The arms carried by the union miners were successfully cached, and they might be used again.[55]

Gradually, in the last days of July and later, men began to defend the union policy and line of action on the streets of the Coeur d'Alene towns without suffering arrest.[56] Letters advancing the prounion point of view began to appear in the *Spokane Review* in August, although one suspects that they were printed only for the purpose of being refuted in subsequent issues. For each prounion letter, three answers were printed, on the average.[57]

The *Spokane Review* tended to marshal antiunion press opinion outside the district. Always inclined to give more space to the owners' case, the *Review* became hysterical when violence broke out. It opened its news columns to the wildest rumors and to the exaggerated details of alleged atrocities, such as the Mission "massacre." Its editorials fulminated day after day against the union's "lawless regime,"[58] the "tyranny of the mob," [59] and "savagery;"[60] and then it turned to a cry for "justice," meaning the punishment of the participants to the extreme penalities of the law.[61] The reaction of the press in general throughout the Northwest tended to follow the lead of the *Review*, since the *Review* was the closest daily paper to the scene of the disturbance which had a wide circulation. The violence was universally condemned and a determination was expressed that law and order must prevail.[62]

Organized labor remained loyal to the union miners in the face of an adverse press. Money and supplies continued to come from many sources, particularly Butte and Spokane.[63] As the union leaders were placed on trial, a widespread campaign was launched to collect a miners' defense fund. On July 27, a big labor rally took place in Spokane at the Haymarket Square.[64] Speakers harangued an audience of a thousand men. George Smith of the

[52] The affidavit of Breen et al., cited above in note 49.
[53] *Spokane Review*, December 22, 1892, p. 5, the closing argument of James H. Hawley before the jury in the Leasure murder trial.
[54] Opinion expressed in a letter, Willey to J. F. Curtis, July 28, 1892, in *Governor's*.
[55] *Spokane Review*, September 3, 1892, p. 2, a quotation from the *Wallace Miner*.
[56] *Spokane Review*, July 24, 1892, p. 2; August 5, 1892, p. 2, for examples.
[57] E. g. a prounion letter by Lucy Anderson in *Spokane Review*, July 31, 1892, p. 3, refuted in letters by Linus Edmunds in issue of August 5, 1892, p. 2; An Observer, August 6, 1892, p. 5; and George W. Owens, August 9, 1892, p. 2.
[58] *Spokane Review*, July 12, 1892, p. 6.
[59] *Ibid.*, July 13, 1892, p. 6.
[60] *Ibid.*, July 14, 1892, p. 6.
[61] *Ibid.*, July 20, 1892, p. 6.
[62] E.g. in a sampling of editorial opinion throughout the Northwest in the *Spokane Review*, July 14, 1892, p. 6, in a column entitled "The Idaho Horror."
[63] *Spokane Review*, July 20, 1892, p. 2.
[64] *Spokane Review*, July 28, 1892, p. 3.

miners' union central executive committee, who had been in Portland when the excitement occurred, made the chief oration. Money was raised; music hall entertainment was furnished between speeches; and resolutions of confidence and support were passed carrying such forceful language that the *Spokane Review* editorialized "The representatives of organized labor in Spokane have gone crazy."[65] The annual convention of the American Federation of Labor met in Philadelphia in December and voted powerful resolutions of support to the miners and appropriated $500 to their defense fund.[66] The Federation also called for a congressional investigation of the whole Coeur d'Alene problem.[67] Organized labor in general accepted the view that the state and federal intervention in the Coeur d'Alenes was an unwarranted suppression of the local government, and that Governor Willey was either the accomplice or the dupe of predatory capitalistic interests.[68]

---

[65] *Ibid.*, July 28, 1892, p. 6.
[66] *Ibid.*, December 14, 1892, p. 2.
[67] *Ibid.*, December 15, 1892, p. 6.
[68] *Spokane Review,* July 28, 1892, p. 3, the Haymarket Resolutions; *ibid.*, September 20, 1892, p. 4, opinions of Captain Jack O'Brien, president of the Federated Trades of Portland, Oregon; *Idaho Daily Statesman,* December 13, 1892, p. 1, report of Samuel Gompers' annual message to the American Federation of Labor convention.

23

Contempt and Conspiracy

W ITH THE miners' union leaders under arrest and the state government in control of the Coeur d'Alene district through the agency of martial law, the problem of how to proceed against the prisoners confronted Governor Willey and his aides. They soon recognized the impossibility of holding hundreds of prisoners indefinitely for trial, even though W. B. Heyburn, spokesman for the Mine Owners' Association, protested against the release of a single prisoner.[1] Governor Willey conferred either personally or by letter and telegram with United States Attorney Fremont Wood at Boise, and General Curtis and Prosecuting Attorney Charles W. O'Neil at Wallace.[2] The outcome of these conferences was a decision to proceed at once with trials in the federal court, because the injunctions issued in May laid the basis for immediate legal action. The state could try its cases later.

By July 18, Albert Hagan was in Boise making a showing before Judge Beatty on behalf of the Helena and Frisco and the Bunker Hill and Sullivan companies. He charged wholesale violation of the injunctions of May 28. Warrants for the arrest of 25 violators were issued by Beatty.[3] United States Marshal Joseph Pinkham hastened to Wallace with the warrants, arriving on the twenty-third.[4] General Curtis delivered the prisoners to Pinkham, 19 from the Wallace guard houses and 6 from the Wardner stockade. Leaving on a Union Pacific train the morning of July 25,[5] the 25 prisoners were conveyed to Boise in Marshal Pinkham's custody and under the guard of the three southern Idaho national guard companies en route to their homes— Boise, Weiser, and Hailey. Company A, of Boise, accompanied the prisoners

---

[1] *Idaho Daily Statesman,* July 19, 1892, p. 5.
[2] Three letters in the *Governor's* file: Willey to O'Neil, July 15, 1892; Willey to Curtis, July 18, 1892; Willey to Wood, July 20, 1892. Also *Idaho Daily Statesman,* July 21, 1892, p. 8, for report of conference of Willey and Wood.
[3] *Idaho Daily Statesman,* July 20, 1892, p. 5; *Spokane Review,* July 20, 1892, p. 2.
[4] *Spokane Review,* July 24, 1892, p. 8.
[5] *Ibid.,* July 26, 1892, p. 1.

all the way, and saw them lodged in the Ada County jail before acknowledging the homecoming demonstration put on by the citizens of Boise.[6]

For a week the union prisoners awaited their trial. It was a busy week, however. Prominent union leaders from Butte came to town and conferred with the defense attorneys.[7] Within labor circles a campaign was set afoot to raise a defense fund for the union miners.[8] By this time Campbell W. Bushnell was under arrest at Wallace and Frank Ganahl had quit the miners' cause in disgust, so that a new and more powerful group of attorneys was now preparing to defend the miners. Patrick Reddy, of San Francisco, California, a one-armed veteran of the Civil War, and noted for his eloquence, wit and sharpness in cross-examination, headed the new circle.[9] James H. Hawley, of Boise, and his partner William Reeves, were also employed in the miners' defense. Hawley had been a pioneer of Idaho in the 1860's, and had made a legal reputation for himself in the territorial days. This reputation was destined to grow even greater, and Hawley, years later, served the state as governor. On their first appearance in court, the new counsel for the defense achieved a minor victory. Judge Beatty admitted the prisoners to bail.[10] Bonds of $1,500 apiece for 11 of the 25 defendants were secured by prominent Boise citizens—chiefly Democrats, including ex-governor Edward A. Stevenson.[11]

The first trial opened in Judge Beatty's court on August 2. Twenty-one of the defendants were charged with contempt of court in the violation of the injunction of May 28 by participating in the attack upon the Helena and Frisco mine and mill on July 11. Six of the defendants were charged with similar contempt for participating in the seizure of the Bunker Hill and Sullivan concentrator the night of July 11 and 12.[12] Judge Beatty, who had issued the injunctions in the first place, now heard all the testimony and the arguments in the case and delivered the decisions and sentences at the end of the trial. It was thus a clear-cut case of judge-made and judge-executed law. And any discussion or evaluation of the proceedings must hang upon the character and caliber of the judge. It is the almost universal opinion of living citizens of Idaho who had dealings with Beatty that he was a mediocre judge, decidedly inferior to the quintet of attorneys who argued before him—Wood, Heyburn, Hagan, Reddy, and Hawley—and that the contempt case was not one of his outstanding performances.[13]

The trial lasted 12 days with public interest running high throughout its duration. The complainants marshalled a great array of witnesses: mine owners, such as Clement, McAuley, Sweeney, Jenkins, De Lashmutt, Gross, and Finch; deputy marshals Hammill, Harris, and Human; nonunion miners, such as John Kneebone, blacksmith at the Frisco, and Percy Summers of the Gem. The violent events of the preceding month were reviewed in great detail. Charles A. Siringo appeared on August 6 and his testimony provided the

[6] *Idaho Daily Statesman*, July 27, 1892, p. 8.
[7] *Ibid.*, July 26, 1892, p. 4; *Spokane Review*, July 26, 1892, p. 1.
[8] *Idaho Daily Statesman*, August 3, 1892, p. 8.
[9] *Ibid.*, July 27, 1892, p. 5.
[10] *Spokane Review*, July 31, 1892, p. 3.
[11] *Idaho Daily Statesman*, August 2, 1892, p. 5.
[12] *Idaho Daily Statesman*, August 3, 1892, p. 8.
[13] Such opinions, among others, were expressed to the writer by Edward Boyce, one of the defendants, and William E. Borah, an interested spectator at the trial.

climax of the complainants' case. The defendants introduced few witnesses and were content to weaken or nullify the opposing testimony in cross-examination. Wood, Hawley, Reddy, and Heyburn presented eloquent arguments at the close of the testimony. The whole chain of violent proceedings from Gem to the Mission constituted a single contempt, argued Wood and Heyburn, and anyone who participated in any part of the sequence was guilty of contempt.[14] Hawley and Reddy in their arguments alleged a long conspiracy on the part of the Mine Owners' Association, beginning with the hiring of detectives, and running through the January shutdown, the April lockout, the injunctions, importation of "scabs" and armed guards, the whole purpose of which conspiracy was to induce a violent resistance. A plaintiff who induces a violation is not entitled to redress.[15]

Judge Beatty considered the testimony and the arguments and delivered his verdict on August 11. From the evidence he concluded that the firing was begun by the miners in the hills, that both explosions at the Frisco were caused by union miners, and that driving the "scabs" out of the country was a definite policy of the miners' union—all of which constituted contempt of the order of the court.[16] Nine of the defendants he found guilty of contempt of court in the violation of the Helena and Frisco injunction, and four others guilty of contempt in the violation of the Bunker Hill and Sullivan injunction.[17] The remaining twelve defendants were dismissed from the charge of contempt. Those adjudged guilty were sentenced to terms in the Ada County jail, as follows: Thomas O'Brien and Joseph Poynton, not exceeding eight months; Thomas Eaton, John Fitzgerald, Dan Harrington, Hugh McGee, John Nicholson, Gus Peterson, Edward Boyce, Thomas Doyle, Thomas Heney, and Fred Dean, not exceeding six months; and Robert Robinson, not exceeding four months. These men were taken to the Ada County jail and began at once the service of their terms.[18]

Before adjourning at Boise, Judge Beatty ordered a special term of the United States Circuit Court to convene at Coeur d'Alene City on August 23.[19] A federal grand jury was summoned and for a week, beginning the twenty-fourth, deliberated over criminal charges brought against the miners' union leaders and members. Many witnesses, including mine owners, nonunion miners, and detective Siringo, appeared before the grand jury. Fremont Wood and Frank Crossthwaite assisted the grand jurors. On September first, the foreman presented his report. Two true bills of indictment had been found by the grand jury. These indictments charged criminal conspiracy to defeat the progress of justice in the United States Circuit Court by violation of the Bunker Hill and Sullivan injunction of May 28.[20] On the first indictment 84 men were listed as defendants. All the leaders, prominent members and well-known abettors of the miners' union were indicted—including, of course,

---

[14] *Idaho Daily Statesman*, August 12, 1892, p. 8.
[15] *Ibid.*, August 12, 1892, p. 8.
[16] *Idaho Daily Statesman*, August 12, 1892, p. 8.
[17] The sentences were announced partly on August 11 and the rest on August 13. *Idaho Daily Statesman*, August 12, 1892, p. 8; August 14, 1892, p. 8.
[18] *Idaho Daily Statesman*, August 14, 1892, p. 8.
[19] *Spokane Review*, August 11, 1892, p. 1.
[20] *Spokane Review*, September 3, 1892, p. 1.

those already imprisoned for contempt of court.[21] The second indictment listed 116 names.[22]

Fourteen prisoners were brought down from Wallace to Coeur d'Alene City at the last of August to stand trial.[23] Included among these defendants were Justices George A. Pettibone and W. H. Frazier; attorney Campbell W. Bushnell; M. L. Devine, Charles St. Clair, John Murphy, Barney Reilley, and J. W. Glass. The first name on the list of defendants in the indictment was Peter Breen, but although Breen was a prisoner at Wallace at the time, he was not placed on trial. Yet the case is filed and must be referred to as *the United States versus Peter Breen et al.* A curious division in the defense counsel occurred at this trial. Defendant Bushnell, who had been the miners' union attorney, was represented by his law partner Frank Ganahl, while the remaining 13 defendants were represented by Hawley and Reddy. A few minor embarrassments resulted from this division, such as when the counsel disagreed occasionally on challenges to prospective jurymen.[24]

The trial jury was completed on September 9. It was made up almost entirely of farmers from Latah County.[25] The trial lasted over two weeks, and was a topic of front page news in the papers of the Northwest. An array of interesting witnesses, including the sensational Siringo again, a sharp fire of cross-examination, and a flood of eloquence in the arguments characterized the trial. George Pettibone was identified by several witnesses as the dynamiter of the Frisco mill, but testimony was contradictory and far from conclusive as to which side fired the first shots in the battle at Gem. The crime charged was conspiracy, and this term required much definition and caused long argument, in the course of which attorney Pat Reddy was credited with a *bon mot* worthy of repetition. "Concert of action alone does not constitute conspiracy," argued Reddy. "The birds sing in concert; but they have no agreement to do so."[26] On September 28, the jury brought in its verdict. Four of the defendants were found guilty: George Pettibone, Mike L. Devine, Charles St. Clair, and John Murphy.[27] The remaining ten defendants were found not guilty and were discharged. Judge Beatty sentenced the guilty quartet to terms in the House of Correction at Detroit; Pettibone, 2 years; Devine and St. Clair, 18 months; Murphy, 15 months.[28]

Immediately, notice of intention to appeal was given by defense attorneys.[29] All through the fall and the following winter, action on the second indictment or upon other defendants named in the first indictment was delayed pending the outcome of the appeal proceedings. On the first and second of February, 1893, four lawyers, Patrick Reddy and Walter H. Smith, for the sentenced men, and Attorney General W. H. H. Miller and Charles W. Russell for the government, met in Washington, D. C., and argued the case

[21] The indictment is filed in U. S. Moscow file 1. The names of the defendants were printed also in *Spokane Review*, September 3, 1892, p. 1.
[22] *Spokane Review*, September 4, 1892, p. 1.
[23] *Ibid.*, September 1, 1892, p. 2.
[24] *Spokane Review*, September 9, 1892, p. 7.
[25] *Ibid.*, September 10, 1892, p. 8.
[26] *Spokane Review*, October 1, 1892, p. 3.
[27] *Ibid.*, September 29, 1892, p. 1; also the original verdict, handwriten in ink, signed by G. W. Tomer, foreman, dated September 28, 1892, and filed in U. S. Moscow file 1.
[28] *Spokane Review*, September 29, 1892, p. 1.
[29] *Ibid.*, September 29, 1892, p. 1.

before the United States Supreme Court. On March 6, Chief Justice Melville W. Fuller delivered the majority opinion in the case, now known as *George A. Pettibone et al. versus the United States.*[30] The indictment, declared Fuller, is defective. Furthermore, the acts committed are not crimes against the United States, but against the statutes of Idaho, and a federal injunction should not be employed to convict of crimes against the state. The decision of the lower court is reversed; the indictment should be quashed; and the prisoners discharged.[31]

As a result of Justice Fuller's decision, no further prosecutions under the indictments of September 1, 1892, were made in Judge Beatty's court. And since a part of the Supreme Court ruling had cast doubt upon the legality of the contempt proceedings, Judge Beatty on March 20 ordered the two contempt prisoners who still remained in the Ada County jail—namely, O'Brien and Poynton—released without completing their full terms.[32]

---

[30] *United States Reports,* Cases Argued and Decided in the Supreme Court of the United States, October terms, 1892-1893, vol. CXLVIII, pp. 197-214, *George A. Pettibone, et. al. versus the United States* (Lawyers' Edition, book 37, Rochester, N. Y., The Lawyers' Coöperative Publishing Company, 1901).
[31] *Ibid.,* pp. 209-210.
[32] *Idaho Daily Statesman,* March 21, 1892, p. 8; *Spokane Review,* March 22, 1892, p. 8.

24

The State Tries
a Case

THE MILITARY and federal authorities worked fairly rapidly in making arrests and in placing the accused on trial. The county officers lagged behind in similar duty. Governor Willey had to prod the county prosecutor into action.[1] It is true that the county took over the custody of certain prisoners, such as Peter Breen, George Pettibone, Webb Leasure, Barney Reilley, and others. Yet the conspiracy trial at Coeur d'Alene City had almost ended before any important steps were taken by the county.

On September 21, a grand jury of Shoshone County began the consideration of criminal charges at the county seat, Murray.[2] All the rest of September and the first week of October the grand jury deliberated. Charles A. Siringo made his final appearance in the district before this body.[3] When the grand jury presented its report on October 6, it became evident that the jurymen had not been idle. Four major indictments had been found against the miners' union leaders and members and sympathizers. All four indictments named the same defendants, a list of 42 persons, including O'Brien, Poynton, Pettibone, Leasure, Breen, Dallas, Eaton, and others. Three of these indictments were for murder; one charged the 42 defendants with the killing of Ivory Bean at the Gem mine;[4] the second accused them of killing John Stanlick at the Gem mine;[5] and the third charged them with the death of Archie McDonald in the explosion of the Frisco mill.[6] The fourth major in-

---

[1] Three letters in *Governor's:* Willey to O'Neil, July 15, 1892; Willey to George B. McAuley, July 28, 1892; Willey to Fremont Wood, August 22, 1892.
[2] *Spokane Review*, October 2, 1892, p. 8.
[3] *Ibid.*, October 4, 1892, p. 2; Siringo, *A Cowboy Detective*, p. 183.
[4] The indictment is on file in the record of *The State of Idaho versus Daniel W. Leasure, alies Web Leasure, et al.*, Idaho Wallace file 95.
[5] This indictment is on file in the record of *The State of Idaho versus Peter Breen et al.*, Idaho Wallace file 93.
[6] Indictment on file in the record of *The State of Idaho versus George A. Pettibone et al.*, Idaho Wallace file 96.

dictment accused the same 42 persons of malicious destruction of property in the explosion of the Frisco mill.[7]

Less important indictments were brought against Joel Warren for bringing a force of armed men into the state of Idaho;[8] against Bernard Reilley for assault upon M. J. Donnelly with intent to commit murder, while both were confined in the military prison at Wallace;[9] and against Richard A. Cunningham upon more than a score of technical charges, including withholding county funds.[10] Altogether, this grand jury in its three weeks session indicted enough people of serious crimes to keep the district court busy for years, if it had attempted to try every person so charged.

The district court under Judge Julius Holleman took up the indictments as soon as they were issued from the grand jury. The immediate problem became where to find an impartial trial jury for these cases in Shoshone County. It was an impossibility. Therefore, when James H. Hawley, on October 11, moved for a change of venue, Judge Holleman granted the request without much argument.[11] In 1892, both Kootenai and Shoshone Counties were included in the same judicial district, so that the miners' cases could be moved to Kootenai County and still be heard by the same judge and prosecuted by the same prosecuting attorney. And so it was ordered. At the same time, some of the county's prisoners were admitted to bail.[12] Peter Breen was set at liberty upon $10,000 cash bail. Breen delivered the cash to the court on October 14, then mounted a swift horse, rode furiously to Wallace (20 miles), and caught the afternoon Northern Pacific train for Missoula and Butte.[13] The story comes from authentic sources that the $10,000 cash bond was provided by Marcus Daly of the Anaconda Copper Mining Company.[14]

On November 22, the district court opened its term in Kootenai County at Rathdrum, the county seat, a town of about 400 inhabitants located in a farming district ten miles north of Coeur d'Alene Lake and about 30 miles east of Spokane.[15] The attorneys gathered for another (and final) major clash before judge and jury. The case of Daniel Webb Leasure (practically always called Webb) on the indictment for the killing of Ivory Bean at the Gem mine was chosen for the first trial. A Kootenai County jury was selected and the trial got under way on November 30.[16]

Leasure's trial was the longest and probably the most interesting of the legal battles which grew out of the Coeur d'Alene labor struggle. The prosecution had a difficult task; it had to prove not only that Ivory Bean was killed

---

[7] Indictment on file in the record of *The State of Idaho versus Thomas O'Brien et al.*, Idaho Wallace file 94.

[8] Indictment on file in the record of *The State of Idaho versus Joel Warren*, Idaho Wallace file 92.

[9] Indictment on file in the record of *The State of Idaho versus Bernard Reilley*, Idaho Wallace file 91.

[10] Indictment on file in the record of *The State of Idaho versus Richard A. Cunningham*, Idaho Wallace file 90.

[11] *Spokane Review*, October 12, 1892, p. 1; the original motions for change of venue in the above seven cases, all dated October 11, 1892, are filed with their respective records, in Idaho Wallace files 90 to 96, inclusive.

[12] *Spokane Review*, October 12, 1892, p. 1; the judge's order for bail, listing the amounts for each defendant, is on file in Idaho Wallace file 93.

[13] *Spokane Review*, October 15, 1892, p. 2.

[14] As related to the writer in an interview at Butte, Montana, June 3, 1936, by Timothy Nolan, a former law partner of Peter Breen, still practising at Butte.

[15] *Spokane Review*, November 23, 1892, p. 1; for a sketch of Rathdrum at this period see *Spokane Review*, December 25, 1892, p. 9.

[16] *Spokane Review*, December 1, 1892, p. 1.

by a bullet fired from the town of Gem, but also that Webb Leasure fired the fatal shot. For such a task, Charles W. O'Neil and his Kootenai County colleague, Robert McFarland, did not seem adequate,[17] so W. B. Heyburn was rushed to the rescue, and he took actual command of the prosecution.[18] A wealth of testimony was offered in this trial, in which the fighting at Gem and the killing of Ivory Bean were described in detail. Yet at the end of the trial it was as impossible as ever to know beyond a question of doubt which side first opened fire on July 11. The situation at Gem on that date was so tense that an accidental shot or even the imagined report of a shot could have precipitated the battle.

A number of amusing incidents were revealed in the course of the trial which offered contrast to the grim nature of the case. One witness, a certain George W. Moore of Mullan, reported a second-hand account of the battle in which Webb Leasure was barricaded behind a beer barrel at Bill Daxon's saloon during the hottest part of the fight. The Gem mine guards were said to have shot off the hoops of the barrel, leaving Webb crouching behind a pile of loose staves.[19] Another prosecution witness, Winfield Erwin, a store employe at Gem, during his cross-examination was asked to point out to the jury a certain location on a large map of the district which hung in the courtroom. Erwin awkwardly stood directly between the jury and the map. "Will you please step aside?" asked O'Neil, "the jury cannot see through you." Quickly Pat Reddy remarked, "I have no doubt but that the jury can see through this witness!"[20] Finally, the defense's alibi for Leasure struck a chord of risibility back in the Coeur d'Alenes even though it may not have appealed to the jury's sense of humor. Webb did not shoot Ivory Bean, because he was at the time lying in a heap in a corner of Daxon's saloon, dead drunk.[21] Inasmuch as Webb had been observed scores—perhaps hundreds—of times in that condition at Mullan and Wallace, the alibi had a ring of truth in it for the home folks.

The arguments before the jury were packed with erudition and eloquence, and they stand as a sort of grand summary not only of the trial but also of the labor conflict which preceded. O'Neil argued that it was sufficient to prove that when Bean was killed Leasure was aiding and abetting a conspiracy, that by preconcerted action an attack was made upon the Gem and Frisco mills, that a mob existed, and that Leasure was a member of that mob.[22] Hawley replied that there was no conspiracy by the miners' union other than a collective defense of their rights, that Leasure was not a member of the union, and that there was a strong possibility that Bean was killed by the bad marksmanship of the Gem guards.[23] Patrick Reddy, continuing the defense argument, traced the long history of the capital-labor struggle from the time of the Black Death in the fourteenth century down to the present. He argued that

---

[17] *Spokane Review,* November 29, 1892, p. 8, both O'Neil and McFarland were reported in poor physical health.
[18] *Spokane Review,* November 30, 1892, p .2.
[19] *Spokane Review,* December 9, 1892, p. 1.
[20] *Ibid.,* December 9, 1892, p. 1.
[21] *Ibid.,* December 17, 1892, p. 1; December 18, 1892, p. 9.
[22] *Spokane Review,* December 21, 1892, p. 2.
[23] *Ibid.,* December 21, 1892, p. 2; December 22, 1892, p. 5.

organized labor is the only answer to organized capital. The Mine Owners' Association provoked the fight, and once it was begun, the miners were only acting in self defense, and their course was justified.[24] To this argument W. B. Heyburn replied with an exposition of the case for law and order, for the security of life and property, which placed limitations upon justifiable unionism. There was a conspiracy which caused Bean's death, and Leasure was a part of it. Heyburn concluded with a call for a verdict of "guilty."[25]

On the twenty-third of December the case went to the jury. After two hours of deliberation the verdict came back: "not guilty." With the end of the Leasure trial the court adjourned for the Christmas holiday, and the rest of the Coeur d'Alene cases went over to the February, 1893, term in Shoshone or the March term in Kootenai.[26]

When the February and March terms came around, the Coeur d'Alene cases received quick disposal. In February, at Murray, Barney Reilley was acquitted of the assault charge—not because he had not committed the assault upon Donnelly, but because the intent to commit murder was not proved.[27] The charges against ex-sheriff Cunningham were not sustained; the jury split six to six.[28] At Rathdrum, in March, the Joel Warren case opened up and then quietly collapsed, since all the attorneys agreed that it would be impossible to prove the charge.[29] Finally, on March 28, the murder indictments were dropped and all prisoners held thereon set at liberty. Peter Breen received a refund of his $10,000 cash bail accompanied by what amounted to an apology from prosecutor O'Neil. There was no evidence, said O'Neil, that Peter Breen took any part in the fighting; on the contrary, he constantly urged moderation and lawful procedures in the crisis.[30]

By the end of March, 1893, all the members of the miners' union who had been charged with crime were at liberty.[31] The 13 convicted of contempt of court had either served their terms or had been released by Judge Beatty; the four convicted of conspiracy had had their sentences reversed by the United States Supreme Court; the one murder charge which went to trial had resulted in acquittal; and all other state indictments had been dropped. Only the federal indictments for conspiracy remained current; the Supreme Court's decision had practically invalidated them; and they were to be dropped definitely in July.

24 *Ibid.*, December 22, 1892, p. 5.
25 *Ibid.*, December 23, 1892, p. 2; December 24, 1892, p. 1.
26 *Spokane Review*, December 24, 1892, p. 1.
27 Original verdict (ms.) signed by the foreman, and dated February 21, 1893, in Idaho Wallace file 91.
28 *Idaho Daily Statesman*, March 15, 1893, p. 8, as told to the *Statesman* by James H. Hawley.
29 *Spokane Review*, March 28, 1893, p. 2; March 29, 1893, p. 1.
30 *Spokane Review*, March 29, 1893, p. 1.
31 *Ibid.*, March 29, 1893, p. 1, for comment on the facts.

25

Political
Reverberations

Iт was inevitable that the Coeur d'Alene conflict should become a political
issue; deep-seated economic questions generally do, and in addition, 1892 was
a campaign year. Already, in 1890, in Shoshone County politics an economic
class line had been drawn. Prominent mine owners, such as John A. Finch,
C. D. Porter, and John Hanley (foreman at the Hunter) went to Boise as
legislators wearing the Republican label. Richard Cunningham, Democrat,
had been swept into office as sheriff on a flood of miners' votes.[1] This political cleavage, already noticeable in 1890, was drawn rigidly in 1892, and it has
persisted with only a few local variations and exceptions to the present day.
Mine owners and their sympathizers have generally been Republicans in Shoshone County, and organized labor when it has been active politically in the
county has generally followed the Democratic party.

A further illustration of the political lineup is found in the party affilia-
tions of the principal figures in the 1892 conflict. On the Republican side were
W. B. Heyburn, Fremont Wood, Governor Willey, General Curtis, Prosecu-
tor O'Neil, the two Pinkhams, and Judge Beatty. Democrats included Frank
Ganahl, Campbell Bushnell, James H. Hawley, Patrick Reddy, Peter Breen,
Sheriff Cunningham, Justices of the Peace Pettibone, Frazier, and Angel.
An illuminating note accompanied the account of the arrests in a Spokane
newspaper: "All but 10 of the Democratic central committee of Shoshone
County are among the prisoners."[2] However, not all the Democrats were in
the union camp. Albert Hagan, one of the Mine Owners' Association attorneys was a Democrat, and so was Sheriff Sims, one of the union's sharpest
opponents.

---

[1] Henderson, Shisch, and Averill, *An Illustrated History of North Idaho*, pp. 1021-1022, for the
tabulated election returns of 1890 in Shoshone County.
[2] *Spokane Review*, July 17, 1892, p. 2.

The Coeur d'Alene labor crisis reached the explosive stage too late to exert any influence upon the national conventions of the Democratic, Republican, or People's parties. But in state conventions in the Northwest, and particularly in Idaho, the Coeur d'Alene situation influenced platform, resolutions, and candidates. The People's party, being a protest movement among farmers and laborers, was more sensitive to the labor situation than either of the old parties.[3] Organized labor strove to inject the Coeur d'Alene and the Homestead issues into the campaign whenever the opportunity arose.

In May, 1892, the Idaho state Democratic convention met at Pocatello. This meeting served only to nominate delegates to the national convention, but it paused long enough to deprecate the federal interference in the labor trouble in northern Idaho, referring doubtless to the injunctions.[4] A similar convention of the Populists a day or two later at Boise condemned both state and federal interference, and went on to express sympathy for the miners "in their unequal struggle."[5]

When the Shoshone County Republican convention met at Osburn, August 2, the mine owners were present in force, with Frank Jenkins of the Bunker Hill as chairman of the county committee. This little convention went to work condemning all acts of lawlessness and the Democratic sheriff (Cunningham, not Sims) and his deputies. The county Republicans likewise praised the actions of Governor Willey and President Harrison.[6] When the Republican state convention assembled at Moscow on August 18, it also condemned lawlessness, but it did not mention the Coeur d'Alene situation specifically. Governor Willey was not renominated; he had to make way for J. W. McConnell of Moscow who had served an extremely brief term (only two months) in the United States Senate in 1891.[7] A. J. Pinkham and George H. Roberts of the Willey administration were also knifed at Moscow. But out of the convention came one nominee from the Coeur d'Alene struggle—James F. Curtis, for Secretary of State. W. B. Heyburn's name also appeared on the party slate, as a prospective presidential elector, pledged, of course, to Harrison.[8]

The Democratic state convention at Boise, August 25, found itself in a predicament. It must condemn Governor Willey's policy, but it could not appeal to the state with a defense of the "lawless" miners. So it compromised, and condemned the state government's actions "after the suppression of all riotous demonstrations and the arrest of rioters." The platform plank went on to denounce specifically "J. F. Curtis, the military satrap now clothed with a little brief authority in Shoshone County." The Democratic gubernatorial candidate was likewise a compromise—John M. Burke, of Shoshone County.[9] Burke was a mine owner and promoter. He had been part owner of the Tiger

---

[3] For resolutions sympathetic to the miners' cause see *Spokane Review*, July 26, 1892, p. 7, People's party, Washington state platform; *Idaho Daily Statesman*, August 19, 1892, p. 8, People's party, Idaho state convention.
[4] *Idaho Daily Statesman*, May 26, 1892, p. 1.
[5] *Ibid.*, May 27, 1892, p. 1.
[6] *Spokane Review*, August 4, 1892, p. 2.
[7] *Spokane Review*, August 19, 1892, p. 1.
[8] *Ibid.*, August 20, 1892, p. 1.
[9] *Ibid.*, August 26, 1892, p. 1.

mine, and he had given his name to the town of Burke. But he was not a member of the Mine Owners' Association, and was not in sympathy with their anti-union labor policy.[10] He could thus appear either as a mine owner or as a friend of union labor, whichever the occasion demanded.

Within Shoshone County the political issues were much more clearly drawn. A vote for the Republican candidates meant a vote in support of the "law and order" regime of Willey, Curtis, Sims, et al. A vote for the Democratic aspirants indicated opposition to the martial law policies and at least a sympathetic attitude toward the miners' union. The sharpest contests centered around the offices of sheriff and the county commissioners. For sheriff the Republicans nominated Donald R. Cameron, a strong "law and order" man; the Democrats forced the issue by putting up Cunningham's chief deputy, Jack K. Waite, whose prounion sympathies were well known.

In the campaign throughout the state two questions arose. The first concerned John M. Burke, Democratic candidate for governor. Where did Burke really stand on the Coeur d'Alene issue? Was he a mine owner? Or did he actually approve the miners' union cause from start to finish? Both sides claimed him in the Coeur d'Alene district; but the mine owners' claim was not for the purpose of furthering his election—it was merely to discredit him among the working class and thus allow McConnell to profit.[11] The second question concerned the conduct of the election under martial law in Shoshone County. Would General Curtis use his authority to embarrass the Democrats? Wild rumors circulated that the Burke and Mullan precincts—Democratic strongholds—would be disfranchised by some military hocus-pocus.[12]

Democratic alarms were unfounded. The election day came and passed with no display of military force in the county beyond the closing of all saloons by order of both the governor and General Curtis.[13] In the presidential canvass, the Weaver electors carried Idaho, due to a preelection fusion of Democratic and Populist presidential tickets. McConnell and the whole Republican state ticket were elected, including Curtis for Secretary of State and Willis Sweet of Moscow for United States Representative. The 1893 legislature, however, was divided; Republicans had a majority in the lower house, while Democrats and Populists controlled the Senate.[14]

Although McConnell carried the state, he ran far behind Burke in Shoshone County. Indeed, the whole Republican state ticket went down in the county voting. Curtis was knifed particularly low. The new county commissioners were two Democrats and one Republican. Cameron, Republican "law and order" man, won the sheriff's star by a majority of one hundred twenty votes over Jack Waite. The county sent two Democratic state senators to Boise, Alexander E. Mayhew and Robert Neill; and of the four state representatives, three were Democrats and one Republican. The remaining county

[10] Burke's position is analyzed in the *Idaho Daily Statesman*, October 18, 1892, p. 4; and *Spokane Review*, November 2, 1892, p. 2.

[11] *Spokane Review*, November 3, 1892, p. 1.

[12] *Ibid.*, November 3, 1892, p. 1.

[13] Letter, Willey to Curtis, November 4, 1892, in *Governor's*.

[14] *Idaho Daily Statesman*, November 23, 1892, p. 1, what purports to be an official tabulation of the state vote.

offices were about equally divided between the parties.[15] Thus, although Shoshone County "went Democratic" on the state ticket and the majority of the legislative offices, yet on the most critical local issue—namely the sheriff's post—the "law and order" candidate won a triumph over the known—too well known—union champion, Mr. Waite.

When the legislature met in January, 1893, several reverberations of the Coeur d'Alene trouble were heard at Boise. Governor Willey retired with a farewell message in which he defended his policy.[16] His successor, McConnell, failed to control the legislature. A coalition between Democrats and Populists in the senate blocked many of the governor's projects and played some strange political tricks before adjournment. The legislature paid the special state expenses in the Coeur d'Alene affair, after cutting the figure from $23,651.60 to $16,000. This sum included the back pay due the Idaho National Guard. However, the legislature refused any compensation to officers who were also in the service of the United States, thus cutting off Captain Ballance.[17] A final devastating stroke by the senate was the defeat of the appropriation for the Idaho National Guard.[18] With no funds for continuing the guard, that organization practically went to pieces in the next few months,[19] and when a new labor crisis arose in the Coeur d'Alenes in 1894, the state found itself without any effective armed forces.

General Curtis, as Secretary of State, throughout his two years' term took a considerable amount of heckling as a result of his experiences in the Coeur d'Alenes. From time to time in 1893 and 1894, prominent union members such as Tom O'Brien and Jack Wallace wrote to Curtis asking him as Secretary of State to institute a search for a rifle or a pistol or other personal possessions alleged to have been lost while the writer was being held prisoner by the state in 1892. Curtis answered each letter courteously, but made no promises.[20] And research does not reveal any recoveries of such losses.

---

[15] *Spokane Review,* November 20, 1892, p. 8, an accurate tabulation of the county vote; also Henderson, Shiach, and Averill, p. 1022.
[16] *Idaho Daily Statesman,* January 5, 1893, p. 7.
[17] *Idaho Daily Statesman,* March 5, 1893, p. 5; French, *The Coeur d' Alene Riots of 1892,* p. 49; State of Idaho, *General Laws of the State of Idaho Passed at the Second Session of the State Legislature* (Boise, Statesman Printing Company, 1893), pp. 178-179, for the provisions of the appropriation act.
[18] *Idaho Daily Statesman,* March 16, 1893, p. 8.
[19] French, p. 48.
[20] Letter, Curtis to W. A. Jones, November 10, 1893; letter, Curtis to John Wallace, January 22, 1894, both filed in the Secretary of State's vault, State Capitol, Boise, Idaho.

26

A More Perfect Union:

The Western
Federation of Miners

T HE 13 MINERS' UNION members and sympathizers, convicted of contempt of court, and sentenced to terms in the Ada County jail, spent an interesting and productive fall and winter at Boise. The jail was crowded so that accommodations were inadequate indoors. Accordingly, the sheriff of Ada County permitted the prisoners to go outside the jail and gave them the liberty of the entire city block on which the jail stood.[1] In the hot summer days of August and September and through the clear bracing autumn weather the Coeur d'Alene miners played ball, pitched horseshoes, and loafed more or less at ease in the open air.[2] Friends and sympathizers and even passers-by stopped for a conversation with the men. Many a harangue did the union leaders deliver before interested audiences on the court house steps or in the shade of the elm trees.[3] James H. Hawley, their lawyer, made frequent visits to the men to talk over their own cases and to report the news from the north. And many long discussions took place among the men themselves. They reviewed the incidents of July and the long train of antecedent events; they considered the mistakes of their strategy; and they planned better organizing and sounder policies for the future. All recognized that the aid of the Butte union and of other labor organizations had been indispensable, and they pondered how to organize labor's forces more effectively for the whole mining West.[4]

At Butte similar discussions were taking place. The Coeur d'Alene struggle had taught some valuable lessons. The long period of special assessments,

---

[1] *Idaho Daily Statesman*, August 14, 1892, p. 8.
[2] *Ibid.*, August 17, 1892, p. 1.
[3] *Spokane Review*, October 21, 1892, p. 1.
[4] *Idaho Daily Statesman*, June 28, 1907, p. 10, report of testimony of Edward Boyce in the William D. Haywood murder trial; Selig Perlman and Philip Taft, *Labor Movements, 1896 to 1932*, p. 172, states: "It was in this prison [the Ada County jail] that the plans for the organization of the Western Federation of Miners were formulated."

first for relief funds, then for legal defense funds, had taxed the Butte Miners' Union severely. It, too, considered how to broaden the base of labor support in another such crisis.[5] Certain steps had already been taken in Montana. The Butte union had enlisted the aid of other labor groups in its immediate vicinity through the Silver Bow Trades and Labor Assembly. But more important was the organization in 1892 of all the miners' unions of Montana into an association called the Montana Miners' State Association.[6] Miners' unions at Granite, Castle, Barker, Neihart, and Black Pine had all joined forces with the Butte union, and in the Coeur d'Alene crisis they had contributed considerable sums to the relief funds. The possibility of expanding this association's activity occurred to the Butte union leaders.[7] An example of successful amalgamation of labor forces was given at Columbus, Ohio, in January of 1890, when the prominent coal miners' unions of the nation combined to form the United Mine Workers of America.[8]

In February and March, 1893, the contempt prisoners were discharged from the Ada County jail. Three of them, at least, went directly to Butte upon regaining their liberty, namely Tom O'Brien, Joe Poynton, and Tom Heney. There in the latter part of March and early April they conferred with the Butte leaders.[9] The outcome of these conferences and of the winter's reflections was the issuance in April of an invitation by the Butte Miners' Union to all the miners' unions of the West to send delegates to a convention at Butte on May 15, 1893.[10] The Montana Miners' State Association had already scheduled a convention for that date and place. It was planned that the two simultaneous conventions would merge into one large gathering.[11]

Several days before the fifteenth of May the miners' union delegates began to converge upon Butte. They came from all the union camps of Montana, the Coeur d'Alene district of Idaho, the quartz gold and lead-silver regions of Colorado, the Tintic district of Utah, and the Black Hills of South Dakota. There were 42 delegates when the last arrivals were counted.[12] A delegation of 16 represented Butte, including such prominent leaders as W. J. Weeks, Sam Williams, Patrick Gallagher, William Cunningham, John Gilligan, and Thomas Malouin. Five men came from the Coeur d'Alenes: Tom O'Brien and Joseph Poynton from Mullan; William J. Wilson from Burke; and George R. Smith and Patrick (Paddy) Burke from Gem.[13] Early arriv-

---

[5] *Anaconda Standard*, May 13, 1893, p. 4; *Butte Bystander* (Butte, Montana) [a labor weekly], May 6, 1893, p. 2.
[6] *Anaconda Standard*, May 13, 1893, p. 4.
[7] *Anaconda Standard*, May 13, 1893, p. 4.
[8] *Spokane Review*, January 25, 1890, p. 1; January 26, 1890, p. 2.
[9] *Anaconda Standard*, March 27, 1893, p. 5.
[10] *Ibid.*, May 20, 1893, p. 4; *Butte Bystander*, May 27, 1893, p. 1; *Butte Miner*, May 20, 1893, p. 1. All these papers print a resolution of the miners' convention which acknowledges the Butte union's invitation, but no copy of the actual letter of invitation has come to light.
[11] *Anaconda Standard*, May 8, 1893, p. 5; May 13, 1893, p. 4.
[12] The record of delegates attached to the original constitution of the Western Federation of Miners, at the headquarters (Denver) of the International Union of Mine, Mill and Smelter Workers, lists 42 delegates by name, distributed as follows: Terry's Peak, S. D., 1; Central City, S. D., 2; Lead City, S. D., 2; Neihart, Mont., 2; Butte, 16; Bannock, Mont., 1; Barker, Mont., 1; Granite, Mont., 5; Aspen, Colo., 1; Creede, Colo., 1; Ouray, Colo., 1; Rico, Colo., 2; Burke, 1; Gem, 2; Mullan, 2; Eureka, Utah, 2. However, *Anaconda Standard*, May 20, 1893, p. 4, accounts for 56 delegates, distributed as follows: Aspen 5, Butte 16, Burke 2, Belt Mountain, Mont., 2, Central City 3, Creede 2, Eureka 2, Gem 2, Granite 8, Lead City 5, Mullan 2, Ouray 1, Rico 3, Terry's Peak 2.
[13] These names listed as delegates on a sheet attached to the original constitution, cited above in note 12.

ing delegates were entertained by labor organizations in Silver Bow County.[14] On one such occasion, a Knights of Labor rally at Anaconda, Peter Breen delivered the oration of the day, while both O'Brien and Poynton spoke briefly.[15]

The miners' union convention began its sessions on Monday, May 15, 1893, at the Butte Miners' Union Hall,[16] and continued through Friday the nineteenth. The sessions were held behind closed doors, and only a few details leaked out to the press. John McLeod, of Terry's Peak, South Dakota, served as chairman; Thomas Malouin of Butte was secretary.[17] Very early the decision was made to organize a broad federation of all the miners' unions of the West, and the rest of the time was consumed with the necessary details of that plan. By Friday evening the constitution and by-laws of the Western Federation of Miners were approved and given to the press.[18] Also the resolutions passed by the convention, and the officers for the year 1893-94. John Gilligan of Butte stood forth as the federation's first president; D .D. Good of Granite, Montana, and John Duggan of Eureka, Utah, were the vice presidents; Thomas Malouin of Butte held the busy position of secretary-treasurer. To celebrate these achievements, a social session was held Friday night in the Union Hall.[19]

An analysis of the original constitution and by-laws of the Western Federation of Miners and of the convention's resolutions reveals the connection—direct, in many instances—between the Coeur d'Alene conflict and the new federation. The preamble to the constitution lists 10 objectives for the new federation. At least half of them refer to issues which were at stake in the Coeur d'Alenes the year before, for example:

> First—to secure an earning fully compatible with the dangers of our employment.
>
> Second—to establish as speedily as possible and forever our right to receive pay for labor performed in lawful money, and to rid ourselves of the iniquitous system of spending our earnings where and how our employers or their officers may designate . . .
>
> Sixth—to prevent by law any mine owner or mining company from employing Pinkerton detectives or other armed forces for taking possession of any mine, except the lawfully elected or appointed forces of the state, who shall be bona-fide citizens of the county and state . . . .
>
> Ninth—to demand the repeal of all conspiracy laws that in any way abridge the rights of labor organization.
>
> Tenth—to procure employment for our members in preference to nonunion men.[20]

The resolutions adopted at this founding convention also show the influence of the Coeur d'Alene crisis upon the convention. In addition to resolutions favoring free and unlimited coinage of silver, government ownership of railroad and telegraph, the eight-hour day, popular election of United States

---

[14] *Anaconda Standard* May 14, 1893, p. 8.
[15] *Ibid.*, May 15, 1893, p. 3.
[16] *Ibid.*, May 16, 1893, p. 6.
[17] *Ibid.*, May 16, 1893, p. 6.
[18] *Ibid.*, May 20, 1893, p. 4, the constitution in abridged form, however.
[19] *Anaconda Standard*, May 20, 1893, p. 4.
[20] The complete constitution and by-laws of the Western Federation of Miners, as of May 19, 1893, are in the archives of the International Union of Mine, Mill and Smelter Workers at its headquarters in Denver. This union generously provided the writer with a copy.

senators, state inspection of mines, the assembled miners vehemently echoed two of the issues of the Coeur d'Alene:

> RESOLVED, That we demand the repeal of all conspiracy laws, and the enactment of laws prohibiting the employment of detectives and armed forces except by the elected or appointed officers of any city, county and state, who shall be bona-fide resident citizens of such city, county and state, for the protection of persons and property, and in all cases of strikes or lockouts that may result from a disagreement between employers and employes.

> RESOLVED, That we are opposed to states maintaining militia companies, and request working-men everywhere not to join such organizations and endeavor to secure legislation that will abolish this great evil.[21]

Concerning the Western Federation of Miners as an organization, a few words of explanation are perhaps desirable. The federation was not a new union, but rather an association of local miners' unions. Thus, the individual miner was a member of his local union, and he was a member of the federation only as that local union maintained its good standing. A per capita tax of $1.00 per member per year was collected from the local union to support the federation.[22]

In regard to strikes, the federation laid down a definite policy of mutual support for the local unions:

> It shall be unlawful for any local Union to enter upon a strike unless when ordered by three-fourths of its resident members and on approval of the Executive Board, who shall have at least thirty days' notice of the action of the local Union; Provided, That when employers refuse to give thirty days' notice, or thirty days' time to consider the proposed change in wages or working time made by them to the local Union, then it shall be lawful for such local Union to strike in order to maintain their position, and they shall be entitled to receive all the assistance which approval by the Executive Board would entitle them to.[23]

Within the framework of the new federation the Coeur d'Alene miners' unions were established as charter members. The Mullan union received charter number 9, Burke was number 10, Gem number 11. The Wardner union was not represented in the convention, but it was included in the organization and numbered 18. Incidentally, the Butte Miners' Union took the charter number 1, and the headquarters of the federation was located in Butte. In the Coeur d'Alenes, as everywhere, the local unions retained their old local constitutions to which were added the Western Federation of Miners charters. The Coeur d'Alene union charters, along with all the charters issued at the original convention, bore the date May 15, 1893.[24]

One can hardly overemphasize the importance of the Western Federation of Miners in the labor history of the West. From the humble beginnings of 1893 with 14 unions and perhaps 10,000 miners (almost half of them in Butte alone), the federation grew within 10 years to 200 unions and somewhere near 50,000 members.[25] Under the leadership of shrewd and aggressive

[21] These resolutions were printed in *Anaconda Standard,* May 20, 1893, p. 4; *Butte Miner,* May 20, 1893, p. 1; *Butte Bystander,* May 27, 1893, p. 1.
[22] Article IV, section 1, Constitution of the Western Federation of Miners.
[23] Article IV, section 2, Constitution of the Western Federation of Miners.
[24] This information on charters and dates came in a letter from John M. Sherwood, Secretary-Treasurer of the International Union of Mine, Mill and Smelter Workers, addressed to the writer and dated Denver, Colo., June 9, 1936.
[25] U. S. Senate, *A Report on Labor Disturbances in the State of Colorado, from 1880 to 1904, Inclusive,* p. 40, quoting from the *Miners' Magazine* (official publication of the Western Federation of Miners), issue of December 29, 1904.

officers, such as Edward Boyce (of Wardner), president from 1896 to 1902, and William D. Haywood, secretary-treasurer from 1901 to 1907, the federation fought a series of bitter industrial battles in the mining states of the West. Some of these strikes exceeded the Coeur d'Alene conflict in duration, in violence, and in magnitude. Some of them were landmarks in the history of American labor, such as Leadville, Colorado, in 1896-97; the Coeur d'Alene again in 1899; Telluride, Colorado, 1900; Cripple Creek, Colorado, 1903-04. Selig Perlman and Philip Taft in their *Labor Movements, 1896 to 1932,* call the Western Federation of Miners "the most militant [union] in the history of the United States."[26] William Hard, who made a brief study of the federation in 1906, after commenting on its fighting qualities, analyzed its fraternal and idealistic aims, and concluded:

> . . . In its attitude toward the working class, . . . the Western Federation has displayed an idealism which has brought a ray of imagination and of sentiment into the life of many an underground toiler. Opening its doors freely and gladly to all workingmen, denouncing all devices for excluding outsiders and for making the trade union a monopoly, cherishing the interests of the unskilled man even above those of his more fortunate comrade, preaching the doctrine of a united working class, calling upon every workman to regard his brother's trials and ambitions as his own, fighting successfully for the establishment of eight-hour laws, offering to the anarchism of certain corporations the only real resistance which that anarchism has ever encountered, the Western Federation of Miners has contributed to the history of Western mining its one flash of social thought, its one deviation from a purely materialistic line of progress.[27]

Finally, however, it is important to notice that in its original form the Western Federation of Miners was not a revolutionary organization. Its original preamble made no eloquent declaration of socialism nor even of working class consciousness. It announced to the world that it sought to maintain friendly relations with the employer, preferring voluntary arbitration and conciliation to strikes.[28] The federation thus began like most American labor unions of that time, as a job protective organization.[29] In its original form, the federation was primarily a craft union of underground miners and muckers. The inclusion of mill and smelter workers into the federation came later, as did also the adoption of Marxian objectives.

---

[26] Perlman and Taft, p. 172.
[27] William Hard, "The Western Federation of Miners," *Outlook,* LXXXIII, May 19, 1906, p. 133.
[28] Preamble to the constitution of the Western Federation of Miners, 7th numbered paragraph.
[29] Perlman and Taft, p. 172, for a similar analysis.

27

Miners' Unions
Renascent

ALTHOUGH MARTIAL LAW ended in the Coeur d'Alenes in November, 1892, the miners' unions in the district remained dormant all winter. There were good reasons for this inactivity. The unions' most prominent leaders were lodged in the Ada County jail; four of the most energetic members were languishing in the federal prison at Detroit; over 200 of the members stood indicted for crimes either by federal or state grand juries; many union members were at liberty only under a considerable bond; and a few were still confined awaiting trial. Within the district, the "law and order" group was dominant with the new sheriff favorable to that point of view and with the Law and Order Leagues still secretly spying and reporting subversive activity.

With the coming of spring in 1893, however, the miners' unions in the Coeur d'Alenes blossomed forth into new life. Certain events of the winter had planted the seed for this renascence. First of all, the acquittal of Webb Leasure at Rathdrum just before Christmas had discouraged the "law and order" group, and thereby given encouragement to the union sympathizers. Beyond question Webb had been in the union camp at Gem and had shouldered a rifle there. The state's failure to convict in such a clear-cut case made prospects bad for further prosecution. And, indeed, there were no further prosecutions by the state on any serious indictment. Then the United States Supreme Court's decision on March 6, 1893, reversing the verdict of the jury in the conspiracy case, also gave comfort to the union side. This decision invalidated the remaining federal indictments and ended prosecutions in the circuit court. Finally, the release of the prisoners in February and March from Boise, Detroit, and Wallace and the subsequent return of union leaders to civil life provided a stimulus to renewed union activity.

Still a further reason for the union renascence lay—strange as it must seem—in the panic of 1893, which struck the mining industry some heavy blows. The metals market weakened in the late winter season; lead and silver

115

prices sagged, then plunged to low levels.[1] The mines of the Coeur d'Alenes began to close in March.[2] By April the situation had become a debacle with banks failing in Wallace and Wardner and half the big mines shut down.[3] How did such an economic tragedy aid the union revival? Simply thus: the nonunion miners who had come in during martial law were the first to go when employment ceased. As mine after mine closed, the population of the district again dwindled until it became essentially the old permanent residents, of whom the workers were still predominantly union members.

On the third of April, three men stepped off a Northern Pacific train at Mullan and commenced the most remarkable tour of the district in its whole history. They were Tom O'Brien, Joe Poynton, and Tom Heney, and they had just returned to the Coeur d'Alenes by way of Butte from their winter residence in the Ada County jail. Bands played; processions marched the streets; there were dancing and banqueting and speech making.[4] Everywhere the returned union leaders went in the district a record-breaking celebration occurred. At Wallace, O'Brien made a speech on the intriguing subject: "The Jail as an Adjunct in Educating Public Sentiment on Great Industrial Questions," a topic upon which he could speak from experience.[5] At Gem, the three unionists were taken from the train at the Granite mill, placed upon a flat car and hauled up through the camp by a crew of forty men wearing union badges and carrying a union banner and an American flag.[6] At Burke, O'Brien was taken from the train and hoisted upon the broad shoulders of a group of union miners and paraded through the town.[7] The *Mullan News* reviewed the eventful tour and concluded: "No men have ever been so honored before in the Coeur d'Alenes."[8]

Tom O'Brien had never been a fire-eater. His leadership of the union, while firm, had never encouraged violence. Now, on his return to the district, his public remarks carried a conciliatory message. "We think it is now time," he said at Mullan, "that the differences existing between ourselves and the mine owners should be amicably adjusted. . . . I have assurances from friends of both parties which lead me to believe that the end is near when we can settle down and work in harmony with our employers."[9] And to these sentiments even the *Spokane Review* could say "Amen!"[10]

The triumphant return of O'Brien, Poynton, and Heney provided the necessary impetus to throw the union activity into high gear. The union halls which opened for the homecoming banquets and dances remained open for the varied uses to which they had formerly been put.[11] Prounion opinions

---

[1] David T. Day (compiler), *Mineral Resources of the United States, 1893,* Department of the Interior, U. S. Geological Survey (Washington, Government Printing Office, 1894), p. 96, for the lead market of 1893; Richard P. Rothwell (ed.), *The Mineral Industry, 1893* (New York, The Scientific Publishing Company, 1894), pp. 311-312, for the silver market of 1893.
[2] *Spokane Review,* March 3, 1893, p. 7, reports the closing of the Bunker Hill and Sullivan on March 1.
[3] *Ibid.,* April 8, 1893, p. 2.
[4] *Spokane Review,* April 5, 1893, p. 2.
[5] *Anaconda Standard,* April 18. 1893, p. 5.
[6] *Ibid.,* April 18, 1893, p. 5.
[7] *Anaconda Standard,* April 18, 1893, p. 5.
[8] *Spokane Review,* April 14, 1893, p. 4, quoted in an editorial entitled "Mr. O'Brien's Reception."
[9] *Ibid.,* April 14, 1893, p. 4.
[10] *Ibid.,* April 14, 1893, p. 4.
[11] *Ibid.,* April 12, 1893, p. 2, a union dance at Wardner.

which had been guarded throughout the winter were expressed openly and aggressively in April. For instance, when Van B. De Lashmutt tried to attribute the mining shutdowns to high wages and asserted that the mine owners should have reopened in 1892 at $3.00 for miners and $2.50 for muckers,[12] he was promptly refuted. Union apologists hastened to point out that the mine owners' troubles were quite largely due to inefficient mining by nonunion men. The Michigan miners practically ruined the Union mine, they said, and they concluded with this blast: "The attempt of the mine owners to run their mines with sheepherders, cowboys, and ranchers has proved a flat failure." They implied that skilled mining labor—meaning union labor—was needed.[13]

Participation of the Coeur d'Alene unions in the convention at Butte at which the Western Federation of Miners was formed has already been discussed. That bit of cooperation was a sign of healthy union activity. It was not until the middle of June, however, that the unions gave indisputable proof of their renewed vitality. On the twentieth of June the miners and muckers at the Frisco mine went on strike, asking $3.50 a day for all men working underground. This strike had been called by Gem Miners' Union No. 11, and it created a furor in the district.[14] The old battle cry had been sounded and pessimistic souls began to prophesy a repetition of 1892. When A. M. Esler heard of the strike and of the muckers' demands, he reacted promptly. He closed down the mine and mill.[15] It was cheaper to close down than either to fight the strike or pay the higher wages. In sympathy with Esler, or else fearing a similar situation, the Gem mine and mill also closed down the same day.[16] Thus, the unions' first attempt to renew the industrial war was met by a counter attack; the repetition of the union wage demand was answered by a revival of the lockout.

Two interesting celebrations took place at Wallace in July, 1893, which show the extent to which the miners' unions had recovered their strength and their standing in the Coeur d'Alene community. The first of these events was the Fourth of July. In spite of the deepening gloom of the panic, the district turned out in force for a gay holiday. Perfect weather prevailed; a big crowd packed the town; and the whole holiday program went through without a hitch from procession to fireworks and dance. The double handed drilling contest was won by Tom Gaffney and Paddy Welch of the Burke Miners' Union. The Declaration of Independence was again declaimed by Justice A. E. Angel, that notorious abettor of the miners' union a year ago. Two orations were delivered, one by W. R. Stokes and the other by Campbell W. Bushnell, miners' union attorney and only 10 months before on trial for conspiracy in the United States Circuit Court.[17]

More significant, and certainly more ominous, was the event of July 11, 1893, in Wallace. The miners' unions in the district declared this holiday and

[12] *Spokane Review*, April 8, 1893, p. 2; similar expressions by De Lashmutt in *ibid.*, January 10, 1893, p. 3; January 15, 1893, p. 5.
[13] *Ibid.*, April 11, 1893, p. 2, a letter signed J. H. Barnes, undated.
[14] *Spokane Review*, June 21, 1893, p. 2.
[15] *Ibid.*, June 23, 1893, p. 1.
[16] *Ibid.*, June 23, 1893, p. 1.
[17] *Spokane Review*, July 6, 1893, p. 6.

celebrated a grim anniversary before the public gaze. It was a memorial service in honor of the three union men who lost their lives in the battle at Gem.
The union forces gathered at Fifth and Cedar Streets and marched 500 strong
up Nine Mile Canyon to the Miners' Union Cemetery. There speeches were
delivered by Campbell W. Bushnell, Charles Lane, W. N. Morphy, and finally Peter Breen, but recently released from half a dozen indictments for
murder, malicious destruction of property, and conspiracy.[18] On this occasion
Breen was reported to have said, "We have given the mine owners a fight to
the finish, and if they are not satisfied we can give them some more. . . .
This is the happiest day of my life, and I am at all times willing to be classed
as one of the dynamiters of the Coeur d'Alenes."[19] After the solemnities at the
cemetery, the union men of the district rallied in a social affair far into the
night at the historic Gem Miners' Union Hall.[20]

[18] *Ibid.*, July 13, 1893, p. 6.
[19] U. S. House of Representatives, 56th Cong., 1st sess., H. Rept. 1999, *Coeur d'Alene Labor
Troubles*, p. 18, quoted in a letter from Governor Frank Steunenberg to Secretary of War Elihu Root,
October 10, 1899.
[20] *Spokane Review*, July 13, 1893, p. 6.

28

The Coeur d'Alene
Scene in 1893

A GENERAL VIEW of the Coeur d'Alenes in July, 1893, reveals a dark and unhappy scene as compared with the prosperous days of '91. The mining industry faced a serious crisis in the panic, and since the Coeur d'Alene district's fortunes rose or fell according to the prosperity or depression of mining, its economic situation was extremely bad. The metals market had collapsed, cutting by 20% to 25% the value of the output of the mines. Silver, which had coasted along through 1892 at around 85 cents an ounce, dropped in June, 1893, to 62 cents.[1] Lead had sold pretty steadily around $4\frac{1}{4}$ cents a pound, running sometimes to $4\frac{1}{2}$ cents. In October, 1892, it went below 4 cents, and through 1893 it continued to fall. By July it had slipped below $3\frac{1}{2}$ cents, and the end was not in sight.[2] The big mines whose operations had been so profitable in 1890, 1891, and even 1892, now stoood on the brink of ruin. They must get concessions from the railroads, or cut wages again, or close down.[3] Concessions were not to be had from the railroads; the owners were sick of battling over the wage question. So they closed down.

After several warnings, particularly after wholesale shutdowns had occurred in Colorado, Nevada, Utah, and Montana, the Coeur d'Alene mines began to close. The Bunker Hill and Sullivan closed on March first,[4] to be followed by the other Wardner mines: Sierra Nevada, Last Chance, Stemwinder.[5] The Morning at Mullan shut down on March 21.[6] The Gem mines followed in June in circumstances already described.[7] The Hunter went in July[8] and the Burke mines in August. The Tiger and Poorman held out the longest, since, being shaft mines, they had a continuous pumping expense whether operating or not, and they preferred to work as long as they could

[1] Richard Rothwell (ed), *The Mineral Industry, 1893,* pp. 311-312.
[2] David T. Day (compiler), *Mineral Resources of the United States, 1893,* p. 96.
[3] *Spokane Review,* January 15, 1893, p. 5, Van B. De Lashmutt's analysis of the situation.
[4] *Spokane Review,* March 3, 1893, p. 7.
[5] *Ibid.,* April 8, 1893, p. 2.
[6] *Ibid.,* March 22, 1893, p. 8.
[7] *Ibid.,* June 23, 1893, p. 1.
[8] *Ibid.,* July 15, 1893, p. 2.

make expenses and a little over. By the middle of August the debacle was complete; the 1893 shutdown was more thorough than the lockout had been in 1892.

On top of the mining suspension came bank failures. Banks at Wardner and Wallace in which Van B. De Lashmutt and George B. McAuley were controlling directors collapsed early in April.[9] Heavy losses were sustained by the business community. De Lashmutt and McAuley suffered not only financial ruin in their banks and mines, but also a severe loss of confidence, since both had heavily overdrawn their accounts before the crash came.[10]

As the mines closed, the working population, now unemployed, tended to drift away from the district. Single men and new arrivals went first. The towns and camps dwindled in size. The permanent residents eked out a living with the aid of wood-cutting, hunting, fishing, and huckleberry picking. Wardner suffered particularly this year. On April 20, a fire broke out which swept away 75 buildings, taking the entire business district and many residences.[11] A contrast is inevitable between the two fires, Wallace in 1890, Wardner in 1893. There was the same warm-hearted sympathy and aid to the sufferers at Wardner, but with the mines closed, bank closed, and half the population gone or going, the Wardner merchants and residents had little incentive to rebuild. Whereas Wallace had sprung up anew out of the hot ashes and smoke, Wardner lingered for long months a desolate half-ruin of a town.

A year had passed since the union uprising. What were the effects of that year upon the industrial battle lines? Just at the moment a temporary truce had been called in the hostilities. The panic had proved stronger than the contesting parties and it was taking its toll from both; there were no wages for the union miners, and no profits for the mine owners. Nevertheless, a deep-seated division existed in the community as a result of the warfare of 1892, a division which was destined to outlive a generation. The whole population of the Coeur d'Alene district had been enlisted upon one side or the other in the conflict, and when new issues arose the people lined up anew in support of the combattant forces more easily than before. Bitter and uncompromising antagonism broke forth upon small provocation, such as the flurry at Gem in June, 1893. Conciliatory advice such as that given by O'Brien could have only a temporary effect.

Out of the warfare of 1892 neither side emerged completely victorious. The owners had suppressed the union, but only temporarily; they had succeeded in operating with nonunion labor, but at unusual expense. Furthermore, they had been but slightly successful in bringing the lawless element to justice. Convictions in the courts had been few; sentences light; and the worst offenders—such as the assailants at the Mission—had never been identified. The union had survived the shocks of martial law, arrests, prosecutions, and boycott in employment. Its resources had been exhausted, but it had revived with stronger organization thanks only to the support from outside the district. Probably the only constructive result of the struggle of 1892

[9] *Spokane Review,* April 8, 1893, p. 2.
[10] *Ibid.,* April 16, 1893, p. 2.
[11] *Ibid.,* April 21, 1893, p. 1.

was the formation of the Western Federation of Miners. The calm of the summer of 1893 was not a permanent peace; it was only a truce. If one looked ahead he could see more of the same bitter warfare looming in the future. And perhaps even more bitter and more destructive.

It is impossible to compute the costs of the 1892 conflict in a neat total of dollars and cents. Many intangible elements enter into the calculations. One can only gather together the known items of special expense, make an estimate of others, and enumerate those intangible quantities. The State of Idaho spent almost $3,000 for military services, over $6,000 for transportation, over $12,000 for the lodging and feeding of prisoners.[12] Its telegraphic bill must have run into the thousands also. Governor Willey lost in political prestige, while General Curtis, and lawyers Heyburn and Hawley gained. The whole state of Idaho suffered a loss of confidence in the eyes of investors and settlers, since the state government seemed incapable of preserving peace.

The United States government spent $34,110.25 in additional military expenditures in the Coeur d'Alenes.[13] That item included the lodging and feeding of prisoners and transportation. About $22,000 was spent in prosecuting the contempt and conspiracy cases.[14] How much Shoshone County spent in keeping its relatively few prisoners, in convening a grand jury and two terms of the district court, and in prosecuting the Webb Leasure case at Rathdrum cannot be known definitely. The sum probably went over a thousand dollars.

The mine owners lost an unknown and unknowable sum in profits during the months when the mines lay idle. They bore also a heavy expense in the hiring of detectives, armed guards, and lawyers. The Frisco company lost a mill in the actual battle. An intangible loss was the alienation of the confidence of a large portion of the community. The union miners lost their wages for the greater part of a year. Wage loss was estimated at $200,000 a month. The union's unemployment continued for about 10 months. Following the July outbreak came the loss of liberty for hundreds of unionists, and loss of repute throughout the Northwest as a result of the circulation of antiunion news and editorials in newspapers. Balancing this loss of repute, however, there was a gain in labor solidarity as shown by relief and defense contributions. As a final ironical thrust, the circuit court in 1895 assessed upon the unions the costs of the injunction suits, totaling over $2,000.[15]

The business community of the Coeur d'Alene towns suffered as heavy losses as any. The burden of the long crisis fell upon storekeepers, saloon keepers, retail traders of all kinds. Bankruptcies followed, but in what numbers or what amounts one can only guess. In addition, the stores and saloons of Gem were subjected to a rain of bullets from the Gem mine on July 11.

A couple of curious incidents complete the picture of the consequences of the Coeur d'Alene labor war. On November 25, 1892, A. M. Esler of the Helena and Frisco company presented the county commissioners at Shoshone

---

[12] *Spokane Review*, January 1, 1893, p. 1; *Idaho Daily Statesman*, January 1, 1893, p. 4; March 5, 1893, p. 5, according to this last report, only $16,000 was appropriated to pay $23,651.60 in claims. French, *The Coeur d'Alene Riots of 1892*, p. 49, reports an additional $7,650 appropriated in 1895.
[13] French, p. 49.
[14] *Spokane Review*, September 29, 1892, p. 1.
[15] The judge's decrees (ms.), dated October 14, 1895, and signed by James H. Beatty are filed in U.S. Moscow files 8 and 9.

County with a bill for damages amounting to $55,145.08. The damages were, of course, for the destruction of the Frisco mill the preceding July. Esler's argument was that the county, although warned of the danger, did not provide adequate protection. The county commissioners refused to pay the bill.[16] When word of the affair got about the county, Adam Aulbach, editor of the *Coeur d'Alene Sun* at Murray, the county seat, wrote and published a sharp little paragraph referring to Esler's bill as "an exhibition of impudence, such as can come only from such an exciter of riots as the black-hearted and lying A. M. Esler."[17]

Mr. Esler responded to the county's rebuff and to Aulbach's blast with suits in the United States Circuit Court. He resorted to the federal court because both he and his company were citizens of Montana. He sued Shoshone County for $100,000 and Aulbach for $15,000. Unfortunately for Esler, he not only failed to collect any damages, but he had to pay the costs in both suits. Judge Beatty found the answer of County Attorney Charles W. O'Neil adequate in one case,[18] and Adam Aulbach succeeded in proving that Esler was a citizen of Idaho in the other.[19]

In the summer of 1893, Mr. John Hays Hammond left the United States for a career in the South Africa gold and diamond mines. He withdrew from the presidency of the Bunker Hill and Sullivan Mining and Concentrating Company, and he took manager Victor M. Clement with him to Africa.[20] In Spokane, Joel Warren set up the Warren Detective Agency in the spring of 1893.[21] Ex-governor Norman B. Willey left Idaho early in the year and went to Blue Canyon, California, to superintend a gold mine. Later, in 1913, his health broken, Willey received a pension from the state of Idaho which kept him the remaining years of his life.[22] Charles A. Siringo, the detective, went on to new adventures and more triumphant exploits throughout the western states. He returned to the Coeur d'Alenes in 1906 and 1907, as the personal bodyguard of James P. McParland.[23]

Of the lawyers who were so prominent in 1892, W. B. Heyburn became United States senator from Idaho; James H. Hawley became governor of Idaho; and Patrick Reddy returned to Idaho in 1899 to defend other union miners in the state courts. Of the miners themselves, Edward Boyce became president of the Western Federation of Miners, holding that office for six years, 1896 to 1902. Peter Breen, of Butte, Montana, became a successful labor lawyer, and in 1899 helped defend union miners in the Coeur d'Alenes. In 1907, Breen came to Boise and assisted E .F. Richardson and Clarence Darrow in the defense of the Western Federation officers accused of the murder of ex-governor Frank Steunenberg. One of those defendants was George A. Pettibone.

---

[16] Esler's complaint in the case of *The Helena and Frisco Mining Company versus the County of Shoshone*, dated June 26, 1893, filed in U. S. Moscow file 31.
[17] Esler's complaint in the case of *Alfred M. Esler versus Adam Aulbach*, dated December 8, 1892, and filed in U. S. Moscow file 16.
[18] Dismissal and judgment (ms.), dated November 15, 1894, U. S. Moscow file 31.
[19] Dismissal and judgment (ms.), dated May 15, 1894, U. S. Moscow file 16.
[20] Hammond, *Autobiography*, I, pp. 116, 187.
[21] *Spokane Review*, April 27, 1893, p. 5.
[22] James H. Hawley, *History of Idaho, the Gem of the Mountains*, pp. 224-225.
[23] Siringo's books, *A Cowboy Detective* and *Riata and Spurs*, tell of his adventures; the former, pp. 492, 496, 501-503, tells of his return to the Coeur d'Alenes.

Bibliography

I

Unpublished Source Materials Used in This Monograph

Valuable unpublished source materials have been used in the preparation of this Monograph. The majority of these manuscripts are located in Boise, Moscow, and Wallace, Idaho.

At Boise, the governor's vault in the capitol contains correspondence files of past governors. About 200 letters by Governor Norman B. Willey are there on file, carbon copies, on executive stationery, and most of them signed. Fifty of these letters, dealing with the Coeur d'Alene situation or the Idaho National Guard, were indexed, and either copied or outlined. This is the *Governor's* file frequently cited in the notes. In addition to letters, the governor's vault also contains perfect copies, original typewritten drafts with signatures and seals, of the three proclamations issued by Governor Willey on June 4, July 13, and November 15, 1892.

The Secretary of State's vault in the capitol yielded only a few letters by James F. Curtis, who held the office in 1893 and 1894. None of the correspondence of A. J. Pinkham was found.

In the library of the Idaho State Historical Society, are located the two significant collections of messages cited in the notes as *Congressional Dispatches* and *Willey Collection.* The former contains 84 telegrams and letters sent and received by the Idaho Delegation in Congress (Senators George L. Shoup and Fred T. Dubois and Representative Willis Sweet), May 23 to July 19, 1892. This collection is typewritten on United States watermarked paper and enclosed in a large envelope bearing the postal franking signature (printed) of the late Addison Smith, for many years United States Representative from Idaho, and through whom, presumably, the collection was acquired by the library. A few of these messages, namely those sent by Governor Willey, are duplicates of originals in the *Governor's* vault or in the *Willey Collection,* and these appear to have been accurately copied. No such check is possible, however, upon the majority of the *Congressional Dispatches.*

The *Willey Collection* is made up of 101 messages, of which all but two were sent by Governor Willey in the period of May 23 to November 15, 1892. A large number of these messages are handwritten in ink or pencil and signed with what appears to be Governor Willey's signature. Many are written on Western Union telegraph blanks, others on executive stationery, still others on letterpress impression paper. All these loose copies have been pasted into a "gummed stub file" letter book, in chronological order. Where possible, these messages have been checked with originals in the governor's vault or with copies in *Congressional Dispatches* or in the newspapers, and the comparison seems to indicate that the items in this *Willey Collection* are accurate and probably genuine. The collection came into the possession of the Idaho State Historical Society through Miss Margaret Roberts, daughter of George H. Roberts, attorney-general in the Willey administration. Miss Roberts says that the book of telegrams was thrown away when the official records were transferred to the new capitol building, and that she saw the book, opened it, read her father's name therein, and kept it.

At Moscow, Idaho, in the office of the clerk of the United States District Court, District of Idaho, Northern Division, are the records of the cases which came before the United States Circuit Court in 1892 and 1893. These Moscow files contain a large quantity of material which exists nowhere else, in the form of complaints, warrants, indictments, affidavits, court orders, motions, exhibits of all sorts. Only the items of greatest value, however, are listed here.

U. S. Moscow file 1, *The United States versus Peter Breen et al.,* contains five envelopes of papers. In envelope 2 are Judge Beatty's instructions to the jury, and the original terms for the surrender of the Gem mill; envelope 4 has the original and complete indictment for conspiracy, plus the Bunker Hill and Sullivan injunction upon which the indictment was based.

U. S. Moscow file 7, *The Coeur d'Alene Mining and Concentrating Company versus the Miners' Union of Wardner, Idaho, et al.,* has also five envelopes of papers. Envelope 1 contains the original restraining order (injunction) of May 7, 1892, with the affidavits of A. B. Campbell, William M. Pipkin and George L. Wolf. Envelope 3 has the important affidavit of Thomas O'Brien and the constitution of the Coeur d'Alene Miners' Union. In envelope 5 are the mine owners' collective affidavit and their letter to Governor Willey, and a copy of the Butte Miners' Union's mortgage upon the union halls in the Coeur d'Alenes.

U. S. Moscow file 8, *The Bunker Hill and Sullivan Mining and Concentrating Company versus the Miners' Union of Wardner, Idaho, et al.,* is almost empty; most of its contents were transferred to file 1.

U. S. Moscow file 9, *The Helena and Frisco Mining Company versus the Miners' Union of Wardner, Idaho, et al.,* has three envelopes. In envelope 1 are A. M. Esler's original complaint and the restraining order of May 28. Envelope 3 contains 13 affidavits of witnesses and participants in the battle at Gem and the attack at the Mission.

U. S. Moscow file 16, *Alfred M. Esler versus Adam Aulbach,* and U. S. Moscow file 31, *The Helena and Frisco Mining Company versus the County of Shoshone, Idaho,* are both small files of relatively unimportant suits.

In the Shoshone County Court House at Wallace, Idaho, are the records of seven cases which came before the district court in the First Judicial District of Idaho, in 1892 and 1893. The Wallace files are not so rich in important documents as are the Boise and Moscow files. Idaho Wallace file 90, *The State of Idaho versus Richard A. Cunningham,* contains nothing of value. Idaho Wallace file 91, *The State of Idaho versus Bernard Reilley,* contains the affidavit of William H. Clagett and W. W. Woods regarding the Law and Order Leagues. Idaho Wallace file 92, *The State of Idaho versus Joel Warren,* has a transcript of a trial in a Justice court which gives valuable information on the Warren incident. Idaho Wallace files 93, 94, 95, and 96, *The State of Idaho versus Peter Breen et al., versus Thomas O'Brien et al., versus Daniel W. Leasure et al., versus George A. Pettibone et al.,* respectively, contain nothing of first importance except the indictments.

At Denver, Colorado, in the office of the International Union of Mine, Mill and Smelter Workers, repose the original constitution and bylaws of the Western Federation of Miners. Through the generosity of Mr. John M. Sherwood, Secretary-Treasurer of the International Union in June, 1936, a copy of this constitution and bylaws was sent to the writer.

In Portland, Oregon, lives Mr. Edward Boyce, former president of the Western Federation of Miners and a participant in some of the events of 1892. On August 3, 1936, the writer, with the permission of Mr. Boyce, submitted to the latter a series of questions in writing, to which he replied under date of August 18, 1936. The letters from Boyce and Sherwood are the only pieces of personal correspondence which have been utilized in this monograph.

II

Printed Materials

Adamic, Louis. *Dynamite, the Story of Class Violence in America* (New York, The Viking Press, 1934), 495 pp.
> Contains a brief notice of the 1892 Coeur d'Alene strike; too brief to be good.

Anaconda Standard (Anaconda, Montana), March to May, 1892; March to May, 1893.
> A valuable newspaper file. However, the important months of June, July, and August, 1892, are lacking in the file at Butte.

Bimba, Anthony. *The History of the American Working Class* (New York, International Publishers, 1927), 379 pp.
> A good survey, written from the Marxian point of view. A sympathetic treatment of the Western Federation of Miners.

Brissenden, Paul Frederick. *The I. W. W. A Study of American Syndicalism* (New York, Columbia University, 1919), 422 pp.
> A good discussion of the Western Federation of Miners as one of the nuclei of the I. W. W.

Brooks, John Graham. *American Syndicalism, The I. W. W.* (New York, 1913), 264 pp.
> A good discussion of the Western Federation of Miners as one of the forerunners of the I. W. W.

Butte Bystander (Butte, Montana), March to May, 1893.
> A small labor weekly which supplements the *Anaconda Standard* as a source of information on the organization of the Western Federation of Miners.

(Butte Miners' Union). "Our Anniversary," *The Miners' Voice,* I (June, 1935), p. 1.
> A brief but valuable retrospective article.

Cody, Edmund R. *History of the Coeur d'Alene Mission of the Sacred Heart* (Caldwell, Idaho, Caxton Printers, 1930), 45 pp.

The Daily Miner (Butte, Montana), June, 1880; June, 1881; June, 1882; May, 1893.
> Valuable for the early history of the Butte Miners' Union.

Durham, Nelson W. *History of the City of Spokane and the Spokane Country, Washington, from Its Earliest Settlement to the Present Time* (Chicago, 1912), 3 vols.
> Follows closely the newspaper accounts.

The Federal Court Reporter, vol. 51.

French, George Edgar. "The Coeur d'Alene Riots of 1892," *Overland Monthly,* XXVI (July, 1895), 32-49.
> A valuable and interesting article. Lieutenant French was regimental adjutant of the Fourth United States Infantry, on duty in the Coeur d'Alenes in 1892.

Foote, Mrs. Mary Hallock. *Coeur d'Alene* (Boston, 1894), 240 pp.
> A sentimental piece of fiction which twists the facts in order to make the story go. For example, the hero is rescued from a horrible death at the Mission by the arrival of U. S. troops. A piece of antiunion propaganda.

Fuller, George Washington. *The Inland Empire of the Pacific Northwest, a History* (Denver, H. G. Lindermann, 1928), 3 vols.

Fuller, George Washington. *A History of the Pacific Northwest* (New York, Alfred A. Knopf, 1931), 383 pp.
> Probably the best general work on the Pacific Northwest. A brief but accurate account of the whole Coeur d'Alene struggle.

Hammond, John Hays. *The Autobiography of John Hays Hammond* (New York, Farrar and Rinehart, 1935), 2 vols.
> A reminiscence 40 years after.

Hard, William. "The Western Federation of Miners," *Outlook,* LXXXIII (May 19, 1906), 125-133.
> A sympathetic analysis of the history and the objectives of the Western Federation of Miners.

Hawley, James H., ed. *History of Idaho, the Gem of the Mountains* (Chicago, The S. J. Clarke Publishing Company, 1920), 4 vols.
> Surprisingly little on the Coeur d'Alene trouble, in view of the fact that Hawley was a participant.

Henderson, John M., Shiach, William S., Averill, Harry B. *An Illustrated History of North Idaho* (- - - Western Historical Publishing Company, 1903), 1238 pp.
> The best local history of Shoshone and other northern Idaho counties in print.

Idaho Daily Statesman (Boise, Idaho), March, 1892, to July, 1893.
> A file of utmost value in tracing the activities at the state capital.

Idaho. Legislature. *General Laws of the State of Idaho* (First and Second Sessions of the State Legislature).

An Illustrated History of the State of Idaho (Composite authorship; editor not named) (Chicago, 1899), 726 pp.
> Contains a good article on the early history of the Coeur d'Alene lead-silver mines by Frank R. Culbertson; otherwise mediocre.

Ingalls, Walter Renton. *Lead and Zinc in the United States* (New York, 1908), 368 pp.

Mullan, John. *Report on the Construction of a Military Road from Fort Walla Walla to Fort Benton* (Washington, 1863), 363 pp.

New York Herald (New York, N. Y.), July, 1892.
> Contains a few items not printed in the western papers, chiefly news dispatches from Washington, D. C.

Perlman, Selig. *A History of Trade Unionism in the United States* (New York, The Macmillan Company, 1929), 313 pp.
> Excellent general survey.

Perlman, Selig, and Taft, Philip. *Labor Movements, 1896-1932* (New York, The Macmillan Company, 1935). [Vol. IV of *History of Labor in the United States,* by John R. Commons and associates] 683 pp.
> Brilliant chapters on the Western Federation of Miners, and an accurate (though brief) account of the Coeur d'Alene trouble.

Rickard, T. A. *The Bunker Hill Enterprise.* (San Francisco, Mining and Scientific Press, 1921), 143 pp.
> Contains a wealth of material (financial and technical) on the company and the mine, but only a little on labor relations.

Rothwell, Richard P., ed. *The Mineral Industry, 1893* (New York, 1894), 894 pp.

Siringo, Charles A. *A Cowboy Detective* (Chicago, 1912), 519 pp.
> Reads like fiction. Perhaps it is.

Siringo, Charles A. *Riata and Spurs* (Boston, Houghton Mifflin Company, 1927), 276 pp.
> More remarkable reminiscences by a remarkable detective.

Smith, Robert Wayne. *History of Placer and Quartz Gold Mining in the Coeur d'Alene District* (unpublished M. A. Thesis, University of Idaho, 1932), 124 numbered leaves.

Spokane Review (Spokane, Washington), January, 1890, to July, 1893.
> The most valuable of all the sources. The only daily newspaper file extant which gives extensive space to happenings in the Coeur d'Alenes.

Stoll, William T. *Silver Strike* (Boston, Little, Brown and Company, 1932), 273 pp.
    Rambling reminiscences by a Mine Owners' Association lawyer, written almost 40 years after the events.

Taggart, Arthur F. *Handbook of Ore Dressing* (New York, John Wiley and Sons, 1927), 1679 pp.

U. S. Congress. House. Committee on Military Affairs. *Coeur d'Alene Mining Troubles,* 56th Cong., 1st sess., H. Rept. 1999 (1900), 132 pp.
    Refers to 1892 events infrequently and only as background for later happenings.

U. S. Congress. Senate. *Couer d'Alene Mining Troubles* (containing a paper, "The Crime of the Century. Worse than Siberian Cruelties under the American Flag," by Edward Boyce), 56th Cong., 1st sess., S. Doc. 25 (1899), 6 pp.
    A few items on early miners' unions in the Coeur d'Alenes.

U. S. Congress. Senate. *A Report on Labor Disturbances in the State of Colorado, from 1880 to 1904,* Inclusive, 58th Cong., 3d sess., S. Rept. 122 (1905), 363 pp.
    Information on early miners' unions in the West.

U. S. Congress. Senate. *Federal Aid in Domestic Disturbances, 1787-1903,* 67th Cong., 2nd sess., S. Doc. 263 (1922), 322 pp.
    A brief sketch of the federal intervention in the Coeur d'Alenes in 1892.

U. S. Geological Survey. *Mineral Resources of the United States, 1893,* David T. Day, compiler (Washington, 1894), 810 pp.

U. S. Geological Survey. Ransome, Frederick Leslie, and Calkins, Frank Cathcart. *The Geology and Ore Deposits of the Coeur d'Alene District.* Professional Paper 62 (Washington, 1908), 203 pp.

U. S. Geological Survey. Umpleby, Joseph B., and Jones, E. L. Jr. *Geology and Ore Deposits of Shoshone County, Idaho,* Bulletin 732 (Washington, Government Printing Office, 1923), 156 pp.

United States Supreme Court Reports, vol. 148.

U. S. War Department. *Messages and Documents,* 1892, vol. I (Washington, 1892), 739 pp.
    Contains the reports of Brig. Gen. Thomas H. Ruger, Brig. Gen. Wesley Merritt, and Col. William P. Carlin. The best account of the military movements in the Coeur d'Alenes in 1892.

Walters, Lois. *Frank Steunenberg and the Mine Riots in Idaho* (unpublished M.A. thesis, University of California, 1932), 97 numbered leaves.
    One chapter on the 1892 episode, and a poor one at that.

The Weekly Miner (Butte, Montana), June to August, 1878; June, 1879; June, 1880.
    Valuable for the beginnings of the Butte Miners' Union.

Wood, Fremont. *The Introductory Chapter to the History of the Trials of Moyer, Haywood, and Pettibone, and Harry Orchard* (Caldwell, Idaho, The Caxton Printers, 1931), 40 pp.
    Contains a brief survey of the 1892 crisis as a background for subsequent events.

Yellen, Samuel. *American Labor Struggles* (New York, Harcourt, Brace and Company, 1936), 398 pp.
    Valuable for the general labor background of 1892, especially the Homestead, Pa., struggle. Does not discuss the Coeur d'Alene conflict.

Index

Idaho Congressional delegation, 59, 75, 78
Idaho National Guard, 48, 59, 60, 70-75, 79, 82-83, 109, 121
Idaho politics, 1892, 106-109
Idaho, state of, admission to union, 10
indictments by Shoshone County grand jury, 102-103
indictments for conspiracies, 99-100
Ingalls, Walter Renton, 3
injunction, temporary, 42-43, 45, 56, 58
injunction, permanent, 59, 97-98

Jenkins, Frank, 24, 26-30, 69, 98, 107
Jerome, T. K., 38, 43, 94
Jones, Walter, 43
June thirteenth, celebration of, Butte, Montana, 14
justices of the peace, 39

Kellogg, Idaho, 6
Kellogg, Noah S., 23
Kellum, Samuel, 35
Kemmer, M. T., footnote 39
Kennedy, Dan. footnote 17
Kneebone, John, 98
Knights of Labor, 86, 112

Lane, Charles, 118
Last Chance Mill, 69
Last Chance Mine, 8, 18, 29, 31, 32, 46, 119
Law and Order leagues, 94-95, 115
lead, 2-4, 119
lead-silver mines, 3, 6, 17
Leadville, Colorado, 13, 114
Leasure, Webb, 86, 102-105, 115, 121
Linn, Thomas A., 60
Livers, John L., 75
Lockout, 37
Lookout station, Lookout Pass, 86
Lucy, Jack, 53
Luddy, W. H., 19
Lund, Olaf. 54

McAuley, George B., 28-29, 32-33, 37, 45, 49, 56, 69, 74, 89, 93, 98, 120
McCarty, E. D., footnote 45
McConnel, J. W., 107-108, 109
McCormick, Cyrus H., 24
McDonald, Archie T., 65, 102
McFarland, Robert, 104
McGee, Hugh, 99
McKinley Tariff Act, 11
McLeod, John, 112
McParland, James P., 122

Malouin, Thomas, 111-112
Marsh, G. W., 85, 89
martial law, 78, 80-84
"Massacre" at the Mission, 71-73, 95, 120
Mayhew, Alexander E., 60, 108
Medical care for miners, 15
Merritt, Wesley, 76-77
military camps in Coeur d'Alene district, 90
military occupation of Couer d'Alene mining district, 79, 81-82, 121
military post, movement to establish, 84, 92
military prisons. See prisons, military.
Miller, W. H. H., 100
Mills. D. O., 24
Milo Gulch, 3
Milwaukee Mining Company, 29
Mine Owners' Association, 21, 28-30, 32-36, 40, 45, 72, 92, 95, 99, 105, 106, 108
Mine Owners' Association ultimatum, 34-36
Mine owners' letter to governor Willey, 48-49
Miners' defense funds, 95-96, 98, 111
miners' grievances, 14-16; medical care, 15
Miners' Union Cemetery, Wallace, Idaho, 118
Miners' Union Hospital, 19, 20-21, 25, 36
Miners' union relief organization, 40, 53, 93-94
miners unions. See names of unions.
mining camps, 4, 9-10
Mission of the Sacred Heart. See Cataldo Mission; "Massacre" at the Mission
Missoula Montana, 8-9, 46
"Mollie Maguires," 66

Monahan, John, 30, 66, 72
Monongahela River, 62
Montana Miners' State Assocation, 111
Moore, F. Rockwood, 69
Moore, George W., 104
Morning mine, 3, 8, 12, 29, 92, 119
Morphy, W. N., 118
muckers.See carmen and shovelers.
Mullan, John, 2
Mullan, Idaho, 37, 70, 77
Mullan Miners' Union, 18, 22, 43, 113
Mullan News, 116
Mullan Road, 2, 9
Mullan Tribune, 10, 38, 94
murder cases, 102-105, 118, 122
Murphy, John, 100
Murray, Idaho, 2, 4, 6-7, 9

Neill, Robert, 108
Nicholson, John, 99
Nolan, Timothy, footnote 16
non-union miners, 39, 41, 44-47, 50, 52-54, 58, 60-61, 63, 65-66, 68-71, 78, 92, 99, 116
Northern Pacific Railroad, 2, 7-8, 32, 44-45, 47, 49, 70, 76-77, 79, 81, 86, 103, 105, 116

O'Brien, Thomas, 35, 39-40, 53, 55-56, 63, 68-69, 70, 85, 99, 101-102, 109, 111-112, 116, 120
Old National Bank of Spokane, 17
O'Neil, Charles W., 75-97, 104-106, 122
O'Rourke, Patrick, footnote 17
O'Rourke, Phil, 23
Osburn, Idaho, 4, 6-7

Page, (Lt. Col.), 85
panic of 1893, 115-116, 119-120. See also bank failures, Wallace and Wardner
parole of prisoners, 87-88
Parsons, George M., 78, 83, 87
Paxson, Frederic Logan, v, vi, vii
payday for troops, 91-92
"peaceful persuasion," 52-53
Peck, Origin O., 23
People's Party (Populists), 107-108
Perlman, Selig, 50-51, 114
permanent injunction. See injunction, permanent
Perry, James, 53
Peterson, Gus, 99
Pettibone, George A., 19, 39, 56, 67, 85-87, 100-101, 102, 106, 122
Pettibone, George A., et al. vs. the United States, 101
Pinkerton detectives, 30, 62, 67, 112
Pinkham, A. J., Quartermaster General, Idaho National Guard, 78, 82, 87-88, 94, 106-107
Pinkham, Joseph, U. S. Marshall, 11, 42-43, 56, 97, 106
Pinney, James A., 42
Pipkin, William M., 41-42
Pocatello, Idaho, 3
Polaris mine, 3
Poorman mine, 3, 8, 29, 34, 56, 83, 88, 93, 119
Populists. See People's Party (Populists)
Porter, C. D., 29, 106
Porter, Peter, 72
Porter, Robert, 29
Powers, William, 19, 25
Poynton, Joseph F., 35, 39, 43, 56, 85, 99, 101-102, 111-112, 116
preambles, 19, 112
pressure upon state government, State of Idaho, 50-51
Pritchard, Andrew J., 2
Prince, Vivian (Captain), 46
prisoners, 83-85, 98, 121
prisoners, guarding of, 82
prisoners, parole system, 87-88
prisoners, release of, 87-88
prisons, military, 87-89
Proclamation of June 4, 1892, by Governor Willey, 49; of July 13, 1892, by Governor Willey, 78, 80-81; of July 15, 1892, by President Harrison, 81; of November 19, 1892, by Governor Willey, ending martial law, 84

130

Wardner, James F., 23
Wardner Miners' Union, 18, 22, 25-26, 113
Wardner News (newspaper), 10, 40
Wardner tramway. *See* Bunker Hill and Sullivan tramway
Warren Detective Agency, 122. *See also* Warren, Joel
Warren, Joel, 44-45, 66, 103, 105, 122
Weeks, W. J., 111
Welch, Paddy, 117
Welch, Mrs. Sarah, 20
Western Federation of Miners, 111-114, 117, 121-122

Willey, Norman B., 10, 47-51, 56, 59, 60, 62, 74-76, 78, 80, 82-84, 86-88, 92, 94, 95, 97, 102, 106-109, 121-122
Williams, R. R., 19
Williams, Sam, 111
Wilson, William J., 111
Witter, A. C., 13
Wolf, George L., 41-42
woodcutting, 53
Wood, Fremont, 63, 88, 97-99, 106
Woods, W. W., 95
Wourms, John, footnote 16

Young, "Brig," 40

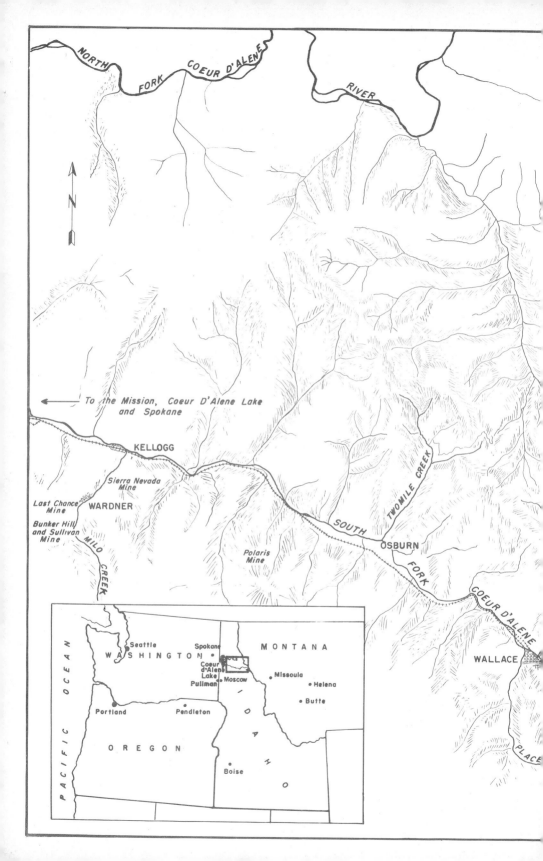